D1535068

Water, Engineering and Landscape

Water, Engineering and Landscape

Water control and landscape transformation
in the modern period

Edited by Denis Cosgrove and Geoff Petts

WITHDRAWN

Belhaven Press
(A Division of Pinter Publishers)
London and New York

Tennessee Tech Library
Cookeville, TN

© Denis Cosgrove, Geoff Petts and Contributors, 1990

First published in Great Britain in 1990 by
Belhaven Press (a division of Pinter Publishers),
25 Floral Street, London WC2E 9DS

All rights reserved. No part of this publication may be
reproduced, stored in a retrieval system, or transmitted by any
other means without the prior permission of the copyright holder.
Please direct all enquiries to the publishers.

British Library Cataloguing in Publication Data
A CIP catalogue record for this book is available from the British Library

ISBN 1 85293 069 1

For enquiries in North America please contact
PO Box 197, Irvington, NY 10533

Library of Congress Cataloging-in-Publication Data
Water, engineering, and landscape: water control and landscape
   transformation in the modern period/edited by Denis Cosgrove and
   Geoff Petts.
       p.   cm.
   Includes index.
   ISBN 1-85293-069-1
   1. Hydraulic engineering—History.   2. Land use—History.
   I. Cosgrove, Denis E.   II. Petts, Geoffrey E.
   TC18.W38   1990
   627'.09—dc20   90–41792
                                                              CIP

Typeset by DP Photosetting, Aylesbury, Bucks
Printed and bound in Great Britain by
Biddles Ltd of Guildford and Kings Lynn

Contents

List of Plates

List of Figures

List of Tables

List of contributors

Morag Bell is Senior Lecturer in Human Geography at Loughborough University. A graduate of Nottingham University, she obtained her DPhil from Oxford and has since studied and published on the geography of development ideas and the human use of environmental resources in Southern Africa.

Keith Boucher is Lecturer in Physical Geography at Loughborough University. He graduated from Bristol University and undertook postgraduate study on Spanish agrarian reform. His published research is in climatology and he is currently studying precipitation and flood events in the Danube Basin.

Robin Butlin is Professor of Geography and Head of Department at Loughborough University. His main research is in historical geography, currently of the fenlands of North-East Cambridgeshire. He is also studying the history of historical geography and the historical geography of the Holy Land.

Denis Cosgrove is Reader in Cultural Geography at Loughborough University. A graduate of Oxford and Toronto Universities, his published research is on the development and representation of landscape in Western culture in the modern period, especially in Italy. He is currently undertaking a comparative study of global images in the 16th and 20th centuries.

Jennifer Elliott is Lecturer in Human Geography and Recreation Studies at Staffordshire Polytechnic. She graduated and gained her PhD from Loughborough University and during graduate research was Honorary Research Associate at Zimbabwe University. She continues to research environmental issues in the developing world.

Pyrs Gruffudd holds a postdoctoral research post at Nottingham University as member of a project on English nationalism, culture and heritage. He obtained his first degree and PhD from Loughborough University with a thesis on landscape and nationalism in inter-war Wales.

Will Hamley is Lecturer in Human Geography at Loughborough University. He holds degrees from Wales and London Universities and researches the growth of science parks in the USA as well as the economic and environmental impacts of hydro-electric power generation in the Canadian North.

Michael Heffernan is Lecturer in Geography at Loughborough University. He graduated from Swansea and his PhD at Cambridge concerned the historical geography of North-Western France. His current research is of French representations of overseas colonies, particularly in North Africa, and of French exploration and geography in the eighteenth and nineteenth centuries.

Geoff Petts is Professor of Physical Geography at Loughborough University. He graduated from Liverpool and obtained a PhD at Southampton. He has published widely on various aspects of fluvial geomorphology and river regulation, specializing on research at the interface of hydrology, geomorphology and ecology.

Neil Roberts is Lecturer in Physical Geography at Loughborough University. He graduated from Oxford and completed a PhD at University College London. His research spans issues of environmental change in the tropics and subtropics, especially in Africa and the Middle East.

Max Wade is Senior Lecturer in Physical Geography at Loughborough University. He is a graduate of Liverpool Polytechnic and took a PhD at UWIST for a thesis on the Gwent Levels. This was the origin of his interest in the ecological impact of landuse changes in lowland Britain and the management of a range of freshwater systems.

Preface

This collection of essays originated in a seminar series held in 1988 among staff and postgraduates in the Department of Geography at Loughborough University of Technology. The seminars included an apparently diverse set of research perspectives but yielded a common interest in questions of the development and management of wetland environments. The authors of these essays, all present or former members of the department, have addressed aspects and instances of the complex interaction between water, engineering and landscape.

Geographers have traditionally accepted a wide brief in their studies of spatial relations and the processes and patterns inscribed into natural and human environments. This has often led to significant divergence in epistemology and method, and at times to dichotomy and mutual incomprehension within our discipline, especially between those committed to physical geography as a natural science and those taking a social scientific or humanities perspective to geography. Despite frequent calls for a unified treatment of the natural environment and human agency within geography, practical evidence of productive dialogue remains relatively rare. It is appropriate, then, and timely in the light of growing public environmental awareness, that from the youngest university geography department in Britain, and from its one university of technology, a collection such as this should emerge. While maintaining the integrity of approach and method specific to the individual contributions, each of these essays directly concerns the ways in which humans have intervened in physical processes, the consequences that have occurred and the geographical landscapes that have resulted.

The work of producing this collection has brought to its contributors greater understanding of, and respect for, both the unity and diversity of the geographical enterprise. If it contributes similarly to its readers it will stand as a fitting monument to the first decade of geography at Loughborough University.

The editors wish to acknowledge and thank Erica Milwain for the cartographic work and Val Pheby for typing parts of the manuscript. Acknowledgement is due to the Royal Geographical Society for permission to reproduce Plate 6.1 and to the Société de Géographie de Paris for permission to reproduce Plate 6.2.

Loughborough
February 1990

CHAPTER 1

An elemental division: water control and engineered landscape

Denis Cosgrove

And God said, Let the waters under the heaven be gathered together unto one place, and let the dry land appear: and it was so. (Genesis 1.9)

These essays concern the relations between two of the four elements traditionally believed to constitute the world: water and earth. They are written by geographers, scholars whose task it is to describe and understand the terrestrial scene and the ways in which it is shaped by human and natural processes. They are informed by our recognition of a significant juncture in human relations with the physical earth. The closing century leaves us immediate heirs to a triumphalist age of apparent mastery over nature: imitators of the divine cosmogony in the scale and success of our interventions in the elemental world. Yet we are witnessing the painful birth of a consciousness that human works may perhaps be less enduring and certainly less harmonious than those described in Genesis. The essays here variously document aspects of our arrival at this juncture, covering an arc of historical time that leads from the beginnings of the modern world in Renaissance Europe, through the steady growth in the geographical and technical scale of European and European-inspired water and land engineering over the past six centuries, to the contemporary desire to constitute a more humble and unified way of conceiving the relations between earth, water and human life. Each essay is a self-sufficient study but together they point to common themes and common questions. These are, on the one hand, conceptual and epistemological, concerning the meanings of water, landscape and engineering within geography as a unified environmental science; and on the other, historical and historiographic, concerning changing European conceptions of and intervention in the hydro-environment since the sixteenth century. They are also speculative, concerning the future development of our relations with land and water. Here we address these themes and questions from a perspective grounded in cultural and historical study. In the closing essay we return to them from a perspective rooted in the natural and applied sciences.

Water, culture and the hydro-landscape

The place of water as one of the four elements of ancient cosmography implies its centrality in physical and organic life. More than wind and fire, it is water that shapes the natural landscape through marine, glacial and above all fluvial action. It is also the *sine qua non* of human life. Omnivorous animals, we have a seemingly infinite scope of choice for solid diet, but water is an invariant human and organic need. The geography of human settlement has always been and remains today shaped in large measure by the distribution of available sources of fresh water. But as with all brute facts of our existence, humans culturally appropriate water, and invest it with meanings (Dardel, 1952). It becomes a metaphor mapped onto other dimensions of human existence, individual and social, material and spiritual. It is through the meanings that we give to water and to its geographical manifestations—in rivers, streams and lakes—that we come to understand it and to exert forms of human control over its inherent nature.

In experience, a key geographical characteristic of fresh water is flow (Bachelard, 1942). Falling from the skies, it gathers in puddles, runs away in streams that follow the lie of the land, soaks into the earth and reappears in larger streams that merge with others and flow in rivers towards the sea. Water is an element of movement, unpredictable, difficult to contain. The river is life, its flow is cleansing. In Judeo-Christian thought, born in a semi-arid physical environment, water is a symbol of salvation, we are born again of water, we are washed in the Jordan River. The Psalms sing thus of running water and redemption: 'As the hart panteth after the water brooks, so panteth my soul after thee, O God' (42:1), 'The Lord is my shepherd; I shall not want. He maketh me to lie down in green pastures: he leadeth me beside the still waters' (23:1–2). But the river is threatening, its waters turn the solid earth to flood and marsh, and so also present in the Psalms is the fear of the uncontrolled waters first experienced in Noah's Flood: 'Save me, O God; for the waters are come into my soul. I sink in deep mire, where there is no standing: I am come into deep waters, where the floods overflow me' (69:1–2). Water is no more freely given than salvation, it demands human vigilance, the imposition of order through human ingenuity, if its benefits are fully to be realized.

Control and appropriation of water have been fundamental to the building of human cultures and civilizations. The Jews themselves were twice taken into bondage by powerful urban societies based on the control of hydro-environments: into Egypt and Babylon. Like other early civilizations of the Old World, in northern India, Southeast Asia, China and Meso-America, these cultures were erected on the surplus produced when great rivers could be managed and their flows diverted into irrigation canals and ditches. The sophistication of technology and social coordination necessary to establish and maintain such systems is such that it has suggested to some scholars the concept of 'hydraulic civilization', a specific type of social formation founded upon centralized state authority with its own forces and relations of production emerging out of water engineering and control:

Where agriculture required substantial and centralized works of water control, the representatives of government monopolized political power and societal leadership, and they dominated their country's economy. By preventing the growth of strong competitive forces, such as a feudal knighthood, an autonomous church, or self-governing guild cities, they were able to make themselves the sole masters of their society. It is this combination of hydraulic agriculture, a hydraulic government, and a single-centred society that constitutes the institutional essence of hydraulic civilization. (Wittfogel, 1956: 153)

Wittfogel goes on to point out that the great majority of the world's historical civilizations have been based on hydraulic agriculture, that they have dominated the global population and that their temporal endurance has generally been far longer than that of civilizations based on rain-fed agriculture. The debates over the appropriateness of the historical and theoretical validity of the Wittfogel thesis need not be rehearsed here. Our focus is principally on Europe, the one world region which has developed a civilization based initially on rain-fed agriculture, and on regions subject to the dominant influence of European culture. Perhaps only in the humid lowlands of Western Europe could the concept of riparian rights fragmenting entitlement over water between the owners of the stream banks make legal sense. It was transplanted to the New World, where it remained an aspect of American policy until its inapplicability to the semi-arid and arid regions of the Far West was realized in the late nineteenth century. None the less, the Wittfogel thesis accurately identifies an intimate link between environmental authority in the form of water control and political power. Indeed, even the Roman Empire, parent to subsequent European cultures, while in no sense a hydraulic civilization, left among its most enduring marks in the landscape the monumental masonry of aqueducts that led water into its cities. The crumbling evidence of Roman hydro-engineering cutting across the wastes of the Roman Campagna became for Renaissance observers signs of the power and glory of Empire as well as mute testimony to the passage of time and human vanity, and thus objects of landscape aesthesis.

The geometrical precision of an aqueduct signifies the engineer's vision of water flow, a bounded channel form that has become the common conception of how even a natural river should appear. In Europe, in other long-settled regions subject to large-scale administration, and increasingly across the world, rivers do indeed appear this way in the landscape: linear features clearly defined by banks and levees, their flow regulated and largely predictable—in short, tamed. Today we find it hard to say what a 'natural' river might look like. But we may be sure that it would be a much less clearly defined geographical feature than the rivers we see and imagine, something more akin to what we observe when water flows over a pavement or beach: multi-channelled, braided, covering a band of land much broader than we customarily think, a rich and diverse woodland habitat for plant and animal life different from that of the areas it drains (Chapter 2). No river of even medium, let alone large, size in Europe is like this; along with the landscapes through which they once so freely flowed, they have all been controlled and engineered. The natural landscape of the river, formerly a wide zone, has been both simplified and concentrated to a network of narrow longitudinal trapezoids whose ecology is as dependent upon continued human intervention as the reclaimed fields that parallel them (Chapter 5). Human order has replaced natural order, imposed according to human visions and human needs. Control goes beyond simply preventing the dangers that free-flowing rivers might represent to human habitation and livelihood. It yields power: motor power for machines—directly in the case of the mill, indirectly in the case of the hydro-turbine—as well as the political power that fascinated Wittfogel. Until a mere two hundred years ago water far outstripped fire or air as the key source of motor power for human technology. If irrigation systems may be claimed as the foundation of ancient civilization, so Marx pointed to the introduction of the watermill as a key force of production in the making of feudal civilization. The modern period of free market capitalism, of European commercial and political expansion, of experimental science and its application, which begins mid-way through the present millennium, is characterized by its own forms of intervention in water flows and its own distinct forms of hydro-landscape. Both core areas of European merchant capitalism, upper Italy and Flanders, witnessed early innovation in the mechanical control of water flows and river regulation. At the opening of the fifteenth century, Lombardy, the Venetian plain and Tuscany, on the one hand, and the Low Countries, on the other, were both landscapes of merchant cities within ill-drained lowland plains, their topographies characterized by slow-flowing and easily flooding rivers.

Water, engineering and the landscape of modernization

In medieval Flanders and Italy, as in the rest of Europe, and indeed in most parts of the world throughout human history, the vast majority of interventions into water flows were local, small-scale and unrecorded. Indeed, the term 'engineering' is probably inappropriate as a designation for such works. Careful use of wetlands such as the 'indigenous' agricultural practices on the dambos of Southern Africa discussed in Chapter 8, is typical of the acute sensitivity of agrarian societies to their resources. Construction of weirs, offtakes of irrigation water along channels, minor dredging for improved drainage, raising embankments to reduce the risk of flooding have for the most part been undertaken at specific points without regard to consequences elsewhere. Today, small-scale and local intervention is often celebrated as ecologically and environmentally more acceptable than the mega-projects which have characterized the modern age. But we should be careful to avoid romanticizing this. Any intervention into a dynamic system like a river will have consequential effects. Those of smaller, more local works will simply be less dramatic. In fact the attempts on the part of local and central government to control such uncoordinated activity testify often to its damage to broader, less localized interests; for example, Venice, like other Italian city states, constantly sought to regulate the unauthorized construction of weirs and other impediments along navigable rivers (Chapter 3). The capital necessarily invested for anything other than minor and local action has meant that integrated and enduring schemes have generally been more carefully planned and monitored in terms of consequences, even if they have been necessarily insensitive to local communities and livelihoods, as was the case of medieval monastic improvements and those documented for the fenland districts in the seventeenth century (Chapter 4). What is certainly true is that the pace and scale of hydro-engineering dramatically accelerated from the later sixteenth century and may be seen as one dimension of 'modernization' in Europe and regions subject to European control. Clearly the great river regulation and wetland reclamation schemes of seventeenth and eighteenth-century Europe: in northeast Italy (Chapter 3), the Low Countries, the lower Loire, the East Anglian Fenlands and elsewhere, must be seen in the context of modernization. It was the emerging centralized state that was able to underwrite, legislatively and financially, drainage consortia, a capitalist land market which could realize the financial gains of improvement in increased land values (Chapter 4), technological innovation in pumps, dredging devices, locks and sluices, and thus engineer a new landscape.

But modernization was as much cultural as it was political, economic and technological. It involved a new way of seeing the world and of conceiving the relations between human life and the natural world (Harvey, 1989). Geographical science, above all, provided new representations of the world in maps and charts based upon Ptolemaic models and the developing sciences of astronomical observation and triangulation. One of the consequences of the new geography was the erosion of the world view inherited ultimately from Aristotle. Not only did astronomical observation challenge the Greek assumption of a geocentric cosmos, but the navigators' demonstration of the true dimensions of the globe revealed the elemental dominance of water over land across its surface. Attempting to explain this apparently useless water volume in terms of Christian belief in an earth designed by God for the benefit of mankind was one of the stimuli to the revised understanding of the hydrological cycle which we accept today. The classical view that earth rarifies to water which rises to air and is refined by the fire of the sun to fall again to earth presupposed a transfer of ocean waters by subterranean means to the land, for it had long been observed that rivers flowed much more constantly than a variable rainfall could account for. But such transfer could not be reconciled with the areal extent of the oceans revealed by circumnavigation. Only a revised estimation of the significance of oceanic evaporation and the capacity of the earth to store water over long periods could reconcile the oceanic extent with a designed earth (Tuan, 1968). Understanding the modern metaphor of a hydrological cycle and the significance of aquifers and ground water were preconditions for large-scale environmental engineering of the modern world.

The great period of European geographical discovery and mapping new worlds overseas was similarly a period of envisioning and making new worlds at home in Europe. Emerging nation-states like France, Britain and Spain required cartographic and statistical knowledge of their territories to tax and defend them, and smaller territories were obliged to emulate them. A statist landscape began to be sketched out in the form of river regulation as well as forts, bastions, military roads, canals, ports and dockyards. The work called upon the specialized skills of the surveyor, cartographer, military engineer and architect. These 'mathematical practitioners' of sixteenth- and seventeenth-century Europe were members of a broad confraternity which included navigators, instrument makers, estate managers, and naval architects (Taylor, 1967). Their work rested upon analytic thought, experimentation and empirical observation as much as book learning (in their case often through vernacular translation of classical texts) to advance understanding. They were practical men, part of a new professionalism generated outside both traditional guild structures and aristo-cratic, ecclesiastical or university-based life. They were to be found especially in the capital and merchant cities like Venice, London, Amsterdam and Frankfurt. Their influence on the scientific and technological revolutions of early modern Europe cannot be discounted (Vickers, 1984). Their links with Protestantism, especially in its Calvinist forms, were often strong. They were employed by merchant traders, commercial landowners as well as the state for their technical skills, above all those of mathematical calculation. Their interaction with the natural world was thus very different from those of both the traditional landowning aristocracy and the peasantry of medieval Europe. For these men human reason, will and technical abilities mattered more than custom, faith and the vagaries of fortune.

It is from these men that new conceptions of hydrology emerged between the sixteenth and nineteenth centuries: the theory and practice of calculating water volumes and flow and the modern understanding of the hydrological cycle. They were the forefathers of the modern engineer, a trained specialist whose professional status came to be formally recognized in European countries during the eighteenth century. In France, for example, Vauban's great military works for Louis XIV inscribing the first outlines of the state landscape in the Canal du Midi and fortress towns like Neuf Brissac were followed by the establishment of a training school for engineers. The École des Ponts et Chaussées was set up to unite the territory of the *ancien régime* by means of great roads radiating from Paris, crossing marshes, climbing hills and bridging rivers. Their planning depended upon the production of high-quality maps and knowledge of environmental conditions. Revolutionary France intensified the work, establishing the École Polytechnique in 1794 to train applied scientists and engineers, further elevating the status of the engineer as midwife to the Enlightenment and Republican vision of a new age of reason in which applied science would master the environment (Berthaut, 1895).

The French Revolution may be regarded as the decisive historical moment in the establishment of the modern age. The two centuries that have followed have witnessed a trend towards gigantism in human engineering of landscape, not only in Europe but across a world which by the turn of the twentieth century was largely subject to European control. Petts (Chapter 2) points to the pioneering work on the Rhine carried out by J.G. Tulla at the height of the Napoleonic period, noting that by the end of the nineteenth century most of the great

European rivers had been channellized and considerably shortened in total length. Dredging, embankment, channel straightening, elimination of braids and islands, building of groynes and other engineering activities improved navigation, bankside agriculture and public health. More dramatically, feats of European engineering like the Corinth and Kiel canals captured the public imagination and served to enhance the status of the engineer. But these were tiny compared with the interventions in territories subject to European expansion—by the end of the century, the Suez and Panama canals had come to signify to Frenchmen and Britons the natural dominion of imperialist powers and the 'white races' over the environments and peoples of other lands. In Chapter 6 Heffernan reveals even more grandiose dreams: to engineer a second Mediterranean in the desert wastes of the northern Sahara. The simpler technologies employed by indigenous communities of colonial territories were regarded as primitive by comparison with the visionary engineering of their European masters. European engineers, whose skills had not only pushed the arteries of European trade across the vastnesses of Asia, Africa, Australia and the Americas but had also secured the health of Europe's great cities by purifying their drinking water, came to be seen as the architects of a brave new world (Goubert, 1989). Their mode of thought was characteristically rational and calculating, regarded increasingly as capable of applying to the chaotic world of human affairs the same reason and objectivity that accounted for their success in controlling the natural world. Thus engineers dominated the new profession of city manager in the United States at the turn of the twentieth century, concerned not only with planning the physical environment of the city, but equally with its social order (White, 1927). Social engineering and domestic science, both late nineteenth-century concepts, indicate the penetration of the rational mode of applied science as the paradigm for human control into all the environments of human life.

In fact engineering, praised for its practicality, could be as speculative as any other sphere of human thought. In the opening years of the twentieth century the future was often conceived precisely in engineering terms, and engineers like Thomas Edison were the heroes of the modern age (Pursell, 1969). Jules Verne's fiction, forecasting extended aerial flight, journeys to the centre of the earth and the bottom of the sea, and ever more rapid travel, testifies to a widely shared vision of conquering space and time through engineering. Between 1890 and 1910, for example, the Niagara falls, which had since their discovery been a symbol of nature's own power and sublimity (McKinsey, 1985), became a focus for American utopian imaginings founded upon the human capacity to control the waters of a natural wonder: 'With power unrivaled thy proud flood shall speed/The New World's progress towards Time's perfect day' (quoted in McGreevey, 1987). A 2.5-mile tunnel from the foot of the Falls, constructed between 1890 and 1895, with vertical shafts from the river to giant turbines, allowed the generation of electricity on a wholly new scale. By 1896 Westinghouse had demonstrated how this new energy could be transmitted over long distances, lighting the streets of New York's cities with the power of distant waters. Schemes for model communities at Niagara, even a vast metropolis—*the world city*, totally eliminating the Falls themselves—suggested by the razor manufacturer King Camp Gillette, speak to the grandeur of the engineering vision at the turn of the century. Its arrogance is perhaps best illustrated in Gillette's figure of 'Man Corporate' which shows a male figure posed like an Edwardian pugilist and garbed like classical Atlas holding a tiny globe. No longer does the world weigh upon a man's shoulders, it is held in the palm of his hand.

Names like Gillette and Westinghouse may given the impression that the modernist engineering vision was only of a capitalist landscape. It illuminated equally the dreams of socialists. The greatest of twentieth century mega-projects for controlling the water element have been the work of the state, inspired by socialist imaginings. Indeed, the era of the great dam is coincident with the cultural movement termed 'modernism' in the early twentieth century and dependent upon the same technology of earth moving and concrete construction as the skylines of the modern metropolis. From the 1930s the land empires of the United States and the Soviet Union vied with each other at mid-century to create the most massive interventions into their continental river systems. America's New Deal saw the wholesale transformation of natural environments in the Appalachian valleys of the Tennessee Valley Authority and in the western deserts with the construction of the Grand Coolie and Hoover dams (Allen, 1952). In the USSR Lenin's vision of communism as socialism plus electrification of the whole country came to be realized in part by the great hydro-electric schemes along the Volga, Dnieper, Don and later the Siberian rivers. The goals of these works were social and ideological as much as environmental, pushing new forms of social life onto an incalcitrant nature rather than seeking adjustment to a prevailing natural order. The great dams of mid-century stood as symbols of national pride and competition, signs of the superiority of each of the competing social systems. As such they were projected into the environments of client states in the former colonial territories (Chapter 7), especially in the post-war era of 'universal modernism':

The belief 'in linear progress, absolute truths, and rational planning of ideal social orders' under standardized conditions of knowledge and production was particularly strong. The modernism that resulted was . . . 'positivistic, technocentric and rationalistic' at the same time as it was imposed as the work of an elite avant-garde of planners, artists, architects, critics, and other guardians of high taste. The 'modernization' of European economies proceeded apace, while the whole thrust of international politics and trade was justified as bringing a benevolent and progressive 'modernization' to a backward third world. (Harvey, 1989: 35)

The 1960s, now regarded as the watershed decade of modernism, was equally the decade of the great Third World dam and river regulation project. It was the decade of Kariba and Aswan, and of similar mega-structural projects in Mexico, Colombia, Ghana, Mozambique and India as well as in the wilderness regions of Canada and eastern Siberia. Engineering control of water would, it was argued, act as the mechanism for a great leap forward into the industrial future for developing countries. As in Europe and America, the engineer was to be the handmaiden of progress. Ignore the centuries of close adjustment of local peoples and their cultures to their environments, bury ancient communities and practices beneath the impounded waters of progress. After all, had not one of the fathers of Modernism told us that history was bunk? The analytic mode of engineering thought separated such 'soft' issues from the hard 'facts' of hydrological management and subordinated them to both futurist visions and technical competence. The costs and benefits of such schemes were conceived and calculated by the same methods as the volumes and velocities of water flows and the forces to be equilibriated in dam construction (Chapter 10).

Modes of discourse and water engineering in the post-industrial world

However caricatured, it is this conception of environmental problems as tractable to disinterested economic evaluation and technical solution alone that has come increasingly to be challenged in the past two decades. Indicative of change is the reduction in scale and sometimes the collapse of mega-schemes of hydro-engineering since 1970. The history of the James River project in Quebec (Chapter 9), and the abandoning of the Gabčikovo–Nagymaros scheme on the Danube (Chapter 11) provide examples within the First World. In the Third World, although a number of large schemes are still under construction, there is increasing scepticism of landscape engineering on the heroic scale. Many of the completed schemes have failed to deliver their promised benefits while burdening their countries with vast debts, unusable electrical power and adverse environmental consequences. Slow-moving irrigation water breeds the snails which cause schistosomiasis, a chronic debilitating blood disease, while fast-flowing regulated rivers have offered improved breeding conditions for the Onchocerciasis fly, threatening river blindness. Engineers themselves, involved in the poorer countries of the world, see the future today more in terms of 'alternative' technologies sensitive to local traditions and capable of being handled by mere mortals rather than 'corporate man'. It is a vision that fits more closely to images of sustainable living on one earth than to the globe as a plaything in the hands of an engineering Prometheus.

As is pointed out in the concluding chapter, the shift in attitudes away from the mega-project has yet fully to manifest itself in the scale of works actually in progress. But there is growing practical recognition of the magnitude and interlocking nature of long-term social and environmental problems associated with large-scale intervention. This is part of a broader change in consciousness. Recognition of the benefits of ecological and cultural diversity and acknowledgement of the integrity of 'otherness' are world-wide phenomena. Weakened confidence in technical solutions to social and environmental relations also signals a broad rethinking associated by some with the end of modernism. No longer are Western forms of historical change regarded as secure models for other cultures and regions. Indeed, we are now rewriting our own history in ways which challenge the heroic, progressive story we have inherited. The favoured term for the new way of conceiving the hydro-environment and its management is 'holism'. Holism, at least in environmental terms, is beset by contradictions, practical and conceptual. It requires that we think large-scale: a major river is a large geographical phenomenon, but it is difficult simultaneously to manage this scale while remaining sensitive to the local character of the consequences of intervention. Is a 'holistic' approach achieved simply by aggregating the specialisms of the widest selection of interested parties, or does it imply new ways of conceptualizing? Both constituting the object and devising practical ways of intervening are rendered problematic by this term. It is by no means easy to replace the unitary modernist vision with an equally coherent post-modern one.

In part the problem presents itself as one of language, or better, of discourse. We may all recognize the interconnectedness of human lives and the non-human worlds in which they are lived, but the ways in which we conceptualize these worlds and the languages with which we describe and explain their workings are not always congruent. In geography, the problem of finding a common discourse between its natural and social science wings has long been a besetting problem. It is not one that can be resolved by a technical solution—for example, by agreeing to a specific set of concepts or methodology—for we frequently mean different things by the same words. Indeed, the very syntax of our arguments reflects characteristically diverse ways of thinking about the world. In this collection of papers physical and human geographers speak with their own voices about similar issues. Common concerns are apparent—they have been signalled in this essay and are taken up again in the closing chapter. But differences between the modes of apprehension and the languages of communication are still apparent and we have no wish to mask them. Even the title world *landscape* is unstable between discourses: for students of the physical environment landscape is a concrete object of study, the integrated ensemble of landforms yielded by earth-surface physical processes; human geographers see landscape as a historically and socially constituted way of signifying environmental relations whose connections with concrete environmental facts are complex and problematic. Similar differences could be indicated in the ways the other two terms—water and engineering—are deployed.

In the past we might have worried about this lack of uniformity in conceptual definition and language. Western science and technology were rooted in philosophical foundationalism, the belief in a concrete reality distinct from mind, capable of unambiguous definition and description in a language transparent to its facts. Today we are less sure of these claims. Rather we support the notion of parallel discourses, each of which yields its appropriate truth, or refraction of truth, but which cannot be subordinated to a meta-language generating a single theory. As these essays demonstrate, the freedom implied by such acceptance of difference does not yield mutual incomprehension but rather enriches our understanding of complex and contextual problems. But, alongside two cheers for the collapse of rigid theoretical and methodological demarcation lines, we introduce a cautionary note. While letting a thousand flowers bloom in the academy may be liberating, the co-ordinated vision required for practical management of engineered landscapes has not lessened, and co-ordination in the field may be less tolerant of difference than in the printed text. When practical decisions are needed open debate can rapidly yield place to authoritarian rule. In this respect the link between water management and power remains unbroken, and the need for visionary engineering is still with us.

References

Allen, F. (1952) *The Big Change: America Transforms Itself, 1900–1950*, New York, Harper & Bros.

Bachelard, G. (1942) *L'Eau et les rêves. Essai sur l'imagination de la matière*, Paris, Jose Corti.

Berthaut, C. (1895) *Les Ingenieurs-géographes militaires 1624–1854*, 2 vols, Paris, Imprimerie du Service Géographique.

Dardel, E. (1952) *L'Homme et la Terre: Nature de la realité géographique*, Paris, Presses Universitaires de France.

Goubert, J.-P. (1989) *The Conquest of Water: The Advent of Health in the Industrial Age*, London, Polity Press.

Harvey, D. (1989) *The Condition of Postmodernity*, Oxford, Basil Blackwell.

McGreevey, P. (1987) 'Imagining the future at Niagara Falls', *Annals, Association of American Geographers*, 77(1), 48–62.

McKinsey, E. (1985) *Niagara Falls: Icon of the American Sublime*, Cambridge, Cambridge University Press.

Pursell, C.W., ed. (1969) *Readings in Technology and American Life*, London, Oxford University Press.

Taylor, E.G.R. (1967) *The Mathematical Practitioners of Tudor and Stuart England*, Cambridge, Cambridge University Press.

Tuan, Yi-Fu (1968) *The Hydrological Cycle and the Wisdom of God: A Theme in Geoteleology*, University of Toronto Press.

Vickers, B., ed., (1984) *Occult and Scientific Mentalities in the Renaissance*, Cambridge, Cambridge University Press.

White, L.D. (1927) *The City Manager*, Chicago, University of Chicago Press.

Wittfogel, K.A. (1956) 'The hydraulic civilizations' in W.L. Thomas, Jr., ed., *Man's Role in Changing the Face of the Earth*, Chicago, University of Chicago Press, pp. 152–64.

CHAPTER 2

Forested river corridors: a lost resource
Geoff Petts

River corridors are dominant features of landscapes. Once characterized by broad seasonally-inundated floodplain ecotones up to 10 km wide (Petts *et al.*, 1989), the corridors of large rivers throughout the mid-latitudes have been confined to a single, relatively straight, channel with narrow riparian zones by a sequence of engineering works over the past 200 years. Both the structural and functional characteristics of river valley landscapes have been drastically altered. Petts (1984) and Brookes (1988) review the wide-ranging environmental effects of river impoundment and channelization, respectively, but neither gives due regard to the once extensive ecotones that formed transitional zones between the terrestrial and aquatic systems. The importance of these dynamic land–water boundaries, for both nature conservation and river management, has been the focus of recent attention (Naiman and Decamps, in press). Dister *et al.* (1990) conclude that a newly oriented policy for developing floodplains is needed to reverse the drastic reduction of biological communities that has occurred over the past two centuries and to provide for the increasing demands of society for recreation, amenity, and nature conservation. This chapter attempts to recon-struct the characteristics of 'natural' land–water ecotones within mid-latitude river corridors, as the basis for subsequent evaluation of historic changes and assessment of the potential values of landscape restoration schemes.

River corridors of mid-latitudes

The rivers of the northern mid-latitudes (about 35–55°N) have evolved in response to palaeogeographic changes since the Devensian glacial maximum (Starkel, 1987), about 20,000 years ago. Documentary evidence indicates that the corridors of most large alluvial rivers (Figure 2.1) were once forested. In Europe, such alluvial forests have been described for the Danube (Karpati and Karpati, 1958), Rhine (Carbiener, 1983; Dister *et al.*, 1990), Rhône (Pautou and Decamps, 1985) and Garonne (Decamps *et al.*, 1988) rivers (see, for example, Figure 2.2). In the conterminous United States, riparian forests once covered 275,000 km² (Swift, 1984). Written and photographic documentation from

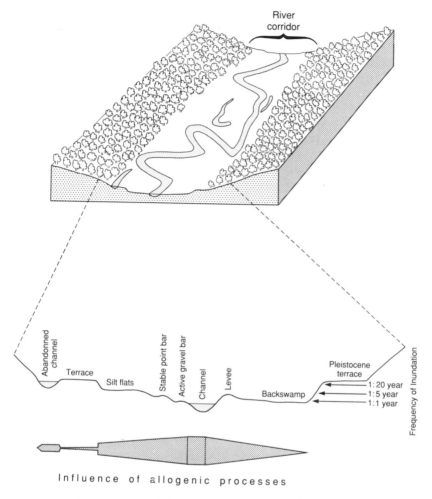

Figure 2.1 General characteristics of natural alluvial corridors. Along large European rivers these were typically up to 10 km wide.

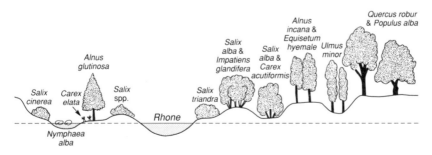

Figure 2.2 Generalized cross-section across the Rhône alluvial corridor, France. (Based on Pautou and Decamps, 1985)

explorers and settlers demonstrates that the floodplain of the Lower Rio Grande, for example, was densely forested (Engel-Wilson and Ohmart, 1978). Thompson (1961) used similar evidence to describe the pristine forest of the Sacramento River corridor which was once 6–8 km wide.

Structure of forested river corridors

Remnants of the once extensive natural forest of the southern Mississippi alluvial plain are characterized by maples (*Acer* spp.), ashes (*Fraxinus* spp.), elms (*Ulmus* spp.) and oaks (*Quercus* spp.) (Robertson *et al.*, 1978). Typically, such alluvial forests display a general lateral zonation, reflecting the transition from semi-aquatic to terrestrial environments. Topography is very important. Slight differences affect the duration of inundation and waterlogging as well as vegetation species composition and distribution. For the River Rhône, Pautou and Decamps (1985) defined three zones: the lowest zone of grasses (Gramineae) and willows (*Salix* spp.); an intermediate willow zone; and a higher-level hardwood zone characterized by elms, ashes, poplars (*Populus* spp.), oaks and maples.

Lateral water flow is an important force in organizing and regulating the function of forests and wetlands within river corridors. Areas lacking the subsidy of lateral water flow develop different functional and structural attributes from those where such a subsidy exists. Inundation is important for maintaining moisture levels, transporting sediments, carrying a nutrient subsidy, imparting hydraulic stresses, and dispersing seeds. However, the rate of lateral channel erosion and deposition, and frequency of avulsion or cutoff are important also, creating disturbance patches and rejuvenating successions related to hydrological status.

Hydrological controls on resource patches

Alluvial forests have a high productivity related to the maintenance of critical soil moisture levels during the growing season; higher or lower moisture values inhibit growth (Gill, 1970). The significance of flooding to maintain adequate growth regeneration has been described, for example, for cypress (*Taxodium distichum*) wetlands (Mitsch *et al.*, 1979; Mitsch and Ewel, 1979; and Brown, 1981). The variable tolerance to flooding of individuals within a species suggests the development of distinct populations with either genotypic or phenotypic differences (Gill, 1970). Strategies for adapting to extremes in both moisture and nutrient availability may be common in riparian woodlands. Inputs of nutrients or nutrient-laden sediments in flood waters during the non-growing season may stimulate growth once the flood has receded. However, the role of the soil may relate to chemical changes consequent upon waterlogging. Changes in pH and oxygen concentrations accompanying water-level changes may affect the

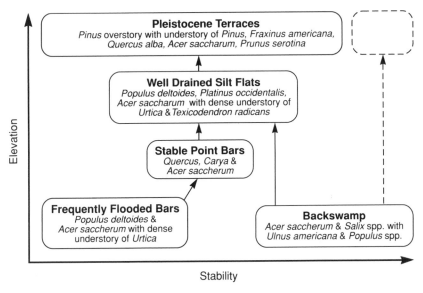

Figure 2.3 Dominant resource patches along rivers in northeast USA. (Based on Morris *et al.*, 1978)

availability of nitrogen, phosphorous and other nutrients, notably iron, manganese and copper.

Resource patches are defined not only by the proportion of the time a site is inundated by flood water but also by the permeability of the soils. Floodplains are composite landforms, with patches of different age and/or sediment type (Lewin, 1978; Petts and Foster, 1985). Trescevskij (1966) reported two distinct patches within the Volga–Don floodplain subject to 30–60 days' spring/summer flooding: clay loam patches with *Populus alba*, *P. deltoides* and *P. balsamifera*, and sandy-silt patches with *P. nigra* and *Acer negundo*. For rivers in northeast USA, Morris *et al.* (1978) describe a river corridor with five resource patches (Figure 2.3), reflecting variations in elevation, stability and sediment type.

Similar distributions are apparent within European river corridors. Along the French upper Rhône, for example, community distribution relates to an allogenic succession influenced by changes of topography and permeability determined by fluvial processes. The succession, from pioneer community on newly-formed alluvial bars to 'climax' woodland on the highest and older parts of the floodplain, relates to floodplain sedimentation (at less than $5\,\mathrm{cm}\,\mathrm{yr}^{-1}$). Raising the land level reduces the frequency of inundation, effectively lowers the water-table, and induces biogeochemical changes within the soil. The succession requires a period of about 40 years. The 'climax' stage has a four-layer structure with a diverse shrub understory and herbaceous ground cover beneath the ash–oak–elm–poplar–willow canopy.

Hydraulic disturbance patches

It has long been established that the diversity of the alluvial plain is related to the regular and repeated rejuvenation of successions associated with channel erosion and deposition. Fluvial erosion causing trees to fall into the river exposing a patch interior, and rejuvenating the 'edge', is important. Over time channel migration destroys large areas of floodplain and creates new ones. The mobility of the river channel is reflected in the age structure of a floodplain (Everitt, 1968) and its biological diversity (Amoros *et al.*, 1987). In rapidly shifting braided channel systems, frequent rejuvenation inhibits long plant successions. Thus, in a braided section of the River Rhône, the riparian zone is dominated by pioneer populations of *Melilotus alba*, *Epilobium dodonaei* and shrubs of *Salix eleagnes*, *S. purpurca*, *S. daphnoides* and *Populus nigra* with *Acer pseudoplatanus* on the floodplain margins (Roux *et al.*, 1989). In less geomorphologically active reaches, hardwood forests develop (see Figure 2.6) with *Fraxinus excelsior*, *Quercus robur* and *Ulmus minor*, but *Alnus glutinosa* persists around abandoned and infilled channels.

River corridor woodland

The evidence demonstrates that wooded alluvial corridors, with seasonally flooded marshlands and a succession of oxbow lakes formed by channel cutoffs, once characterized the 'natural' landscapes of the mid-latitude forest, prairie and semi-arid zones. Within the water–land ecotone, biota are adapted to more or less regular 'pulses' (Gill, 1971) that may occur at short (less than one-year), moderate (one- to ten-year) and long intervals, and their optimum functions depend on them (Naiman *et al.*, in press). In many countries, technological advances leading to land-drainage, dam-building and channelization have drastically altered the hydrological and hydraulic processes necessary to sustain the land–water ecotone.

Human impacts on river corridors

on ground so flat and marshy, that at certain seasons of the year it is inundated to the house-tops, lies a breeding place of fever, ague, and death,
. . . a dismal swamp, . . . teeming with rank, unwholesome vegetation,
. . . an ugly sepulchre, a grave uncheered by any gleam of promise;
. . . a place without one single quality to commend it.

Thus Dickens (cited in Stevens *et al.*, 1975) described the Mississippi–Ohio river confluence at Cairo in 1842. Eleven years later, Ellett (1853: 303–4) wrote:

The banks of the Ohio and Mississippi, now broken by the current and lined with fallen trees, ready to be sweipt by the next freshet into the channel, there to form dangerous snags, may yet, in the course of a very few years, be cultivated and adorned down to the water's edge. In the opinion of the writer, the grass will hereafter grow luxuriantly along the caving banks; all material fluctuations of the waters will be prevented, and the level of the river's surface will become nearly stationary. Grounds, which are now frequently inundated and valueless, will be tilled and subdued; sandbars will be permanently covered, and, under a uniform regimen of the stream, will probably cease to be produced. The channels will become stationary . . . The Ohio first, and ultimately the Missouri and Mississippi, will be made to flow forever with a constant, deep, and limpid stream.

To achieve this objective, Ellett proposed the integrated development of 'great artificial reservoirs', channel straightening and enlargement, bank protection and embanking. The extracts from Dickens and Ellett illustrate the general attitude to floodplains in the nineteenth century, the period during which most alluvial corridors throughout Europe and the USA where drastically altered, to the detriment of the natural resources. Natural river corridors were seen to lack economic value; and present hazards to navigation and human health. In England, for example, levels of mortality three or four times higher than in the healthiest communities, characterized low-lying parishes bordering the River Thames due to plasmodium maleria transmitted by anopheline mosquitos (Dobson, 1980).

Europe

Throughout Europe, floodplain deforestation began about 2500–1000 BP (Wiltshire and Moore, 1983) and although much of the lowlands had experienced a long history of farming by Roman times some riparian forests remained uncleared along large rivers until the mid-eighteenth century. For example, along the lower Rhine, large woods with beaver (*Castor*) were present at this time (Van Urk and Smit, 1989). By 1750, the art of improving rivers for navigation by constructing pound locks—a product of the Italian Rennaissance—making artificial channels, and using stone dikes and groynes was well established. Rapid advances in hydraulics provided a new theoretical basis for river engineering and a platform for the technological developments necessary to control major rivers. Increased navigation during the eighteenth century and canal engineering led to the clearance of riparian vegetation to create towpaths.

The channelization of the braided Alsatian section of the Rhine, initiated in 1817 by Johan Gottfied Tulla, began the creation of truly 'engineered' river corridors. His often quoted statement that 'As a rule, no stream or river needs more than one bed!' became general policy for hydraulic engineers. The regulation of the River Theisz (Tisza), beginning in 1845, drained 12.5×10^6 ha of floodplain marsh and shortened the river course by 340 km. Major draining works were complete on most European rivers by 1880 and these were supplemented by systematic and regular dredging. Channelization has continued throughout the twentieth century. Along the Garonne through Toulouse the shoreline length has been reduced from 11.4 km to 7.2 km (Decamps *et al.*,

1989). Within the Belgian Meuse, the number of islands has been reduced from 56 to 25, and 96 per cent of the bank is artificial (Micha and Borlee 1989). River regulation by dams has further contributed to the alteration of river corridors by regulating river flows (Petts, 1984), thereby reducing or eliminating the water, silt, organic matter and nutrient subsidies to the ecotone. Dam-building technology was well established by the end of the eighteenth century. In a global context, Europe experienced a relatively high rate of dam construction until 1880. Activity increased between 1900 and 1940 but the peak was between 1950 and 1970. Many rivers have been converted to chains of run-of-river impoundments. For example, the Rhône between the Genissiat Reservoir and the Mediterranean—a distance of 470 km—is controlled by a series of 20 low-head hydro-power dams.

USA

In the USA, extensive deforestation and other human impacts have been not only more recent but also more dramatic than in Europe. Along the Sacramento River, California, the clearing of the riparian forests was one of the first of a series of actions that drastically modified the landscape during the Anglo-American period, beginning in 1848 (Thompson, 1961). Along the lower Rio Grande, the corridor was deforested between 1850 and 1900 to provide timber for building materials and fuel, grazing land for livestock and land for cultivation. On the Red River, Triska (1984) reports that large timber rafts were cleared between 1830 and 1875, and between 1880 and 1920 over 300,000 snags (downed trees) were removed. Similarly, on a 1600 km reach of the lower Mississippi, 800,000 snags were removed during a 50-year period from 1870 (Sedell et al., 1982).

Riparian woodlands in the contiguous 48 states now occupy less than 120,000 km^2 (Swift, 1984). In many states, riparian vegetation has been reduced in area by more than 80 per cent. Along one 74 km reach of the Gila River, the 40 km^2 cottonwood–willow (*Populus fremontii* and *Salix goodingii*) forest was reduced to 6 km^2 between 1945 and 1975 (Swift, 1984). The area of riparian hardwood forests along the Mississippi in southeast Missouri declined by 96 per cent between 1780 and 1975 as a result of lumbering and drainage for agriculture (Korte and Fredrickson, 1977). By 1977 the riparian woods along the Sacramento River occupied just 1.5 per cent of their former coverage, being restricted to fragments less than 100 m wide (Henke and Stone, 1978). Of the four predominant floodplain forest types (Klopatek et al., 1979), the elm–ash forests have been most severely affected.

Over only 150 years, channelization in the USA has reduced the length of main river by at least 320,000 km—about 5 per cent (Swift, 1984). By 1973, almost the entire middle Mississippi River (see Figure 2.4) was lined with artificial levees, 196 km of bankline revetment to prevent bank erosion, and over 800 dikes, having a total length of 146 km, project out from the river banks into the river to

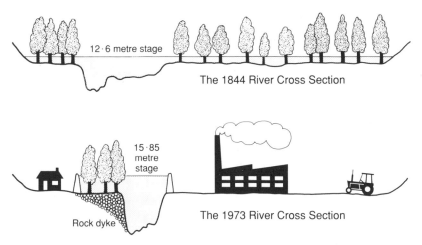

Figure 2.4 Generalized cross-section across the Middle Mississippi River, USA, for a discharge of 36,790 m³ s⁻¹. (Based on Henke and Stone, 1978)

maintain a navigable channel (Stevens *et al.*, 1975).

Large reservoirs proliferated in the USA during the first half of the twentieth century. During the 1930s the construction of large dams and the grouping of multipurpose projects within entire river basins became New Deal symbols of the efficient application of engineering techniques to water management. The Hoover Dam on the Colorado, 221 m high, and its reservoir, Lake Mead, which contains 27×10^9 m³ of water, were symbols of American technological prowess, an approach later also adopted competitively by other countries. The fully integrated development of entire basins was first implemented for the Tennessee Valley. Today, large reservoirs have inundated more than 25,000 km of main river (Swift, 1984) and the extent of smaller impoundments is unknown.

Problems consequent on human intervention

Intensification of engineering works along many European valleys was in response to increasing flooding often believed to have been caused by upland deforestation and land drainage (Hermann *et al.*, 1890). During the nineteenth century, these human impacts may have been exaccerbated by natural climatic fluctuations, notably the humid phases of 1840–50 and 1880–5 (Probst, 1989). In the USA an observed increase in flood frequency and magnitudes during the early nineteenth century was attributed to the extension of cultivated lands, artifical levees, and channel cutoffs along the rivers (Ellett, 1853). On the middle Mississippi at St Louis, the highest recorded flood (36,000 m³s⁻¹) occurred in 1844. However, as pointed out by Strauser and Long (1976), clearance of snags (fallen trees) and riparian vegetation probably contributed to channel widening (from 1,110 m in 1821 to 1,630 m in 1888) and increased braiding (Stevens *et al.*,

1975). These channel changes may also have contributed to raised flood levels. Early river engineering works were partly responsible for the cycle of increasing intensity of intervention. Sediment problems and channel changes induced by engineering works and land-use changes throughout the catchments, demanded further engineering controls. At a small scale, the use of flash locks caused scouring of the channel bed immediately below the weir; the eroded sediment formed a bar below the scour hole and reduced water depths. Similar problems were associated with narrow-arched bridges (Fortune, 1988). Prior to the late nineteenth century channelization was undertaken to force the river to erode a new, uniform and straight bed. However, in most cases channel-bed erosion went far beyond that intended. In Europe, Tulla had planned to retain floodplains as flood storage areas for high-magnitude events (Dister *et al.*, 1990), indicating that the magnitude of incision consequent upon straightening was not anticipated. There are many recent examples of channelization having led to subsequent incision within and upstream of the channelized reach (Brookes, 1988).

Dams and gravel extraction often caused channel incision downstream. Bed degradation of more than 1 m is not uncommon below dams and a considerable length of river can be affected (Petts, 1984). Downcutting of the channel can be equally dramatic below gravel workings (Lagasse *et al.*, 1988). Since 1850, low water levels have fallen by about 1 m on the lower Rhine due to dredging (Van Urk and Smit, 1989) and by 1.8 m at Worms in West Germany (Dister *et al.*, 1990). However, often degradation has resulted from the complex interaction of several factors. Along the Arve River, France, hillslope reforestation, the introduction of check weirs to reduce bedload transport, creation of reservoirs for water supply and hydro-power, and gravel extraction for the aggregate industry have all contributed to a narrowing of the active alluvial tract from 120 m to 50 m, and bed incision by up to 10 m, between 1970 and 1984 (Piery, 1987). Channel degradation not only reduces the frequency of floodplain inundation but also lowers groundwater levels in the alluvial aquifer so that large areas of floodplain can be drained.

Ecological changes

The hydrological and geomorphological characteristics of mid-latitude rivers have changed dramatically since 1850 and it is likely that in Europe at least anthropogenic changes may have been significant over a longer time scale (Petts *et al.*, 1989). In addition to the direct changes resulting from deforestation and land drainage, woodland corridors have been altered indirectly by river regulation. Drainage of the alluvial plain and its isolation from the main river have had wide-ranging effects on the aquatic, semi-aquatic and terrestrial biotopes of river corridors. Lowering groundwater levels and the elimination of the flood season have caused ecological change usually to a less diverse, and certainly less dynamic, system (Bravard *et al.*, 1986; Amoros *et al.*, 1987).

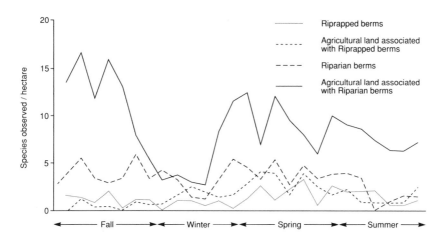

Figure 2.5   Numbers of bird species recorded in different habitats along the Sacramento River, USA. (Based on Pautou and Decamps, 1985)

The direct and indirect changes of riparian woods have had dramatic effects on wildlife (Figure 2.5). Along the Sacramento River, deforested areas have 93 per cent fewer birds and 72 per cent fewer species than forested ones (Henke and Stone, 1978). Insectivorous species often suffer severe losses (Conine *et al.*, 1978). The loss of gravel bars has eliminated nesting sites for Little Tern (*Sterna albifrons*) and Stone Curlew (*Burhinus oedicnemus*) on the upper Rhine (Dister *et al.*, 1990). Several species, such as Goossanders (*Mergus merganser*) and Shoveler duck (*Anas clupeata*) have seriously declined in number. In England and Wales, a decline of otter (*Lutra lutra*) populations has been related to the clearance of bankside trees, especially ash (*Fraxinus*) and sycamore (*Acer*) (Macdonald *et al.*, 1978; Macdonald and Mason, 1982).

During the nineteenth century the Red River in Louisiana was characterized a range of aquatic habitats created by large organic debris (Triska, 1984). Debris jams of trunks up to 36 m long and 1.75 m diameter reduced the channel width from 185 m to 40 m, inducing bed aggradation of up to 7 m in places, and creating backswamp lakes, many over 30 km in length. Typically, data indicate that one downed tree may have occurred as frequently as every 3 m of river bank (Sedell and Froggatt, 1984).

Removal of riparian vegetation and fallen trees not only reduces the diversity of marginal habitats (Shields and Nunally, 1984). The consequent increase in aquatic primary production causes a shift in the energy base of the lotic systems from allochthonous organic matter—a combination of coniferous and deciduous litter—to algae and macróphytes. Moreover, total carbon inputs are reduced. Hesse *et al.* (1987) reported an 80 per cent reduction of organic carbon in the Missouri during the period 1892–1982 and little organic debris is now found in sediments of the lower Rhine (Van Urk and Smit, 1989).

Changes in organic matter transport are of particular significance to biota, for example by altering the distribution of invertebrate feeding groups (Vanote *et al.*, 1980). However, the increased water temperatures and channel substrate characteristics also impact biota. Temperature changes are particularly significant for trout (Barton *et al.*, 1978), not least because lengthening of the warm period increases competition for habitat, especially with cyprinid fishes.

However, the isolation of backwater and floodplain areas from the main channel probably has impacted fish stocks most severely (Welcomme, 1979; Petts, 1984; Lelek, 1989) by eliminating spawning habitats and refuges during periods of lethal and/or critical water quality. Fish species that spawn on gravel bars and on inundated floodplains have been severely affected, for example, in the Dnieper (Zalumi, 1970) and Volga (Eliseev and Chikova, 1974). Competition from species with less specific spawning substrate requirements is also important. On the Rhine, for example, Lelek (1889) noted that the decline of the artisanal fishery coincided with nineteenth-century river channelisation works.

Value of wooded river corridors

The rapidity with which deforestation and river regulation took place during the eighteenth and nineteenth centuries reflected a broader Western modernism, with its belief in controlling environments perceived to have zero economic value. Such works indicate a desire to create positive economic values from the 'wastelands'—more agricultural land to feed the growing populations and controlled routeways for navigation—and to minimize costs of floods and disease, especially malaria by eliminating mosquito habitats.

The forested and wetland ecotones along natural rivers clearly have a major impact on hydro-systems, influencing hydrology, water quality, primary stream productivity, channel morphology and habitat diversity (Petts, 1990). They also have exceptional value for wildlife conservation and are important for recreation and amenity not least in an age of increasing recognition of wilderness values (Martin and Inglis, 1984). Ten values of natural floodplains can be defined; all except one of these relate to wooded river corridors.

1. Flow regulation is an important function of natural swamps and seasonal floodlands which reduce flood peaks and increase low flows, possibly preventing exceptional 'drought' conditions, in the river downstream. However, high flow resistance causes water levels to be increased in comparison to smooth, straight canalized channels (Knight, 1989). Some forested floodplains create particular problems for flood control—for example, where dense growths of phraetophytes, such as salt cedar (*Tamarix chinensis*), impede flood waters, accelerate sedimentation and trap flood debris (Graf, 1980).

2. Water quality can be significantly regulated by both alluvial forests and floodplain swamps. Swamps are efficient phosphorous sinks (Mitsch, 1978; Sloey *et al.*, 1978) and in one case study, Brown *et al.* (1978) reported that 98 per cent of phosphorous and 90 per cent of nitrogen were removed by vegetation uptake, utilization in food chains, and adsorption to sediments. Riparian woods

are also effective water-quality filters (Yates and Sheridan, 1983; Peterjohn and Correll, 1984; and Pinay and Decamps, 1988) utilizing or transforming 90 per cent of the nitrogen and 80 per cent of the phosphorous in shallow and deep throughflow.

3. Water temperature is often cited as a major factor influencing the distributions of aquatic invertebrates and fish, especially trout (*Salmo* spp.) (see, for example, Gray and Eggington, 1969; Scarnecchia, 1988). Riparian vegetation provides shade, regulating temperature fluctuations (see Barton *et al.*, 1978).

4. The balance between autotrophy and heterotrophy is influenced by riparian vegetation in two ways. First, riparian woods contribute to primary stream productivity through shading which effects both stream temperature and light availability to drive primary production. Second, riparian and floodplain vegetation contributes an important source of organic matter to streams (Brinson, 1976; Edwards and Meyer, 1987a; 1987b). A complex mosaic of coniferous and deciduous overstory, understory, and herbaceous ground cover provides a sequence of different organic matter inputs. Rich and diverse populations of aquatic invertebrates are keyed into the timing and varied quality of this detrital food base (Meehan *et al.*, 1978).

5. Channel morphology is also affected by riparian vegetation. Marginal vegetation stabilizes river banks and channel deposits (Wolman and Gerson, 1979). Gill (1970) reviews the flooding tolerance of woody species including examples, mainly from Europe, recommending the restoration of *Salix* spp. and *Populus* spp. for bank protection. Woody debris can also have an important influence on channel-bed morphology (Keller and Tally, 1979; Keller and Swanson, 1979; Marston, 1982).

6. Aquatic habitat opportunities are created by inputs of organic material, and these are important for biological diversity at both meso and micro scales. Marginal trees, exposed roots and overhanging banks provide important cover. Downed trees sustain habitat diversity along the channel margin and provide sites for nitrogen fixation; oviposition, pupation and emergence of invertebrates; fish refugia and rearing sites for young.

7. Fish production is directly affected by riparian vegetation as organic inputs establish the basic components of the food chain which eventually lead to the fish themselves. Moreover, Welcomme (1979) has demonstrated that most natural floodplain rivers have diverse and abundant fish faunas, giving rise to important fisheries. The life cycle of many riverine fish species depends on access to seasonally inundated wetlands or floodplain lakes, for spawning, rearing juveniles, and so on.

8. Important wildlife habitat is created by the riparian woodlands, especially for birds (Decamps *et al.*, 1988; see also Figure 2.5). Indeed, vegetation and vertebrate surveys (Barclay, 1978) typically indicate that natural river corridors have high numbers of species and high relative abundances. The remnant oak–elm (*Quercus–Ulmus*) forests on the Rhine have especially dense bird populations of 285 breeding pairs per 10 ha (Dister *et al.*, 1990). The distribution, volume, density and vertical stratification of vegetation influences avian species

diversity but open water, swamps, dead standing and fallen trees along forest edges are also very important adding structural complexity to the habitat. Along the Rio Grande, Texas, for example, at least 11 species of amphibians and reptiles, 13 bird species and three mammals are *dependent* upon the riparian habitats for their existence (Schmidly and Ditton, 1978).

Beaver (*Castor canadensis*) in North American rivers make significant contributions to the maintenance of this diverse hydro-system: felled trees create disturbance rejuvenating plant successions and dams increase ponding (Hair *et al.*, 1978). Where beaver have increased after near-extinction at the turn of the century, they have markedly increased water area, the length of the land–water interface, and the width of the ecotone (Naiman and Decamps, in press).

9. Timber from riparian woods, characterized by high productivity, can be of economic value (Purseglove, 1989). Polled trees that are evenly cut to form a crown about 2.5 m above ground level, just beyond the reach of grazing animals, are a traditional resource. Pollard willows, cut on a 7–10 year cycle, are commonly used for firewood and fodder. Willows (*Salix* spp.), aspen (*Populus tremula*) and alder (*Alnus* spp.) provide hardwood pulp for paper mills. 'Withybeds' of *Salix viminalis* were once common in England; willows were cut to ground level each winter to produce willow rods for basket making. Reeds (*Phragmites*) and rushes (*Scirpus*) provide materials for thatching and basket making, and grasses (such as *Phalaris arundinacea*) can be regularly cut for cattle forage. Ash (*Fraxinus*) and oak (*Quercus*) are traditional sources of timber, and, of course, *Salix alba coerulea* is the cricket bat willow!

10. Landscape quality is enhanced by the presence of water (Dearden, 1987). Water surfaces are strongly prospect-oriented, while marginal reeds and rushes can provide striking refuge elements. Riparian woods are important refuges by the very nature of their fabric, providing numerous entry points, concealment from view and shelter (Appleton, 1975). These aesthetic values, together with the outstanding conservation qualities of riparian zones, give them an important, although perhaps economically unquantifiable, value to society.

Prospect

The cardinal rule of riparian ecosystem management is to protect the external forces that regulate the ecosystem. (Brown *et al.*, 1978: 27)

Natural river corridors contain a diverse range of habitats reflecting the mosaic of resource and disturbance patches and the age, or successional stage, of each. This scenario is illustrated in Figure 2.6. The corridor is highly productive and can sustain a considerable biomass as long as the physical forces responsible for the high rate of energy flow and productivity remain intact. In mid-latitudes, the natural river corridors were characterized by seasonally flooded forests; their biological diversity was sustained by the flooding regime, channel migration and associated geomorphic processes.

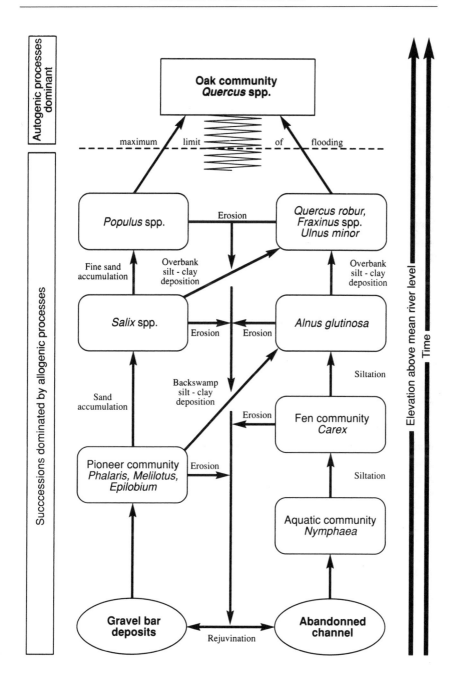

Figure 2.6 Succession of resource and disturbance patches within the Rhône river corridor, France. (Based on Pautou and Decamps, 1985)

Many studies on landscape evaluation have concluded that the degree of naturalness is of universal appeal. However, the concept of naturalness is itself problematic, given the long history of land-use change and water management. For many, neat well-organized engineered landscapes, composed of uniform patches within a homogeneous matrix, are both attractive and natural. This perception of landscape has been influenced by the European tradition of landscape gardening, inherited from seventeenth- and eighteenth-century designers like le Nôtre and Brown. The view of these engineered river corridors as natural landscapes may be a major constraint on the restoration of alluvial forests.

Furthermore, along some rivers restoration of riparian woods may be difficult because of two scientific problems—the inherent change in soil conditions and competition from exotic species. As a consequence, the abandonment of agriculture rarely results in succession to the former, natural, condition. With forest fragmentation, monopolistic species establish, impoverishing the forest flora. On the Rhône, *Ailanthus glandulosa* or *Robina pseudacaria* replace the very diverse 'climax' communities (Pautou and Decamps, 1985). Moreover, following abandonment, autogenic successions are initiated which succeed to alder (*Alnus glutinosa*) woodland after 10–50 years.

In the semi-arid areas of southwest USA, an exotic phraetophyte, salt cedar (*Tamarix chinensis*), introduced in the mid-eighteenth century, has probably spread over 40,000 km² of riparian land (Robinson, 1965), especially along regulated rivers (Williams, 1978), replacing the native cottonwood–willow communities. Although covering a large area, salt cedar woods have a relatively low value for wildlife habitat and recreation (Swift, 1984).

Along the lower Rio Grande, agriculture has declined due to falling discharges, resulting from consumptive uses upstream, and soil salinification reducing productivity. However, the native cottonwood–willow community was unable to recolonize the corridor due to soil changes, lack of annual flooding and seed propagation, reduced moisture levels and changed water quality (Engel-Wilson and Ohmart, 1978). Salt cedar has invaded and now forms monotypic stands with often over 90 per cent ground cover and low relative foliage volume. In comparison with cottonwood–willow forests, the impact on avian populations has been severe: diversities and densities have been reduced, the latter by up to 90 per cent.

Ecotone restoration

Notwithstanding the potential difficulties outlined above, the restoration of land–water ecotones can have a positive affect on landscape. Determination of the minimum and optimum areas for restoration is an area of current research activity. Decamps *et al.* (1988) showed that even a narrow woodland corridor can have considerable benefit for sedentary and migratory birds, not least in providing access routes for new colonizers to island woods on the hillslopes. A riparian wood 20 m wide appears effective in reducing nitrate losses to rivers from intensively cultivated land (Pinay and Decamps, 1988). Recently, Arnold *et al.* (1989) recommended that a restored floodplain should be at least five times the channel width.

For river corridors, 'size' must be supplemented by information on the significance of shape and connectivity, and the interaction between different patches. Along the Sacramento Valley, Henke and Stone (1978) demonstrated that agricultural land associated with woodland buffer zones up to 100 m wide was beneficial for birds, sustaining natural numbers but fewer species. Conine *et al.* (1978) concluded that relatively large densities of riparian species could be maintained if strips of riparian vegetation are restored at 1 km intervals. Furthermore, they suggest that the effects of deforestation and replacement with agricultural land may be mitigated to some degree by creation of forest-edge habitats in conjunction with artificial irrigation or drainage canals, as long as they are lined by weedy margins (see Chapter 5).

However, cosmetic landscaping, such as tree planting, without appropriate management of the hydrological and geomorphological processes, will not lead to sustained river restoration. This is indicated clearly in Figure 26, which shows that within the ecotone, the mosaic of ecological patches is dependent upon allogenic processes and driven by hydrodynamic forces. Removal of hydraulic disturbance, hydrological pulses and the water, sediment and nutrient subsidies, allows succession to a relatively low diversity of autogenic process-dominated patches. Thus, Binder *et al.* (1983), referring to streams in Bavaria, West Germany, recommend the preservation of the natural dynamics of the river corridor, including abandoned channels, as well as the restoration of forests and wetland meadows. Similarly, Dister *et al.* (1990) recommend the restoration of flooding to formerly inundated areas in a programme for restoring the Rhine.

Opportunities in the UK

In the European Community, it is estimated that by the year 2000 the area of agricultural land contributing to surplus production will be 12×10^6 ha (Arnold *et al.*, 1989). Since it is now accepted that the application of zero economic values to natural environments is inappropriate for sustainable land and water management, land–inland water ecotones come to have particular values. With the growing awareness of environmental quality, opportunities will arise for restoring river corridors in the UK. Recent research suggests that greatest benefits result from creating buffer zones at least 20 m wide along water courses, separating intensive agricultural land from riverside pasture including water meadows, and sometimes enclosing abandoned channels or artificial ones. The buffer zones, requiring about 2 ha of land for every kilometre of river bank, should link more extensive woods each of at least 3 ha within the river corridor. These should include willows (*Salix* spp.) and alder (*Alnus glutinosa*) with ash (*Fraxinus excelsior*), sycamore (*Acer pseudoplatanus*), elms (*Ulmus* spp.) and oak

(*Quercus robur*) on higher, drier sites. Major objections to restoring riparian and floodplain woods relate to the possible negative impacts on flood control (Graf, 1980) and to the uncertain hydrological and hydraulic consequences of alternatives to traditional channel designs (Newson, 1986). However, river corridors have many positive values and creative conservation offers opportunities to develop their natural resource potential while mitigating negative effects on flooding.

The largely cosmetic conservation measures of this decade have been beneficial in attracting public interest in river corridors. Research is needed to quantify the controls on ecotones along large rivers and to analyse their physical and biological functions. Questions of patch size, arrangement and connectivity must be addressed and the minimum and optimum process conditions to sustain different patch combinations must be defined. Landscaping and forest management must be integrated with policies for flow regulation and for maintaining geomorphological and hydro-chemical processes if naturally dynamic and diverse river corridors are to be restored on a sustainable basis.

References

Amoros, C., Reygrobellet, A.L., Bravard, J.P. and Pautou, G. (1987) 'A method for applied ecological studies of fluvial hydrosystems', *Regulated Rivers*, 1, 17–36.

Appleton, J. (1975) *The Experience of Landscape*, London, Wiley.

Armstrong, A.C. (1978) *A Digest of Drainage Statistics*, Ministry of Agriculture Fisheries and Food, Field Drainage Technical Report 78/7, London, HMSO.

Arnold, U., Hottges, J and Rouve, G. (1989) 'Removing the straight-jackets from rivers and streams', *German Research*, 1, 22–4.

Barton, D.R., Taylor, W.D. and Biette, R.M. (1978) 'Dimensions of riparian buffer strips required to maintain trout habitat in southern Ontario streams', *North American Journal of Fisheries management*, 5, 364–78.

Barber, K.E. and Coope, G.R. (1987) 'Climatic history of the Severn Valley during the last 18000 years' in K.J. Gregory, J. Lewin and J.B. Thones, eds, *Palaeohydrology in Practice*, Chichester, Wiley, pp. 201–16.

Barber, K.E. and Twigger, S.N. (1987) 'Late Quaternary palaeoecology of the Severn Basin' in: K.J. Gregory, J. Lewin and J.B. Thornes, eds, *Palaeohydrology in Practice*, Chichester, Wiley, pp. 217–50.

Barclay, J. (1978) 'The effects of channelisation on riparian vegetation and wildlife in south central Oklahoma' in R.R. Johnson and J.F. McCormick, eds, *Strategies for Protection and Management of Floodplain Wetlands and Other Riparian Ecosystems*, Washington, DC, US Department of Agriculture, Forest Service, pp. 129–38.

Bilby, R.E. and Likens, G.E. (1980) 'Importance of organic debris dams in the structure and function of stream ecosystems', *Ecology*, 6(5), 1107–13.

Binder, W., Jurging, P. and Karl, J. (1983) 'Natural river engineering—characteristics and limitations', *Garten und Landschaft*, 2, 91–4.

Binder, W. and Grobmaier, W. (1978) 'Bach- und Flussläufe—Ihre Gestalt und Pflege', *Garten und Landschaft*, 1, 25–30.

Bravard, J.P., Amoros, C. and Pautou, G. (1986) 'Impacts of civil engineering works on the succession of communities in a fluvial system: a methodological and predictive approach applied to section of the Upper-Rhône River', *Oikos*, 47, 92–111.

Brinson, M.M. (1976) 'Organic matter losses from four watersheds in the humid tropics', *Limnology and Oceanography*, 21 (4), 572–82.

Brookes, A., Gregory, K.J. and Dawson, H. (1983) 'An assessment of river channelisation in England and Wales', *Science of the Total Environment*, 27, 97–122.

Brookes, A. (1987) 'The distribution and management of channelised streams in Denmark', *Regulated Rivers*, 1, 3–16.

Brookes, A. (1988) *River Channelisation*, Chichester, Wiley.

Brookes, A. (1990) 'Restoration and enhancement of engineered river channels: some European experiences', *Regulated Rivers*, 5, (1); 45–56.

Brown, S. (1981) 'A comparison of the structure, primary productivity, and transpiration of cypress ecosystems in Florida', *Ecological Monographs*, 51, 403–27.

Brown, S., Brinson, M.M. and Lugo, A.E. (1978) 'Structure and function of riparian wetlands' in R.R. Johnson and J.F. McCormick, eds, *Strategies for Protection and Management of Floodplain Wetlands and Other Riparian Ecosystems*, Washington, DC, US Department of Agriculture, Forest Service, pp. 17–31.

Brown, M. and Dinsmore, J.J. (1986) 'Implications of marsh size and isolation for marsh bird management', *Journal of Wildlife Management* 50, 392.

Buckland, P.C. and Edwards, K.J. (1984) 'The longevity of pastoral episodes of clearance activity in pollen diagrams: the role of post-occupation grazing', *Journal of Biogeography*, 11, 243–9.

Carbiener, R. (1983) 'Le Grand Ried central d'Alsace: écologie et évolution d'une zone humide d'origine fluviale rhénane. *Bulletin of Ecology*, 14, 249–77.

Conine, K.H., Anderson, B.W., Ohmart, R.D and Drake, J.F. (1978) 'Responses of riparian species to agricultural habit conversions' in R.R. Johnson and J.F. McCormick, eds, *Strategies for Protection and Management of Floodplain Wetlands and Other Riparian Ecosystems*, Washington, DC, US Department of Agriculture, Forest Service, pp. 248–62.

Darby, H.C. (1983) *The Changing Fenland*, Cambridge, Cambridge University Press.

Dawson, M.R. and Gardiner, V. (1987) 'River terraces: the general model and a palaeohydrological and sedimentological interpretation of the terraces of the lower Severn' in K.J. Gregory, J. Lewin and J.B. Thornes, eds, *Palaeohydrology in Practice*, Chichester, Wiley, pp. 269–306.

Dearden, P. (1987) 'Concensus and a theoretical framework for landscape evaluation', *Journal of Environmental Management*, 34, 267–78.

Decamps, H., Fortune, M. and Gazelle, F. (1989) 'Historical changes of the Garonne River, southern France' in G.E. Petts, H. Moller and A.L. Roux, eds, *Historical Change of Large Alluvial Rivers: Western Europe*, Chichester, Wiley, pp. 249–68.

Decamps, H., Fortune, M., Gazelle, F. and Pautou, G. (1988) 'Historical influence of man on the riparian dynamics of a fluvial landscape', *Landscape Ecology*, 1, 163–73.

Dister, E., Gomer, D., Obrdlik, P., Petermann P. and Scheider E. (1990) 'Water management and ecological perspectives of the upper Rhine's floodplains', *Regulated Rivers*, 5 (1). 1–16.

Dobson, M. (1980) 'Marsh fever—the geography of malaria in England', *Journal of Historical Geography*, 6 (4), 357–89.

Edwards, R.T. and Meyer, J.L. (1987a) 'Metabolism of a sub-tropical low gradient blackwater river', *Freshwater Biology*, 17, 251–63.

Edwards, R.T. and Meyer, J.L. (1987b) 'Bacteria as a food source for black fly larvae in a blackwater river', *Journal of the Benthological Society of North America*, 6, 241–50.

Eliseev, A.L. and Chikova, W.M. (1974) 'Conditions of fish production in the lower reach of the V.I. Lenin Volga hydro-electric station' in B.S. Kuzin, ed. *Biological and Hydrological Factors of Local Movements of Fish in Reservoirs*, New Dehli, Amerind, pp. 193–200.

Ellett, C. (1953) *The Mississippi and Ohio Rivers*, Philadelphia, Lippincott, Grambo and Co.

Engel-Wilson, R.W. and Ohmart, R.D. (1978) 'Floral and attendant faunal changes on the lower Rio Grande between Fort Quitman and Presidio, Texas' in R.R. Johnson and J.F. McCormick, eds, *Strategies for Protection and Management of Floodplain Wetlands and Other Riparian Ecosystems* Washington, DC, US Department of Agriculture, Forest Service, pp. 139–47.

Everitt, B.L. (1968) 'Use of the cottonwood in an investigation of the recent history of a floodplain', *American Journal of Science*, 266, 417–39.

Fisher, S.G. and Likens, G.E. (1973) 'Energy flow in Bear Brook, New Hampshire: an integrative approach to stream ecosystem metabolism', *Ecological Monographs*, 43, 421–39.

Forman, R.T.T. and Godron, M. (1981) 'Patterns and structural components for a landscape ecology', *Bioscience*, 31, 733–40.

Fortune, M. (1988) 'Historical changes of a large river in an urban area: the Garonne River, Toulouse, France', *Regulated Rivers*, 2 (2) 179–86.

Gill, C.J. (1970) 'The flooding tolerance of woody species—a review', *Forestry Abstracts*, 671–88.

Gill, D. (1971) 'Damming the MacKenzie: a theoretical assessment of the long-term influence of river impoundment on the ecology of the MacKenzie River Delta' in: *Proceedings of the Peace-Athabaska Delta Symposium*, Water Resources Centre, University of Alberta, Edmonton, pp. 204–22.

Graf, W.L. (1980) 'Riparian management: a flood control perspective', *Journal of Soil and Water Conservation*, July–August, 158–61.

Gray, J.K.A. and Eggington, J.M. (1969) 'Effect of woodland clearance on stream temperature, *Journal of the Fisheries Research Board, Canada*, 26, 399–403.

Green, F.H.W. (1980) 'Current field drainage in northern and western Europe', *Journal of Environmental Management*, 10, 149–53.

Gregory, K.J. and Lewin, J. (1987) 'Palaeohydrological synthesis and applications' in K.J. Gregory, J. Lewin and J.B. Thornes, eds, *Palaeohydrology in Practice*, Chichester, Wiley, pp. 341–56.

Hair, J.D., Hepp, G.T., Luckett, L.M., Reese, K.P. and Woodward, D.K. (1978) 'Beaver pond ecosystems and their relationships to multi-use natural resource management' in R.R. Johnson and J.F. McCormick, eds, *Strategies for Protection and Management of Floodplain Wetlands and Other Riparian Ecosystems*, Washington, DC, US Department of Agriculture, Forest Service, pp 80–92.

Henke, M. and Stone, C.P. (1978) 'Value of riparian vegetation to avian populations along the Sacramento river system' in R.R. Johnson and J.F. McCormick, eds, *Strategies for Protection and Management of Floodplain Wetlands and Other Riparian Ecosystems*, Washington, DC, US Department of Agriculture, Forest Service, pp. 228–35.

Hermann, Klein J. and Thome (1890) *Land, Sea and Sky* (translated by J. Minshull), London, Ward, Lock and Co.

Hesse, L.W., Hergenrader, G.L., Lewis, H.S., Reetz, S.D. and Schlesinger, A.B. (1982).

The Middle Missouri River The Missouri River Study Group, Norfolk, NE, USA.

Karpati, J. and Karpati, V. (1958) 'The periodic rhythm of the floodplain forests in the flood area of the Danube between Vac and Budapest', *Act. Bot. Acad, Sci. Hungar.*, 8, 59–91.

Keller, E.A. and Swanson, F.J. (1979) 'Effects of large organic debris on channel form and fluvial process', *Earth Surface Processes*, 4 (4) 361–80.

Keller, E.A. and Tally, T. (1979) 'Effects of large organic debris on channel form and fluvial processes in the coastal Redwood environment' in D.D. Rhodes and G.P. Williams, eds, *Adjustments of the Fluvial System*, Dubuque, I.A., Kendall-Hunt, pp. 169–97.

Knight, D.W. (1989) 'Hydraulics of flood channels' in K. Bevan and P. Carling, *Floods*, Chichester, Wiley, pp. 83–106.

Korte, P.A. and Fredrickson, L.H. (1977) 'Loss of Missouri's lowland hardwood ecosystem', *Trans. N. Amer. Wildl. Nat. Resour. Conf.*, 42, 31–41.

Klopatek, J.M., Olson, R.J., Emerson, C.J. and Jones, J.L. (1979) 'Land use conflicts with natural vegetation in the United States', *Environmental Conservation*, 6 (3), 192–200.

Lagasse, P.F., Winkley, B.R. and Simons, D.B. (1980) Impact of gravel mining on river system stability, *Journal of the Waterways Port Coastal and Ocean Division ASCE*, 106, 389–404.

Leach, R. and Leach, P. (1982) 'Roman town and countryside' in A.M. Aston and I. Burrow, eds, *The Archaeology of Somerset. A review to 1500 AD*, Taunton, Somerset County Council, pp. 69–71.

Legendre, L. and Demers, S. (1984) 'Towards dynamic biological oceanography and limnology', *Canadian Journal of Fisheries and Aquatic Sciences*, 41: 2–19.

Lelek, A. (1989) 'The Rhine and some of its tributaries under human impact in the last two centuries', *Canadian Special Publication of Fisheries and Aquatic Sciences*, 106, 469–87.

Lewin, J. (1978) 'Floodplain geomorphology', *Progress in Physical Geography*, 2 (3), 408–37.

Lewis, G. and Williams, G. (1984) *Rivers and Wildlife Handbook*, Royal Society for the Protection of Birds, Conservation Planning Department, Royal Society for Nature Conservation.

Lovejoy, R.E. and Oren, D.C. (1978) 'The minimum critical size of ecosystems' in R.L. Burgess and D.M. Sharpe, *Forest Island Dynamics in Man-dominated Landscapes, Ecological Studies*, 41, Springer-Verlag, pp. 7–12.

Macdonald, S.M., Mason, C.F. and Coghill, I.S. (1978) 'The otter and its conservation in the River Teme catchment', *Journal of Applied Ecology*, 15, 373–84.

Macdonald, S.M. and Mason, C.F. (1982) 'Some factors influencing the distribution of otters (*Lutra lutra*)', *Mammal Reviews*, 13, 1–10.

Marston, R.A. (1982) 'The geomorphic significance of log steps in forest streams', *Annals of the Association of American Geographers*, 72, 99–108.

Martin, V. and Inglis, M. (1984) *Wilderness: the Way Ahead*, Forres, Findorn Press.

Meehan, W.R., Swanson, F.J., and Sedell, J.R. (1978) 'Influences of riparian vegetation on aquatic ecosystems with particular reference to salmonid fishes and their food supply' in R.R. Johnson and D.A. Jones, eds, *Importance, Preservation and Management of Riparian habitat*, Washington, DC, USDA Forest Service, Technical Report RM–43, pp. 137–45.

Micha, J.-C. and Borlee, A.-C. (1989) 'Recent historical changes of the Belgian Meuse' in G.E. Petts, H. Moller and A.L. Roux, eds, *Historical Change of Large Alluvial Rivers: Western Europe*, Chichester, Wiley, pp. 269–96.

Mitsch, W.J. (1978) 'Interactions between a riparian swamp and river in southern Illinois' in R.R. Johnson and J.F. McCormick, eds, *Strategies for Protection and Management of Floodplain Wetlands and Other Riparian Ecosystems*, Washington, DC, US Department of Agriculture, Forest Service, pp. 63–72.

Mitsch, W.J., Dorge, C.L. and Wiemhoff, J.R. (1979) 'Ecosystem dynamics and a phosphorous budget of an alluvial cypress swamp in southern Illinois', *Ecology*, 60, 1116–24.

Mitsch, W.J. and Ewel, K.C. (1979) 'Comparative biomass and growth of cypress in Florida wetlands', *American Midland Naturalist*, 101, 417–26.

Morris, L.A., Mollitor, A.V., Johnson, K.J. and Leaf, A.L. (1978) 'Forest management of floodplain sites in the northeastern United States' in R.R. Johnson and J.F. McCormick, eds, *Strategies for Protection and Management of Floodplain Wetlands and Other Riparian Ecosystems*, Washington, DC, US Department of Agriculture, Forest Service, pp. 236–42.

Naiman, R. and Decamps, H. in press *The Roles of Ecotones in Aquatic Landscapes*, Cambridge, Cambridge University Press.

Naiman, R.J., Melillo, J.M. and Hobbie, J.E. (1986) 'Ecosystem alteration of boreal forest streams by beaver (*Castor canadensis*)', *Ecology*, 67, 1254–69.

Newson, M.D. (1986) 'River basin engineering-fluvial geomorphology', *Journal of the Institution of Water Engineers and Scientists*, 40, 307–24.

Pautou, G. and Decamps, H. (1985) 'Ecological interactions between the alluvial forests and hydrology of the upper Rhône', *Arch. Hydrobiol.*, 104 (1) 13–37.

Peterjohn, W.T. and Correll, D.L. (1984) 'Nutrient dynamics in an agricultural watershed: observations on the role of a riparian forest', *Ecology*, 65, 1466–75.

Petts, G.E. (1984) *Impounded Rivers: Perspectives for Ecological Management*, Chichester, Wiley.

Petts, G.E. (1987), 'Timescales for ecological change in regulated rivers' in J. Craig and J. Kemper, *Regulated Streams: Advances in Ecology*, New York, Plenum, pp. 257–66.

Petts, G.E. (1990) 'The role of ecotones in aquatic landscape management' in R. Naiman and H. Decamps, eds *The Roles of Ecotones in Aquatic Landscapes*, Cambridge, Cambridge University Press, Chapter 11.

Petts, G.E. and Foster, I.D.L. (1985) *Rivers and Landscape*, London, Edward Arnold.

Petts, G.E., Roux, and Moller, H., eds (1989). *Historical Changes of Large Alluvial Rivers, Western Europe*, Chichester, Wiley.

Piery, J.-L. (1987) 'Channel degradation in the middle Arve River, France', *Regulated Rivers*, 1 (2), 183–88.

Pinay, G. and Decamps, H. (1988) 'The role of riparian woods in regulating nitrogen fluxes between the alluvial aquifer and surface water: a conceptual model', *Regulated Rivers* 2, 507–16.

Pinay, G., Decamps, H., Arles, C. and Lacassin-Seres, M. (1989) 'Topographic influence on carbon and nitrogen dynamics in riverine woods', *Arch. Hydrobiol.*, 114 (3), 401–14.

Priestley, J. (1931) *Historical Account of the Navigable Rivers and Canals throughout Great Britain*, reprint, Newton Abbott, David and Charles, 1969.

Probst, J.-L. (1989) 'Hydroclimatic fluctuations of some European Rivers' in G.E. Petts, H. Moller and A.L. Roux, eds, *Historical Change of Large Alluvial Rivers: Western Europe*, Chichester, Wiley, pp. 41–56.

Purseglove, J. (1988) *Taming the Flood*, Oxford, Oxford University Press.

Robertson, P.A., Weaver, G.T. and Cavanaugh, J.A. (1978) 'Vegetation and tree species patterns near the northern terminus of the southern floodplain forest', *Ecological Monographs*, 48, 249–67.

Robinson, T.W. (1965) 'Introduction, spread and areal extent of saltcedar (*Tamarix*) in the Western States', *United States Geological Survey, Professional Paper* 491-A.

Roux, A.L., Bravard, J.-P., Amoros, C. and Pautou, G. (1989) 'Ecological changes of the French upper Rhône River since 1750' in G.E. Petts, H. Moller and A.L. Roux, eds, *Historical Change of Large Alluvial Rivers: Western Europe*, Chichester, Wiley, pp. 167–82.

Scarnecchia, D.L. (1988) 'The importance of streamlining in influencing fish community structure in channelized and unchannelized reaches of a prairie stream', *Regulated Rivers*, 2 (5), 155–67.

Schmidly, D.J. and Ditton, R.B. (1978) 'Relating human activities and biological resources in riparian habitats of western Texas' in R.R. Johnson and J.F. McCormick, eds, *Strategies for Protection and Management of Floodplain Wetlands and Other Riparian Ecosystems*, Washington, DC, US Department of Agriculture, Forest Service, pp. 107–16.

Sedell, J.R. and Frogatt, J.L. (1984) 'Importance of streamside forests to large rivers: the isolation of the Willamette River Oregon, USA, from its floodplain by snagging and streamside forest removal', *Verhandlungen Internationale Vereinigung für Theoretische und Angewandte Limnologie*, 22, 1828–34.

Sedell, J.R., Everest, F.H. and Swanson, F.J. (1982) 'Fish habitat and streamside management: past and present' in *Proceedings of the Society of American Foresters, Annual Meeting*, Bethesda, Maryland, Society of American Foresters, pp. 244–55.

Shields, F.D. and Nunally, N.R. (1984) 'Environmental aspects of clearing and snagging', *Journal of Environmental Engineering, ASCE*, 110 (1), 152–65.

Simberloff, D.S. and Abele, L.G. (1976) 'Island biography theory and conservation practice', *Science*, 191, 285–6.

Sloey, W.E., Spangler, F.L. and Fetter, C.W. (1978) 'Management of freshwater wetlands for nutrient assimilation' in R.E. Good, D.R. Whigham and R.L. Simpson, *Freshwater Wetlands: Ecological Processes and Management Potential*, New York, Academic Press, pp. 321–40.

Starkel, L. (1987) 'The evolution of European rivers—a complex response' in K.J. Gregory, J. Lewin and J.B. Thornes, eds, *Palaeohydrology in Practice*, Chichester, Wiley, pp. 333–9.

Stevens, M.A., Simons, D.B. and Schumm, S.A. (1975) 'Man-induced changes of middle Mississippi River', *Journal of the Waterways Harbors and Coastal Engineering Division, ASCE*, 101, WW2, 119–33.

Strauser, C.N. and Long, N.C. (1976) Discussion of Stevens *et al.* (1975), *Journal of the Waterways Harbors and Coastal Engineering Division, ASCE*, 102, WW2, 281–2.

Swift, B.L. (1984) 'Status of riparian ecosystems in the United States', *Water Resources Bulletin*, 20(2), 223–9.

Thompson, K., (1961) 'Riparian forests of the Sacramento Valley, California', *Annals of the American Association of Geographers*, 51 (3), 294–315.

Trescevskij, I.V. (1966) 'Afforestation in the river floodplains of drought regions in the Volga–Don basin', cited in Gill (1970).

Triska, F.J. (1984) 'Role of wood debris in modifying channel geomorphology and riparian areas of a large lowland river under pristine conditions: a historical case study', *Verhandlungen Internationale Vereinigung für Theoretische und Angewandte*

Limnologie, 22, 1876–92.

Vannote, R.L., Minshall, G.W., Cummins, K.W., Sedell, J.R. and Cushing, C.E. (1980) The river continuum concept. *Canadian Journal of Fish and Aquatic Science* 37, 130–7.

Van Urk, G. and Smit, H. (1989) 'The lower Rhine: Palaeoecological analysis' in G.E. Petts, H. Moller and A.L. Roux, eds, *Historical Change of Large Alluvial Rivers: Western Europe*, Chichester, Wiley, 167–82.

Ward, J.V. (1989) 'The four-dimensional nature of lotic ecosystems', *Journal of the North American Benthological Society*, 8 (1) 2–8.

Welcomme, R. (1979) *Fisheries Ecology of Floodplain Rivers*, London, Longman.

Williams, G.P. (1978) 'The case of the shrinking channels—the North Platte and Platte Rivers, Nebraska', *United States Geological Survey Circular*, 781.

Wiltshire, P.E.J. and Moore, P.D. (1983) 'Palaeovegetation and palaeohydrology in upland Britain' in K.J. Gregory, J. Lewin and J.B. Thornes, eds, *Palaeohydrology in Practice*, Chichester, Wiley, pp. 433–51.

Wolman, M.G. and Gerson, R. 1978. 'Relative scales of time in watershed geomorphology', *Earth Surface Processes*, 3, 189–208.

Yates, P. and Sheridan, J.M. (1983) 'Estimating the effectiveness of vegetated floodplains/wetlands as nitrate-nitrite and orthophosphorous filters', *Agricultural Ecosystems and Environment*, 9, 303–14.

Zalumi, S.G. (1970) 'The fish fauna of the lower reaches of the Dnieper: its present composition and some features of its formation under conditions of regulated and reduced river discharge', *Journal of Ichthyology*, 10, 587–96.

CHAPTER 3

Platonism and practicality: hydrology, engineering and landscape in sixteenth-century Venice

Denis Cosgrove

Venice's relationship with water is as old as the city itself, and as continuous. Water determined the city's existence, its physical presence as much as its maritime trading economy (Lane, 1973). A primary concern of Venetian policy was always to secure the lagoon in which it stood. Venice was threatened by human enemies, to be sure, but more constantly by flood, siltation and disease which could render the Republic's immediate environment uninhabitable. The Venetian lagoon is a creation of dual sets of hydraulic forces, riverine forces emanating from the land (*terraferma*), and marine forces emanating from the tidal gulf at the northern head of the Adriatic sea (Farinelli, 1984). The relations between these two unpredictable elements had to be controlled if the Most Serene Republic was to endure and prosper (Plate 3.1). As the defining frame of Venetian time and space (Tenenti, 1974; Muir 1981), the lagoon stood central to the greater world over which Venetians had to exert control if physical survival, let alone material prosperity, were to be assured. It is little wonder that their practical actions in securing the lagoon were read by Venetians in the broadest philosophical terms. In this chapter I examine some of the practical hydrological policies adopted by the Venetians during the sixteenth century and the broader theoretical and speculative discourses with which these policies were intimately woven. In doing so I do not imply that Venetians were unique, nor that they were especially successful in water management, but rather that their actions exemplify a necessary connection which cultures always seek to establish between their practical interventions in the elemental world—here water and earth—and their deepest cosmological assumptions (Tuan, 1989). Engineering is always to a degree visionary.

The Venetian Hydro-environment

The city of Venice is essentially a collection of islands built up on the levees created by fresh water channels in the lagoon (Goy, 1985; 1989). The actions of wind and tide have produced a discontinuous line of sand and mud banks (*lidi*) behind which rivers reaching the marshy and ill-defined Adriatic coast branch

Plate 3.1   The struggle of elements, between water and land (Engraved frontispiece from Bernado Trevisan, *Della laguna di Venezia* . . . ., Venezia, 1718)

into countless channels, channels which also provide the main arteries for sea water to be spread twice daily across the resulting lagoon. Thus Venice was provided with its main internal and external transportation networks, its sewage system and, through the difficulty of navigating these channels, its prime defence against invasion. The fate of the Genoese fleet, lured into the hazardous lagoon waters in 1389 and defeated by the Venetians' superior knowledge of local navigation, signified the achievement of Venetian mercantile hegemony over European trade in the eastern Mediterranean. But this aquatic environment is radically unstable and any human intervention can increase that instability, introducing the need for further intervention on an increased scale. Actions of the sea, particularly when wind and tides combine to produce a storm surge in the northern Adriatic, demand protection of the *lidi* and can pond back lagoon waters with the result of flooding the city (ASV, 1983). More continuously, the variable regimes of the rivers entering the lagoon produce changes in channel courses and the volumes of fresh water spreading over its surface area of some 55,000 ha. The major rivers have their origins in the Alps and carry large sediment loads. Their velocity slackens with the marked gradient change as they reach the flat Venetian plain, resulting in substantial deposition. The northern lagoon is also fed with fresh, clear water from a dense network of small streams originating in the line of springs (*risorgive*) that crosses the plain parallel with the mountain foothills. These are particularly numerous in the province of Treviso. Human action both within the lagoon and beyond exacerbates an inherently changeable hydrological situation. Within the lagoon reclamation of higher banks, dredging of channels and construction of salt beds and fish traps restricted and altered the dispersion of water. On the mainland, navigation locks, weirs, water offtakes for irrigation, inputs of water from land drainage and, above all, deforestation in the upper Alpine headwater catchments have similarly altered the volumes and regularity of runoff entering the lagoon. Such intervention is as old as human settlement in the region, but inevitably it has intensified over the course of historical time, particularly with medieval monastic land settlement and later the actions of independent city-states.

Over the actions of the sea tides and the wind Venetians had little control except to fortify the defences along the *lidi* with stone breakwaters, wooden palisades and tamarisk planting to protect the lagoon from sea surges which they did under the authority of the Republic's Savii ed Esecutori alle Acque. The lagoon's banks and channels and the rivers entering it presented another matter. It was here that the foundations of Venetian water control policy in the sixteenth century were erected, to: (1) redirect major river systems away from the lagoon and allow them to enter the sea directly to north and south, in Venetian terms to separate sweet (fresh) and salt water, thus reducing the variables of environmental change and the principal cause of siltation; (2) ensure the unencumbered flow of sea water across the lagoon, enhancing its scouring effects on channels and its cleansing action, and reducing the risks of malaria associated with stagnant waters; (3) regulate and protect water channels on the *terraferma*, to drain marshlands and irrigate dry lands. Hydraulic intervention on the Venetian mainland was in part consequential on the policies adopted in the lagoon, for by altering river channels problems of flooding and seepage were exacerbated. Mainland intervention was necessary also to secure unencumbered navigation along the rivers which carried Venice's critical trade with Italy and Europe and, from the late fifteenth century, to satisfy the city's growing demands for food production in secure regions. This policy contained a central contradiction, between, on the one hand, the concerns of Venice to preserve the lagoon as the foundation of its physical existence and its maritime trading role, and, on the other the interests of the *terraferma* as an agricultural region. For both of these aims the control of water was critical, but to secure either one threatened the other. Invariably the conflict was finally settled in favour of the urban/lagoon interest. However, as Venice began to shift over the course of the later sixteenth and seventeenth centuries from a sea trading to an agrarian *rentier* economy so these conflicting interests became as much part of internal debates over the future of the Republic as of debates between city and *terraferma* (Bouwsma, 1984). Put another way, the external land interest, traditionally subordinate to the internal city interest, came increasingly to be incorporated into the latter and thus enmeshed within the central strategic questions of state. It was during the sixteenth century that the contradiction became clearly articulated, most dramatically in the great debate between the *terraferma* landowner Alvise Cornaro and the city engineer Cristoforo Sabbadino (Escobar, 1980; AA.VV., 1980). Then, too, the administrative structures and broad strategy that would determine water control policy for the rest of the Republic's history were constructed. It was equally a period of intense discussion of the theory and practice of environmental intervention, a discussion captured within the terms 'liberal' and 'mechanical' arts. In what follows we shall consider the structures, strategy, theoretical and practical debates that made up Venetian hydrological activity in the sixteenth century.

Administration and action

Until the later years of the fifteenth century, Venetian state policy on hydraulic matters had been conducted through *ad-hoc* and short-lived committees established by the Senate. Membership was generally confined to the noble class and the empirical knowledge gained during their investigations scattered on the committees' dissolution. From 1439, when an attempt was made to collect all written materials, and the following year, when doctors and engineers met to discuss a public health crisis resulting from fresh water in the lagoon, Venetians began to recognize the need for co-ordinated intervention and technical expertise rather than aristocratic amateurism. Towards the end of the century Marco Cornaro, charged to investigate problems of timber supply for shipbuilding, observed the effects of deforestation on erosion in the upper river channels and the consequences for sediment loads. He pointed to the need for adequate gradients to prevent excess deposition and to the effects of deposits entering the lagoon as flow ceased (Escobar, 1980: 105–6).

From the early years of the sixteenth century, partly in response to Cornaro's work, the Venetian Republic adopted a course of centralized control over water matters. The Senate established a series of ministries (*magistrature*) with responsibility for the environment, and through them a systematic planning policy which was largely in place by mid-century. Reflecting the centralized view from the lagoon city which characterized Venetian policy (Ciriacono, 1983), the first of these was the Savii alle Acque (1501) to which was added the Esecutori alle Acque in 1531 (Mozzi, 1927). This joint authority took responsibility on behalf of the state for all waters within and entering the lagoon. Its brief therefore extended across the lagoon itself, to the sea defences of the *lidi* and up the courses of the rivers entering the lagoon. In 1556 was added the Magistratura ai Beni Inculti (MBI) whose remit was to increase grain production by bringing infertile land into cultivation. Much of this land lay in the immediate environs of the lagoon, in the provinces of Padua, Treviso, Vicenza, Verona and the Polesine where problems of waterlogging had been exacerbated by the actions of the water ministry. Where the flows involved directly entered the lagoon, this reclamation ministry had to refer its decisions to the water ministry. To bring land into cultivation where this was not the case, either by drainage or irrigation, the MBI had final authority under the Senate, because the Republic had declared all flowing water to belong to the state. In 1574 a third ministry, the Provveditori sopra i Beni Communali, completed the central administration by assuming responsibility for communal lands. These areas, many of them waterlands, were then coming under increasing pressure for private appropriation as the profits to be made from drainage improvement and cultivation attracted the attention of Venetian and mainland patrician entrepreneurs.

The structure of all three ministries was similar. They were headed by *provveditori*, executive officers chosen by and responsible to the Senate. *Provveditori* came from the Venetian noble class, a class which at this time was defining itself increasingly by its non-involvement with the 'mechanical arts' as opposed to the liberal arts of intellectual and humanist learning (Ventura, 1964). They were advised by a corps of technicians, *proti*, who came from outside the nobility and represented an emerging professional class whose competence lay in understanding how things worked. Each of the ministries remained in existence until the end of the Republic in 1796, keeping detailed records, including a rich heritage of maps and plans deposited in the State Archives (Romanelli & Moreschi, n.d.).

The key to Venetian hydrological policy in the sixteenth century came to lie in the physical delimitation of the lagoon as a salt water environment by diverting two great river systems out of the lagoon: to the north the Piave and Sile rivers, to the south the Brenta and Bacchiglione. One of the first acts of the Water Ministry was to supervise the rerouting of the Brenta at Dolo. This involved a new channel (the Brenta Nova) running south to a point where it met the Bacchiglione, whose channel was straightened below Bovolenta and then took the two parallel canalized courses directly to the sea at Brondolo south of

Chioggia. Recommended by Marco Cornaro, this work was completed in 1507, leaving a reduced flow entering the lagoon at Mestre and Fusina. A century later the amount of Brenta water entering the lagoon was further restricted by a second new channel, the Brenta Novissima, constructed south from Mira. Its high levees delimited Venetian space by defining a clear edge between the land where reclamation and cultivation could take place, and the lagoon wherein all impediments to the free flow of tidal waters had been officially prohibited since 1545. In the case of the northern Piave/Sile system the process of diversion was more complex and prolonged. Cristoforo Sabbadino, engineer to the Water ministry, proposed in 1555 the uniting of the two rivers, and both he and others recognized the need for a systematic plan to regulate the numerous small streams that entered the northern part of the lagoon. However, his plan was not realized until the second half of the seventeenth century when the Piave was diverted to enter the sea near Caorle (1664, 1684) and the Sile directed in a new channel defining the northern lagoon edge and led to the sea via a former bed of the Piave (1663). Various schemes for diverting smaller streams, the Marzenego, Zero, Dese, Meolo and Vallio, remained unrealized at the fall of the Republic.

This overall scheme did not come about without opposition and debate, articulated most clearly in the correspondence between Alvise Cornaro and Cristoforo Sabbadino (AA.VV., 1980). Cornaro, while not himself a noble, was a landowner who had made a fortune from the reclamation of his estates near Padua. Closely involved with the humanists of the Venetian Renaissance, he approached the issues of the lagoon and rivers from a philosophical perspective, ennunciating principles of human intervention in the natural world which had their origin in classical learning and Renaissance beliefs in the dignity and capacity of man. Sabbadino, the greatest of the sixteenth-century hydrological engineers working for the Venetian Republic, consistently expressed his belief in practical understanding of natural processes. While both men recognized the need to arrest the degradation of the lagoon through siltation, Sabbadino opposed Cornaro's interpretation of Adriatic sea levels and its patterns of marine circulation, and also the latter's proposals to reclaim lands within the lagoon itself to help solve the food supply problem. In Sabbadino's view such a solution would break the 'natural' shape and water balance of the lagoon and lead ultimately to the fall of a republic designated by nature as a maritime community.

Actions to stabilize the *lidi* or to keep the interior of the lagoon free of impediments were intended to sustain an existing situation. However, diversion of rivers on the scale proposed by Sabbadino was itself a highly active intervention, although one whose impact was felt primarily on the *terraferma*. It involved digging new channels which were considerably longer than existing ones, constructing embankments to contain them, especially as increased length reduced gradient and thus increased deposition, constructing aqueducts to take the new courses over smaller streams and installing pumps and sluices to join tributaries to the main flow. One of the major consequences of such radical changes to the hydrographic map of the *terraferma* was an increase in the areas

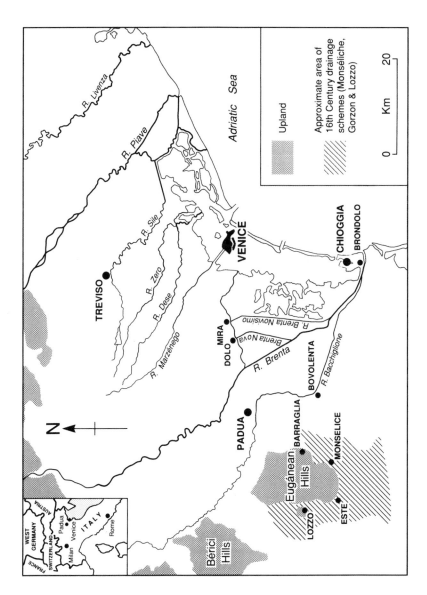

Figure 3.1   The Venetian *terraferma*, general location map showing drainage areas

of land subject to inundation from both the interrupted drainage of lesser streams and from spring flood waters whose frequency and devastation were increased by the sedimentation of raised stream beds of the major rivers. These, of course, were matters close to Cornaro's heart and they made more urgent the work of the reclamation ministry, for whose establishment Cornaro was the prime mover, particularly at a time when the Republic was seeking to increase the production of grain from its land territories.

The first 50 years of the Ministry for Uncultivated Lands saw the establishment of three great drainage schemes (*ritrati*) along the courses of the Brenta and Bacchiglione: the Monseliche, Gorzon and Lozzo projects in the provinces of Padua and Vicenza, and numerous small diversions for irrigation and drainage in the more northerly Treviso, Vicenza and Verona provinces based on the *risorgive*-fed streams. (Figure 3.1). Between 1500 and 1700 reclamation produced up to 50,000 ha (Ventura, 1968) of newly cultivable land and called on the skills of a new breed of technical professionals. These were the *periti* or engineers, men like Cristoforo Sorte, Giacomo Gastaldo and Gianbattista Remi whose practical engineering expertise, recorded in the plans, maps and documents deposited in the state archives, should not obscure their own contribution to a growing theoretical discourse about water, land and environmental management. It was they, above all, whose advice informed the broader policy statements of the aristocratic *provveditori*. The Venetian view of hydro-engineering and landscape emerged from the interation of these two mentalities, their differences and shared assumptions.

Hydrological principles

In 1557 the *Provveditore ai Beni Inculti*, Nicolò Zen, prefacing the written declaration of the great reclamation scheme at Monseliche declared 12 principles which underpinned this and all Venetian hydraulic interventions:

1. The sea is the deepest water on the earth's surface.
2. The sea level at Brondolo (the point where the diverted Brenta reached the sea) should be the levelling base-line.
3. Fresh water should be kept out of the lagoon.
4. Straight channels drain the most effectively.
5. Turbidity increases if flow slows—in depressions (*valli*), lagoons and the sea.
6. Confluence of rivers raises the level of flow and the risks of flooding.
7 Rivers with constant drainage to the sea have constant turbidity.
8. Rivers carrying no sediment do not raise their beds, make levees or extend deltas into the sea.
9. Banked and canalized rivers have more constant depth, ease navigation and drain best to the sea.
10. Navigation channels are more easily maintained with clear than with turbid waters.

11. Dikes for land drainage are more efficient when separated from turbid flows.

12. Drainage channels meeting turbid waters near the sea are raised over time and threaten flooding (Zen, 1557).

Most immediately striking in this list of principles are its empirical warranty and its lack of process statements. Quite clearly Venetians had observed closely the bahaviour of river flow and sediment load characteristics. Almost certainly Zen was basing his statement on the work of his ministry's engineers. We may observe in the notebooks of *periti* like Christoforo Sorte attempts to measure channel size and water volumes with carefully drawn cross-sections and detailed mathematical calculation. However, a process theory of water flow in the sense that we would recognize today, a science of 'hydrometry', measuring the relationship between water depth, speed of flow and sediment-carrying capacity, was beyond the intellectual and technical capacity of sixteenth-century Venetians. The inherently dynamic nature of water flow required a theory of velocity. However, the Renaissance based its scientific theory on Euclid's *Elements* and its engineering on Vitruvius's *Architecture*. From Euclid came the emphasis on separation, analysing individual elements: channel size, water volume, level of flow. But Euclidian geometry did not encompass velocity. From Vitruvius came the architectural concept of engineering: of the machine as *fabrica* (Brusatin, 1980), essentially an aesthetic and moral conception of articulated individual elements whose ultimate models were the macrocosmic world and the microcosmic human body. Here again the thinking was static rather than dynamic, for the machine was not conceived in terms of work, that is, in terms of *mechanism*, but rather architectonically, as a body whose animating spirit came from outside itself.

Naturally, the Venetians recognized the *need* to understand water flow as a continuous phenomenon. Attempts to measure velocity are increasingly apparent in writing from the later sixteenth century (Escobar, 1980: 87). It became the subject of academic interest in the next century, in the work of B. Castelli at the University of Padua, but proper handling of flow characteristics waited upon the seventeenth-century discovery of the calculus. However, Castelli's narrow emphasis on aspects of flow and channel characteristics rather than on the broader context of rivers and their drainage basins has led Ciriacono (1983) to accuse the Venetians of falling behind the Dutch engineers who adopted a more dynamic environmental view in their river regulation schemes. But it is unfair to suggest that Venetians did not adopt a holistic perspective, and indeed one that would commend itself in some respects to a twentieth-century view of environmental interaction. Cristoforo Sorte, for example, produced a text in 1593 proposing the large-scale regulation of the upper Adige River, including a diversion into Lake Garda, the straightening of its channel below Verona and the reclamation of large *valli* areas in the lower Veronese (Sorte, 1593). He pointed out the need to control deforestation in the higher Alpine catchment areas, a region he knew well from his survey work on the Venetian borders with

Austria. In an earlier essay on landscape painting (Sorte, 1580) he included a short discussion of the water cycle which in some measure escaped Aristotelian constraints (Tuan, 1968), revealing a critical theoretical mind in one of the central figures in practical Venetian hydrology, a man who had worked on drainage and irrigation schemes of all scales for half a century. Sorte's combination of empirical knowledge and more speculative and theoretical environmental understanding reveals the extent to which the mechanical and liberal arts and the class groups with which they were associated in Venice were drawn into interaction through the great hydraulic schemes of the sixteenth century.

Platonism and environment

The apparent lack of a broader environmental vision in Zen's statement comes in part from the principle of separation which informs it. Separation was to be maintained between water and land, between fresh and salt waters, between clear and turbid flows, between individual channels, between lagoon water and river water, and between city and *terraferma*. Separation is a guiding principle whose intellectual origins become clearer when we examine another part of the statement:

in the plan [*ritratto* for Monseliche] we should proceed in three stages in imitation of Almighty God, who in the construction of the world [*fabrica del mondo*] separated first the heavens from undifferentiated matter [*materia confusa*], then separated the earth from water and finally made the earth bear particular things: animals, trees and plants. . . . Therefore in three divisions may we carry this scheme forward to completion. (Zen, 1557)

The three stages were, respectively: raising the water above the earth (the principle of separation of elements) by means of pumps and other machines; moving the waters and traffic over them by means of channels, sluices, locks and such devices; and finally ordering and regulating the particulars of the scheme, that is, its continued supervision, operation and maintenance. In modelling the work so explicitly on the divine creation of the world Zen is, I believe, doing more than paying lip-service to the terminology of the Counter-Reformation. He is proclaiming the reclamation as a cosmogony, modelled on the first cosmogonic act, a work of human reason and power. God, the 'Great Artificer', himself employed the principle of separation to define the four elements from the chaos of the First Day of his Creation. Zen's reference to the *fabrica del mondo* indicates his familiarity with a broad contemporary discourse that pulled together philosophical speculation and the mechanical arts of everyday practical life, a discourse popular within certain groups of the Venetian noble class which found acceptance also among the new professions, particularly the 'mathematical practitioners': engineers, cartographers, surveyors and above all, architects (Barbieri, 1983).

Zen's phrase, *fabrica del mondo*, returns us directly to the architectural mode of thinking to which we have already referred. A *fabrica* was primarily a visual concept: an articulated whole whose parts together formed perfection. The archetypical *fabriche* were the universe itself (*farbica del mondo*) and the human body (for example, as described by Vesalius or displayed for public gaze in the anatomy theatres of Padua and Bologna (Ferrari, 1987)). Each of these was conceived in a dual sense. The *fabrica* was immobile until animated by spirit. Unless so animated it was a 'machine' (*macchina*), a passive model of perfection which could be imagined or even pictured but which was inactive. Humans created *fabriche*, above all in architecture. Architecture was the 'queen of the arts', a broad engineering activity through which humans intervened in the construction of the world and transformed the natural environment. Success in environmental engineering rested on knowledge of fundamental principles outlined in Vitruvius's classical work, the *Ten Books of Architecture*, and on Euclidian principles of mathematical and proportional relations also to be found in the cosmos and the human body. Thus in the architectural treatises of the Vitruvian writers from Alberti to Palladio we find the ideas of the building or engineering work as a lesser universe, and its beauty and perfection consisting in so complete an articulation of the parts that nothing might be added or taken away without diminishing the work.

The greater world of the cosmos and the lesser world of the human body are, of course, animated by the divine spirit, the love of God. The human spirit of reason and faith should follow those models:

And indeed, if we consider this great machine of the world, with how many wonderful ornaments it is filled, and how the heavens, by their continual revolutions, change the seasons according as nature requires, and their motion preserves itself by the sweetest harmony of temperature; we cannot doubt, but that the little temples we make, ought to resemble this very great one, which, by his immense goodness, was perfectly completed with one word of his . . . (Palladio, 1570).

Thus Andrea Palladio, the sixteenth-century architect whose work in the Venetian *terraferma* brought him into direct contact with contemporary hydrological and engineering works, writes of his work. Many of his villas were built on reclaimed and newly irrigated lands, and his wooden bridge designed to withstand the violence of the River Brenta at Bassano still stands testimony to his understanding of the forces of water movement. For over a century the Vitruvian text had been interpreted in platonic terms, drawing upon the cosmological writings of the *Timaeus*. The divine mind had created the world according to ideal principles of separation and order, symmetry and proportion, and had made man, a lesser world or microcosm, according to the same principles. The Vitruvian figure of the human body enclosed within circle and square was taken to represent this microcosm, and suggested the nature of God's ideal proportions. The inscription above the entrance to the Platonic academy read 'None without knowledge of mathematics may enter here', a statement which appears on the frontispiece of Nicolò Tartaglia's 1537 text, *La Nova Scientia* (*The*

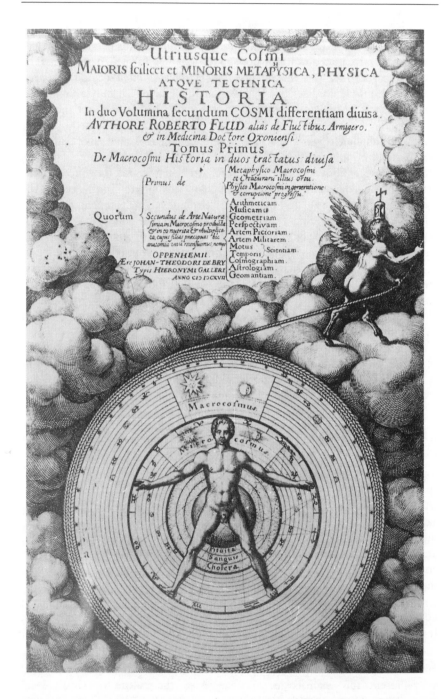

Plate 3.2   The machine of the world: macrocosm and microcosm are set in circular motion by time (Title page from Robert Fludd, *Utriusque cosmi maioris scilicet et minoris metaphysica, physica atque technica historia . . .*, Oppenheim, 1617)

New Science) written by the first translator of Euclid into Italian and published in Venice. Mathematics and, above all, Euclidian geometry were regarded as the secret texts of God's creation, the intellectual discourse through which the pure principles of the divine mind became available to human reason. The numerous texts on mathematics, geometry and proportion written and used by surveyors and engineers in sixteenth-century Venice acted as the theoretical as well as the practical handbooks of environmental engineering (Cosgrove, 1988).

The model for human intervention in the environment was therefore the great world of nature which we not only experience through the senses, but may understand through human reason (Plate 3.2). Little wonder that the first great 'machine' of the Renaissance was Brunelleschi's *fabrica*, the great dome of Florence cathedral whose imaginitive conception rather than its engineering realization gave it spirit or animation and so impressed contemporary observers and commentators (Brusatin, 1980). This platonic interpretation of engineering is perfectly apparent in the translation and commentary on Vitruvius composed by the Venetian patrician humanist Daniele Barbaro, himself owner of an estate in the province of Treviso where water courses were diverted and regulated to supply fountains and rice fields. Published in 1567 and illustrated with architectural engravings prepared by Palladio, Barbaro's commentary adopts a clearly holistic philosophy:

The world is made up of two great parts: the heavens and all that is comprised within the heavens, which today people when dividing the spheres call the region of the elements, and the skies . . . the world is thus a great body and the summary concept of all things because it is perfect, and a thing is perfect when nothing is lacking and nothing may be added. (Barbaro, 1567: 367)

The summary form of the cosmos was the circle, the pure platonic form, a form which unites opposites and resolves the separation of elements. The motive spirit of the cosmos may also be understood by human reason in ideal Euclidian terms: circular or revolutionary motion is observable in the circulation of the earth and the heavenly bodies giving the passages of time in night and day and the seasons. Barbaro (1567: 440–1) describes circulation thus: 'the circle moves and is stationary at its centre, the circumference both ascends and descends, its circumference is convex and concave, its diameter moves quickly and slowly at the same time'.

Circular motion allowed the philosophical understanding of the humanist liberal arts to be related to the more practical applications of the mechanical arts. It is the clue to the manufacture and use of human machines:

They [machines] originate from necessity which moves men to accommodate themselves to their needs; nature instructs them, offering examples . . . from which many machines derive their principles . . . the continuous revolution of the world which Vitruvius refers to as a 'machination', and thus also calls the machine of the world. . . . The form and principle of machines is circular motion. (Barbaro, 1567: 441)

Making machines for human intervention in nature is thus grounded in intellectual understanding of nature itself. Only 'vile mechanicians' fail to understand this higher significance of the principles of motion, but the *proti* and *periti* of the Venetian ministries like Sabbadino and Sorte were increasingly distinguishing themselves from mere mechanicians—the ordinary obedient labourer—as they read and discoursed the same literature as humanist patricians

Plate 3.3 Machine for lifting water using circular motion (Engraving from Daniele Barbaro, *I dieci libri dell'architettura di M. Vitruvio* . . ., Venice, 1567)

like Barbaro, Fracastori and Cornaro. Thus the distinction between the liberal and mechanical arts was blurring in practice at the very time that the aristocracy was seeking to use it as a measure of its own exclusivity (Brusatin, 1980: 39, 63). Barbaro's own discussion of mechanical principles is illustrated in the Vitruvius by engravings of machines he has observed on the *terraferma*: machines designed to lift and transport water and drain land (Plate 3.3). He specifically mentions his own observation of water wheels, Archimedean screws and other rotational machines along the course of the Brenta River, part of the regulation activities of the Venetian water and reclamation ministries.

Practicality

The engineers working for the Venetian government were practical men rather than humanist thinkers. We should not expect them to engage in the higher flights of Platonic speculation, or debates about the Aristotelian scheme of elements and planetary hierarchies. But their work did demand sophisticated understanding of geometrical and mathematical principles. It involved accurate levelling, surveying irregular areas, calculating water volumes and stresses and designing pumps, sluices, land cuts and acqueducts. Moreover, there is considerable evidence that they self-consciously sought to distinguish themselves from Barbaro's 'vile mechanicians', that they did seek more sophisticated understanding of the liberal arts. Silvio Belli, for example, a Vicentine surveyor, lectured to the Olympic Academy in Vicenza on mathematics, engaging esoteric and neo-Platonic matters of mystical proportion (Wittkower, 1949). Cristoforo Sorte, first *perito* of the Venetian reclamation ministry, had been educated in the Este court at Mantua by Giulio Ramano, and his essay *Osservazione nella Pittura* draws upon a wide range of humanist thinking, its style consciously modelled upon classical and humanist writers. Giacomo Gastaldo, the greatest Italian cartographer of the sixteenth century, also worked as a surveyor-engineer for the same ministry and was closely related to the humanist circles surrounding Gianbattista Ramusio, collecting geographical information on the European discoveries. Gastaldo wrote his own commentary on Ptolemy's *Geography* (Milanesi, 1984; Gastaldo, 1562). Finally, we know that the architect Palladio had received a humanist education in the house of the Vicentine noble humanist, Giangiorgio Trissino, had visited and studied the sites of ancient Rome and was fully prepared as a collaborator in Barbaro's Vitruvius project (Wittkower, 1949; Barbieri, 1983).

   In the light of this recognition of a convergence of the liberal and mechanical arts, of Platonism and practicality, we may return to Zen's text for the Monseliche reclamation scheme. The principles of separation have to be read in a broader context: that of an overarching unity. God's creation was a single conception, of which the key sign was the geometrical figure of the circle and whose principle of motion was circularity. The circle signified perfection and its use in human works (*fabriche*) rendered them a reflection of divine order and harmony. Venice, mythologized as an ideal republic, thus revealed its own perfection in the application of circular form and its spirit in revolutionary motion. When Zen compares the drainage of land and the regulation of rivers to the original creation he is thus implying more than a casual similarity. His metaphor speaks to a notion of correspondence between macrocosm and microcosm which will yield perfection and efficacy in the work. It is an aspect of the utopian thinking that characterizes so much of Venetian discourse at this time (*Architettura e Utopia*, 1980). The employment in the work of machines whose own motion is circular may also be interpreted in a hierarchy of correspondences which relate the mere drainage pump to the entire regulation scheme and ultimately to the Republic and the whole of Creation, via the concept of the machine.

In the course of the original cosmogony as understood from the *Timaeus* and Genesis accounts, God had constructed the unity of his work by separating the planetary spheres, arranging them in hierarchical order. He had similarly separated the four elements that go to make up the earthly sphere. Two of these, water and earth, were those that presented themselves to the Republic, and their confusion together in the lagoon and hinterland represented an imperfection— the most serious threat to the proclaimed order of the state. In the lagoon water had to be priviliged for it represented the crucial defence of the city and, equally, its lifeline to the markets which provided Venetian wealth. On the *terraferma* land was the greatest resource, one whose importance was increasing, again for the strategic security of the Republic's population in providing its food supply, and also in terms of the investments of the Venetian nobility which were growing rapidly on the mainland. In both cases the balance of water and land was critical and human intervention was required to sustain a single unitary order. According to contemporary belief, a perfect order was possible only by applying principles of harmony and proportion directly derived from the fundamental structures of the cosmos.

Land and Sea in Venetian Destiny

This elemental separation and recombination of land and water related in a fundamental way also to two visions of Venice, two discourses within the nobility which assumed intense political significance in the second half of the sixteenth century. Traditionally Venetians had seen the role of their Republic as a maritime trading nation whose destiny lay in the *Stato da Mar*, the sea empire. Venetians historians and political commentators regarded this as a divinely ordained mission, a natural consequence of Venice's site and situation (Muir, 1981). But in the aftermath of Venice's near-loss of its land territories in the first decade of the century, its fear over the consequences for trade of the Atlantic navigations and the slow erosion of its hegemony in the eastern Mediterranean by Turkish advance, this destiny appeared less certain and an alternative vision began to be advanced. This was that the Republic's true destiny might lie on the mainland, as a land state whose wealth would be realized in 'holy agriculture' (Sartori, 1981). Such a position accorded well with many features of noble Venetian intellectual life at this time: with the arcadian and pastoral turn in patrician culture and the imperial reconstruction of the city as heir to the mantle of ancient Rome. The debate over which of the elements of land and sea was most appropriate for the realization of the Republic's destiny became linked to political struggles within the noble oligarchy, struggles which reached their peak in the post-Lepanto crisis of the year 1582–3 between the *vechi* and the *giovani* (Bouwsma, 1984: 226ff; Findlay, 1980). The latter group of nobles, who came to control the city after 1583, represented the turn to the *terraferma*. They were led by Leonardo Dona, who himself had extensive land holdings on the mainland and was thus much affected by reclamation and drainage. They deployed the scholarship of late Renaissance humanism and the technical skills of the new engineers in relation to matters of direct political concern (Bouwsma, 1984: 238), forging a close link between Platonism and practicality.

Conclusion

From the apparently mundane world of river channels and drainage pumps to the arcane and arcadian worlds of neo-Platonic philosophy and further to the great matters of state by the opposed groups of the *vechi* and *giovani* may seem a great distance to travel. But they were related in the intellectual and practical lives of sixteenth-century Venetians. The environmental challenges presented by the lagoon and its tributary rivers, like all challenges of the natural world, are mediated for humans through their intellectual and spiritual beliefs and predelictions. Like the Venetians, we believe today that we take an objective and dispassionate view of the natural environment and the demands it places upon us. The formal separation of natural science and metaphysics reinforces that belief. Yet as philosphers of science now recognize, we are no less able to separate philosophical beliefs and cultural assumptions from our science and technology than were early modern Venetians. Like them, and despite our claims to reason and consistency, our landscape engineering is marked by contradiction: between separation and holism, analysis and synthesis.

References

AA.VV. (1980), *Alvise Cornaro e il suo tempo*, Padua.
ASV (Archivio di stato di Venezia), (1983), *Laguna, lidi, fiumi: cinque secoli di gestione delle acque*, Mostra documentaria (Exhibition of sources and documents, catalogue).
Architettura e utopia nella Venezia del cinquecento (1980) Milano, Electa.
Barbaro, D. (1567) *I dieci libri dell'architettura di M. Vitruvio tradotto et commentati da Mons. Daniel Barbaro eletto patriarca d'Aquileia, da lui riveduti et ampliati; et hora in piu commoda forma ridotti*, Venice, de'Franceschi & Chrieger.
Barbieri, G., 1983, *Andrea Palladio e la cultura veneta del rinascimento*, Rome, Il Veltro.

Bouwsma, W.J. (1984) *Venice and the Defence of Republican Liberty: Renaissance Values in the Age of the Counter-reformation*, Berkeley, University of California Press.

Brusatin, M. (1980) 'La macchina come soggetto d'arte' in *Storia d'Italia*, Annali 3: 'Scienza e technica', Turin, Einaudi, pp. 31–77.

Ciriacono, S. (1983) 'Fiumi, canali e lagune nello stato veneziano (Sec. XV–XVIII). Un riesame comparativo', mimeo, Instituto Internazionale di Storia Economica 'Francesco Datini', Prato.

Cosgrove, D (1988) 'The geometry of landscape: practical and speculative arts in sixteenth-century Venetian land territories' in D. Cosgrove and S. Daniels, eds, *The Iconography of Landscape: Essays on the Symbolic Representation, Design and Use of Past Environments*, Cambridge, Cambridge University Press, pp. 254–76.

Escobar, S. (1980) 'L'acqua tra controllo teorico e controllo sociale' in *Storia d'Italia*, Annali 3: 'Scienza e technica', Turin, Einaudi, pp. 85–153.

Farinelli, F. (1984) 'A proposto di una recente opera sull'evoluzione morphologica della laguna veneta e sulle origini di Venezia', *Rivista geografica italiana*, 91, 429–37.

Ferrari, G. (1987) 'Public anatomy lessons and the carnival in Bologna', *Past and Present*, 117, 50–106.

Findlay, R. (1980) *Politics in Renaissance Venice*, London, Ernest Benn.

Gastaldo, G. (1562) *Universale descrittione del mondo*, Venice, Pagano.

Goy, R. (1985) *Chioggia and the Villages of the Venetian Lagoon*, Cambridge, Cambridge University Press.

Goy, R., 1989, *Venetian Vernacular Architecture. Traditional Housing in the Venetian Lagoon*, Cambridge, Cambridge University Press.

Howard, D. (1980) *The Architectural History of Venice*, London, Batsford.

Lane, F.C. (1983) *Venice: A Maritime Republic*, Baltimore, MD, Johns Hopkins University Press.

Milanesi, M. (1984) *Ptolomeo sostituito: studi di storia delle conoscenze geografiche nel XVI secolo*, Milano, Unicopli.

Mozzi, U. (1929) *I magistrati veneti alle acque ed alle bonifiche*, Bologna, Biblioteca alle Acque.

Muir, E. (1981) *Civic ritual in renaissance Venice*, Princeton, NJ, Princeton University Press.

Palladio, A. (1570) *The Four Books of Architecture* (trans. Isaac Ware, 1738), facs., New York, Dover, 1965.

Romanelli, F.C. and Moreschi, C.M. (n.d.) *Laguna, lidi, fiumi: esempi di cartografia storica commentata*, Venice, Ministero per i beni culturali e ambientali.

Tenenti, A., 1974, 'The sense of space and time in the Venetian world of the fifteenth and sixteenth centuries' in J.R. Hale, ed., *Renaissance Venice*, London, Faber.

Sartori, P.L. (1981) 'Gli scrittori veneti d'agraria del cinquecento e del primo seicento tra realta e utopia' in A. Tagliaferri, ed., *Venezia e la terraferma attraverso le relazione dei rettori*, Milan, Giuffrè.

Sorte, C. (1580) *Osservazione nella pittura*, reprinted in P. Barocchi, ed., *Trattati d'arte del cinquecento: fra manierismo e contrariforma*, Vol. 1, Bari, 1960.

Sorte, C., 1593, *Modo d'irrigare la campagna di Verona e d'introdur piu navigationi per lo corpo del felicissimo stato di Venetia . . .* Verona, Girolamo Discepolo.

Tuan, Yi-Fu (1968) *The Hydrological Cycle and the Wisdom of God*, Toronto, University of Toronto Press.

Tuan, Yi-Fu (1989) *Morality and Imagination: Paradoxes of Progress*, Madison, University of Wisconsin Press.

Ventura, A. (1964) *Nobiltà e popolo nella società veneta del' 400 e '500*, Bari, Laterza.

Ventura, A. (1968) 'Considerazioni sull'agricoltura veneta e sulla accumulazione originaria del capitale nei secoli XVI e XVII', *Studi storici*, 9, 674–722.

Wittkower, R., 1949, *Architectural Principles in the Age of Humanism*, London, Warburg Institute.

Zen, N. (1557) 'Termine del ritratto di Monseliche' (6.8.1557), printed in *Il summario di tutte le legge et parti ottenute nel illustrissimo et serenissimo Senato in materia delle beni inculti*, Venice, Griffio, 1558.

CHAPTER 4

Drainage and land use in the Fenlands and Fen-edge of northeast Cambridgeshire in the seventeenth and eighteenth centuries

Robin Butlin

Introduction

This chapter examines the historical geography of habitation and management of the Fenlands and Fen-edge region of northeast Cambridgeshire in the seventeenth and eighteenth centuries. However, the history of this small area of the East Anglian Fenlands not only is indicative of local events and experiences but reflects a wider contemporary northwest European experience of management and control of wetlands. These experiences have certain common elements, including the continuous threats to life and livelihood from North Sea storm surges, the related problem of river floods, the complexity of drainage administrative bodies, frequent conflicts of interest between users of the wetlands, and a similar history of search for and application of new drainage engineering techniques.

Attempts at land reclamation had been made in East Anglia since at least Roman times, but the change from late feudal to early capitalist sytems of land evaluation in the early seventeenth century led to renewed attempts, at varying scales, to improve both land drainage systems and the profitable use of land. These processes involved much conflict and tension, especially between those who depended on traditional use-rights of common resources in the Fens, such as fishing, fowling, turf-cutting, and livestock-grazing, and those who, increasingly for profit, attempted to appropriate those rights through reclamation and agricultural improvement schemes. These conflicts of interest were extremely complex, involving a heterogeneous set of relationships among people and with a hazardous natural environment.

The study area and its physical geography

The particular study area is part of the catchment area of the River Great Ouse, the original and now extensively modified southern drainage channel of the Fens (Figure 4.1). The Fens form a 1,300 square mile (3,400 km^2) basin, floored by Jurassic clays and boulder clay, surfaced with much altered and modified peat and silt. The sub-sea-level surface of this basin is punctuated by islands (such as the Isle of Ely) of Upper Jurassic clays, Greensand, Gault and Chalk Marl, and

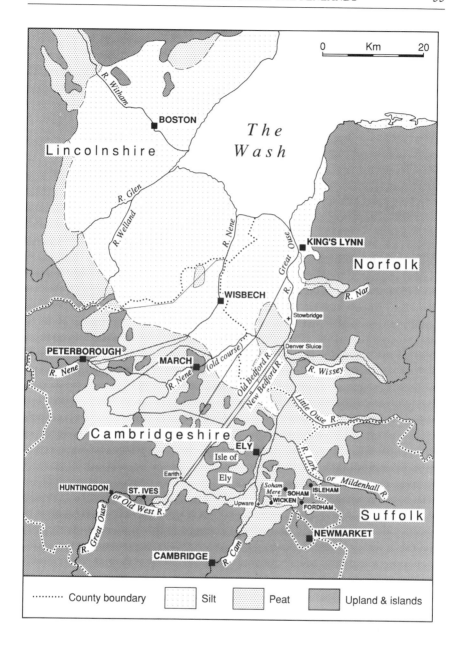

Figure 4.1 The Fenland

it is rimmed to the west by Jurassic limestones and to the south and east by chalk. The soils of the Fens are a product of late- and post-glacial events, and in general terms are very young, especially those of the peat fens. Of particular importance to the study of Cambridgeshire east and south of the Isle of Ely are the peats of the 'black' fens; the residual soils of former meres or lakes, especially Soham Mere; and a variety of soils developed on the lower slopes of the Fen-edge uplands.

The Great Ouse originates in Northamptonshire, whence it flows, originally by means of a very tortuous course, to the North Sea at King's Lynn. Its main Fenland tributaries—the Cam, Lark, Little Ouse, Wissey, and Nar—come from the chalk to the east and south. The Cam and the Lark (or Mildenhall River) are of central importance in this particular study. The other main drainage channels of the Fens are the rivers Nene, Glen, Welland and Witham. The fen rivers have a total catchment area of about 6,000 square miles (15,500 km^2), and discharge into an area one-fifth of that size. This fact is of critical importance to the history of land use and drainage in the region. Vast quantities of water are discharged from the uplands, particularly in winter, into the Fenland basin, whose peats are floored by impervious fen clay, and whose coastal end is barred by silts whose height, partly due to the shrinkage of the inland peats after drainage, is about 10–15 feet (3–4.5 m) above sea level. The peats themselves are generally no more than about 5 feet (1.6 m) above sea level. In the study area between the Lark and the Ouse the peats are slightly below sea level. The relative relief of the peat fens is thus very small, and comparatively slight differences in height have in the past frequently been the dividing line between safety and disaster, life and death.

The natural state of watercourses and their behaviour is of considerable relevance here. The Ouse itself, for example, before the main drainage works of the seventeenth century, had a major meander (now called the Old West River), to the south and east of the Isle of Ely. This system experienced natural processes of river channel development which were major impediments to effective drainage and navigation, including the collapse of banks, trees falling into the watercourses, the growth of aquatic plants and weeds, and the development of gravel and sand bars at the confluence of rivers and streams. Additionally there were large areas of water—lakes and meres, especially in the southern part of the Fenland—which prevented cultivation, though they did offer considerable possibilities for fishing. Human negligence affected the efficiency of water flow, both through failure to clear and maintain channels and ditches and through the erection of a variety of structures such as mills, weirs and staunches. Much of the history of the changing landscape of the fens is therefore the history of success and failure to modify the watercourses of the region.

Additionally important factors in the history of the occupation and management of the Fens have been the hazards resulting from the difficulties of enabling the major drainage channels to discharge fresh water into the sea—the outfall problem—related to the effect of storm surges from the North Sea, which have frequently resulted in sea water flooding and accentuated blocking of fresh water discharge. (Darby, 1983; Gottshalk, 1971–7).

Settlements of the study area

The main settlements in the study area are the parishes of Wicken, Isleham, Fordham and Soham. They lie northeast of the city of Cambridge and north of Newmarket (see Figure 4.1). The parishes vary in size and in physiography. The largest of them is Soham, 12,999 acres (5,261 ha), followed by Isleham, 5,230 acres (2,116 ha), Fordham, 4,204 acres (1701 ha) and Wicken 3,965 acres (1604 ha). They are all located on the fen-edge, abutting the chalk upland in the southeast of the Fens. With the exception of Fordham, each contains substantial areas of low-lying peat fenland. The villages themselves are naturally on the slightly higher ground, at an elevation of about 16–50 feet (5–15 m), but their lower reaches, especially the fenland sections below sea level, have never been totally secure from the hazards of frequent flooding.

The geological bases of the parishes are lower chalk, gault clay, greensand and gravels. The fen areas are for the most part fen peat, on the surface of which quite large meres or lakes, about 32 feet (10 m) deep, were formed. Soham Mere, for example, whose drainage commenced in the early seventeenth century, was located immediately to the west of Soham, and formed an important part of its medieval and early modern economy. The topography and hydrological configuration of this area has been significant in the past, particularly in relation to communication and access. Soham, for example, is on a peninsular site, and the hamlet of Barway to the northwest was formerly an island, connected to the mainland and to Ely, like Soham, by a narrow and perilous causeway.

Drainage and land use in the seventeenth century

Before the seventeenth century, the Fens were in a largely untamed state, their natural products—fish, eels, birds, timber, turf, reeds and sedge—used by the inhabitants of settlements based on higher ground. Cattle, sheep, and horses were grazed, often on the base of intercommoning, on the silt lands and the fen pastures which normally dried out in the summer.

At the beginning of the seventeenth century the Fenland was essentially a largely undrained medieval landscape, the character of which had been described by Camden (1586: 407):

The inhabitants of this and the rest of the fenny Country . . . were called Girvii in the time of the Saxons; that is according to some men's explanation, fen-men; a sort of people (much like the place) of brutish uncivilis'd tempers envious of all others whom they term Upland men, and usually walking aloft upon a sort of stilts: they all keep to the business of grazing, fishing and fowling. All this country in the winter-time, and sometimes for the greatest part of the year, laid under-water by the rivers Ouse, Grant, Nene Welland, Glene, and Witham, for want of sufficient passages. But when they keep to their proper channels, it so strangely abounds with a rich and rank hey . . . that when they've mown enough for their own use, in November they burn up the rest to make it come thicker . . . Besides, it affords great quantities of turf and Sedge for firing, Reeds for thatching; Elders also and other water-shrubs, especially willows either growing wild, or else set on the banks of rivers to prevent their overflowing . . .

Conditions of land use and drainage during the seventeenth century epitomize conditions in the Fenland generally. Richard Atkins, in his description of the southern part of the Great Level in 1604, states that: 'The fens of Soham to be accounted five Miles deep from the Town to the River, and are said to be 30 or 40 miles about by old William' [the fenreeve]. Soham Mere 'is a Mile broad, and two Miles long. It continually loseth from the Land, so as one about 20 Years taking a Lease of *Qu.Eliz.* of the Waste of the *Mere*; another hath since taken another Lease between the former and the *Mere*' (he is referring to the gradual reclamation of the Mere). 'Isleham—hath three common Fens, whereof that next the Town is best; they be not full of Sedge and Reeds, but plain and good feed'. The fens at Fordham were used mainly for peat-cutting (turbary), especially the lower parts, and the fens here were frequently drowned by 'a brook that serves two or three mills breaking its banks'. At Wicken the fens were 'about $1\frac{1}{2}$ Mile Long, but very narrow' (Baddeslade, 1725: 74).

The economy of the fen-edge parishes discussed here not only comprised large areas of low-lying fenland, but also involved a dual upland/lowland system of agricultural production. The villages themselves were on elevated dry sites and, until the early nineteenth century (longer in the case of Soham), were surrounded by open arable and pasture fields, moor and meadow. Soham and Isleham each had four large open arable fields, Fordham six, and Wicken a smaller area of arable contained in three common fields. The holdings within the open fields were generally very small—in parcels of half an acre or less—and widely scattered. The total size of holdings varied, of course, with status, but an examination of inventories for the period gives a strong impression of the predominance of freeholders with small to medium-sized holdings, a large number of cottagers and landless poor, and a small number of large landowners. The dynamics of peasant land holding and inheritance customs in this region have been documented in detail by Spufford (1974; 1976), who highlights the contrasts between the rates of decrease in size and the relative viability of peasant holdings on the uplands and in the Fens. The absence of large estates in northern Cambridgeshire is an important factor in the agrarian history of the region, accounting, for example, for the lateness of large-scale enclosure of the open fields and the constant reassertion and defence of rights of common. The cropping systems used involved rotations of wheat, oats, barley, and maslin, and there was a close link between crop and animal husbandry, shown in the folding of sheep.

During the course of the seventeenth century a combination of circumstances led to intensive efforts to render the Fens more productive. They included an increased general interest in England in the more intensive (and profitable) use of 'waste' land, with consequent changes in property rights and greater investment of capital in land, and the application of new engineering techniques to achieve more efficient land drainage: a combination, in effect, of necessity with opportunity. Lindley (1982: 4–5) has put it succinctly:

the case for internal colonisation was couched in the same terms as that for external, as coincidently serving the national interest and satisfying the profit motive. Successful drainage enterprises brought in effect the addition of a new province to England. National interests were served in a number of ways: drained fenland increased the area of tillage; it accommodated the surplus population of neighbouring regions; it increased the area of the country that could contribute to the taxes of Church and State; it contributed to national pride by freeing the kingdom 'from the imputation of laziness and want of industry' levelled at it by foreigners for allowing large areas of the country to remain nonproductive; and it made a significant contribution to national self-sufficiency.

Such experiences and motives were not unique to England or other low-lying parts of Britain: they were common to many coastal regions of Western Europe—fast developing as the core area of a growing world capital system— and may also be linked to the growth of national consciousness, particularly among the Dutch. As Schama (1988: 34) has stated:

The notion of a communal identity retrieved from the primal flood and made watertight in conditions of peril was not just a matter of heroic metaphor or exemplary allegory . . . the period between 1550 and 1650, when the political identity of an independent Netherlands nation was being established, was also a time of dramatic physical alteration of its landscape.

While the struggle to rescue and reclaim the East Anglian Fenland cannot be seen in quite such dramatically patriotic terms, there is no doubt that the narrative of reclamation and drainage in that region is threaded with notions of proud national achievement and even divine purpose (though the opposite view was taken by some opponents of the new drainage schemes).

The need to increase the amount of arable land in England via the extension of the cultivable area and intensification of productivity was a reflection of the rapid increase in population in the late sixteenth and early seventeenth centuries, notably of London, with direct economic effects on the producing agricultural regions of the east and southeast. The preambles to several of the enabling Acts for drainage indicate this clearly. The purpose of the 'Pretended' Act of May 1649 for draining the Great Level was:

to protect the Level from frequent overflowing and to make it profitable and of advantage to the Commonwealth the owners commoners and inhabitants and fit to bear cole-seed and rape-seed in great abundance which is of singular use to make sope and oyls within this nation to the advancement of the trade of clothing and spinning of wooll, and much of it will be improved into good pasture for feeding and breeding of cattel and for till to be sown with corn and grain and for hemp and flax in great quantity for making all sorts of linen ('L.G.', 1906: 61).

Rapid price inflation encouraged investment in land in the hope of high returns on money invested by individual speculators, and this, together with the prospects of swelling the royal coffers, led to the first major attempts at comprehensive regional drainage schemes for the Fens. Earlier schemes in the late sixteenth and early seventeenth century had foundered because of lack of co-ordination between the owners of small estates, lack of capital, inadequate and inefficient means of drainage, and, to a degree, because of legal difficulties of appropriating large areas of common land to individual ownership.

The first major scheme was approved in 1630, whereby the fourth Earl of Bedford, who owned 20,000 acres (8,100 ha) of land in the Isle of Ely, contracted to drain the very large area of the southern Fenland, later called the Bedford Level, within a period of six years. The earl was to receive 95,000 acres (38,400 ha) of the drained land in return for his investment of capital and entrepreneurial activity. Forty thousand acres (16,200 ha) of this would be subject to a tax to meet the cost of drainage maintenance, and 12,000 acres (4,900 ha) were to be allocated to the Crown. This legal contract is of some importance in understanding the history of land drainage and appropriation in the Fens, for it was devised to circumvent the interests and rights of commoners, represented traditionally by the Court of Sewers, and promoted the vested interests of the Crown and the main landowners. In 1631, 13 additional speculators or 'adventurers' joined in the investment of capital in the undertaking. The adventurers employed the Dutch engineer Cornelius Vermuyden, whose main strategy for the agreed purpose of transforming the wetlands into arable, meadow, and pasture was the cutting of new, straight, artificial channels.

The channel of the Great Ouse was shortened and straightened by means of the Bedford River—a straight cut from Earith to Salter's Lode: 21 miles (34 km) instead of the 30 mile (48 km) natural course, and with a sluice at each end (see Figure 4.1). Eight other major cuts were made in the rivers of the southern Fenland. In 1637 a Court of Sewers at St Ives declared that drainage had been effectively carried out, and that the adventurers were entitled to their allocations of land. In the following year, however, this was overturned by the Privy Council, for there were many objections on the grounds that some of the supposedly drained areas were still flooded in winter. A modification to the allocation was made by the Court of Sewers at Huntingdon in 1638 which gave a higher proportion of the allotted land to the Crown, and a slightly smaller proportion to the undertakers (Darby, 1983: 70).

Drainage work remained in abeyance from 1638 until 1649, mainly because of the Civil War, but resumed thereafter. In 1642 the Great Level of the Fens had been divided by Vermuyden into three areas, the North, Middle, and South Levels (the area of this study being in the South Level), and these divisions were formally adopted by the Board of the Bedford Level in 1697. A second major cut—the New Bedford River or Hundred Foot Drain—was made in 1651 southeast of the Bedford River (renamed the Old Bedford River). Between these two parallel drainage channels was an additional safety feature: the Ouse Washes (the area between the two artificial rivers), which could be used as an overflow area at times of extreme flooding. Additional cuts, sluices and embankments were made and constructed in the period 1649–53, including the Denver Sluice, constructed in 1652, in theory to keep the waters of the Hundred Foot River out of the South Level, but in practice to solve the problem created by Vermuyden's error in constructing the bed of the Hundred Foot River 8 feet (2.5 m) above that of the Great Ouse, with consequent flooding of the South Level (Summers, 1976: 75).

Vermuyden's system for the drainage of the Fens was based on gravitational principles, assuming that the relative relief of the region would enable gravitational discharge of the water to the Wash. He incorporated techniques previously used in Holland and in Italy, including the construction of dikes, straight cuts, and sluices as developed in Holland, and various measures developed in Italy for the prevention of severe channel bank erosion under conditions of faster-flowing rivers. The verdict on Vermuyden's system is that it

worked satisfactorily for a time after its completion in 1653, and would have continued to work had not the lowering of the land-surfaces through the shrinkage of the peat-lands especially, and of the silt-lands to a lesser degree, destroyed the one simple factor on which the system was based, namely gravitational discharge. When this discharge ceased to function a new technology, involving the mechanical raising of water, was bound to be needed just as it had been necessary earlier in the Netherlands for similar reasons. (Harris, 1957: 321)

Many aspects of the problems and possibilities of both the new drainage schemes are evidenced in the manorial and drainage administration records for Fordham, Isleham, Soham and Wicken. The drainage of Soham Mere was, for example, a matter of much comment and interest. The meres of the Fens were not part of the adventurers' and undertakers' drainage contracts, and Soham Mere, being Crown land, was drained by agreement, a new drain being cut for the purpose which went through tunnels constructed under Soham New River, the Mildenhall River, and the Wissey River to Downham Eau and the sluices of the Ouse near Stow Bridge. Vermuyden's drainage scheme had embanked the four rivers of the southern Fenland (the Cam, Mildenhall, Lark Little Ouse and Wissey) and spaced the embankments so that they could function as overflow catchments.

He had constructed Downham Eau to bypass Denver Sluice and take these rivers' floodwaters to the Ouse at Stowbridge (Darby, 1983: 81). Formerly used for fishing, eel-catching, reed- and turf-cutting, the drained Mere was used for pasture and arable land. ('L.G.', 1906: 67). It had been subject to gradual reclamation during the Middle Ages, and was finally drained by the end of the seventeenth century. A document on the effects of drainage of the Mere on the tithes of the vicar of Soham in the late seventeenth century gives a contemporary view of the consequent changes, referring to

the late improved ground of the fens of the Meer. The Meer was formerly water in general, and greatest profit came through the fishing, which is now converted to arable and pasture, and will be planted there flax, hemp, corn. There will be fed there cows, mares, geese, hogs and sheep, and houses will be built thereon. (PCC Soham M.2*, 26 April 1686)

The present-day landscape of Soham Mere, especially when seen from the air (Plate 4.1) testifies to its history of drainage. Small ditched fields mark the former

Plate 4.1   Soham Mere, Soham, and Soham North Field. This view from the west shows very clearly—in the lower half of the photograph—the former extent of Soham Mere, with its distinctive, light-coloured, immature lake-bed calcareous soil. Immediately above the lake is the North Field, a surviving open field now managed in severalty but never enclosed by Act of Parliament or other means. Soham itself is seen between the North Field and the Mere, to the south (right of photograph). Cambridge University Collection: copyright reserved

limits of the Mere, some of these dating from the fourteenth century, whereas the larger fields deriving from the major drainage plan begun in 1664 are to be seen in the centre of the Mere around the main central drain, the 12-foot ring bank and supporting counter-bank (Taylor, 1973: 197–8).

While Vermuyden's large-scale schemes have attracted much attention, it is necessary to stress the importance of the subsequent drainage work, particularly in respect of the critical problems of land shrinkage consequent upon Vermuyden's gravity-based system which stretched into the eighteenth century and involved new legal instruments as well as new drainage techniques.

Opposition to drainage in the seventeenth century

Fenland drainage in the seventeenth century was not without opposition. Strong resistance came from the fen-dwellers because of the anticipated and real loss of rights of common (including grazing, peat-cutting, fishing and fowling) through enclosure of the drained land. They also contended that the capitalist investors had deliberately exaggerated the 'backward' state of the Fens in their submissions to Parliament in order to further their own ends (Lindley, 1982: 6). Opposition came not only from the small landowners and cottagers but also from some of the larger landowners, partly on the grounds that the new reclaimed pastures would reduce the rents on their upland pastures. Opposition to interference with navigation and transport was particularly strong from such towns as Cambridge and King's Lynn. There was also resentment of the presence of strangers involved in the schemes, including the Dutch drainage engineers and Dutch and Scottish prisoners used as labourers.

The nature and chronology of opposition to drainage and consequent enclosure of common land is complex. Most vociferous were the Fenland commoners. Their rights of common pasture were being removed, and the condition of the pastures was in some instances actually worsened by the drainage schemes, causing them to be flooded for longer periods than before. Although year-round freedom from flooding was not entirely beneficial (the silt deposited by winter floods having an improving effect on the soils of the pasture areas), the commoners and some landowners of the southern Fenland claimed that the drainage schemes of the mid-seventeenth century benefited the less productive areas of the northern Fens at the expense of the southern (Lindley, 1982: 11–12). Common characteristics of anti-drainage and anti-enclosure protest and riot included: restrained and discriminating violence against property and drainage works; anxiety to seek legitimation through royal and legal support; a community basis for action, and common cause between the 'middling sort' and the poorer inhabitants (Lindley, 1982: 57–71).

In May 1632, during the first phase of large-scale land reclamation, there was a riotous protest in Soham against the enclosure by Sir Robert Heath, a friend of Vermuyden, of 500 acres (200 ha) of common land, involving the levelling of the enclosure. He had secured an Exchequer award in 1632 for the improvement of 2,000 acres (810 ha) of fenland: 1,500 acres (610 ha) in Metlam Fen and 500 acres (200 ha) in Barroway (Barway) Fen. The award had stated that Heath should enjoy all the waste fens and commonable grounds on the west side of the river cut made by the adventurers from Soham Mill to the River Ouse and between the mill and the river abutting Wicken Fen and Soham Mere. Heath had enclosed the 500 acres in early May 1632, but the enclosures were destroyed and subsequent enclosure attempts frustrated by the commoners (Lindley, 1982: 83).

As the major drainage projects progressed, further attacks occurred: embankments, for example, were destroyed by commoners at Wicken in May 1638. After the end of the Civil War, during the Commonwealth and Protectorate, the attempts at fenland drainage were resumed, as was the commoners' opposition. The proceedings of the meetings of the adventurers for June 1653 state that the Adventurers' works about Swaffham and Soham had been thrown down by 'unruly people' (CRO R59/31/9/6), a reference to the levelling of enclosures and the filling in of drainage channels. The protests continued in 1654 and 1655, with major damage in the summer of 1655 to growing crops caused by the damaging of sluices and consequent flooding in the southern Fenland (Lindley, 1982: 184–5).

Protests in the southern Fenland seem to have diminished after the Restoration in 1660, and Holmes (1985: 172) suggests that this was the result of increased Parliamentary sanction for the resumed and new drainage schemes, epitomized in the 1663 Act for the Bedford Level, by means of which the localized authority of the Courts of Sewers was replaced by that of the Bedford Level Corporation, which gave substantially increased legal protection to the project. This legislation, Holmes (1985: 179) argues, gave the operations of the drainers

a legitimacy superior to that of Council directives or decrees of Commissioners of Sewers. The fenmen's pattern of action suggests that they accepted the force of the 'full and final confirmation' embodied in statute, and the theory of parliamentary sovereignty that sustained it.

The transfer of the administration of drainage in the southern Fenland (the North, Middle and South Levels) to the Bedford Level Corporation in 1663, marks not only the recognition that the scale of the drainage problem required a larger-scale and legally more powerful authority than the Commissions of Sewers, but also the transition from localized, decentralized, self-governing bodies to the more centralized authority of Parliament. The first Commission of Sewers had been established by authority of the Crown in the thirteenth century, with the direct authority to implement good maintenance practices and fine those who were negligent by means of local juries: the Courts of Sewers. In the fifteenth and sixteenth centuries, central legislation clarified and extended their functions and purposes. Their powers were, however, largely confined to overseeing maintenance and periodic improvement of existing watercourses and drainage systems. The basic interest was land drainage, though the interests of navigation were also served (Darby, 1983; Owen, 1967; 1973).

The new Bedford Level Corporation was invested by Act of Parliament with powers of taxation for drainage revenue and confiscation of land for arrears of drainage. Its members were the original adventurers, or their heirs, who had invested in southern Fenland drainage. New officials were appointed, including area drainage superintendents, an engineer, surveyor, treasurer and registrar, and this new body took responsibility for drainage and navigation. The drainage of the Bedford Level was thus placed on a firmer administrative footing; nevertheless, it struggled constantly against a chronic shortage of funds (Summers 1976; 90–1).

In addition to protests and destructive actions, the drainage records are full of complaints about the failure to maintain channels and ditches, the erosion of banks, problems with low bridges across watercourses, and conflicting interests over navigation and other river uses (especially as a result of the construction of weirs). The minutes of the Adventurers' Proceedings for April 1663 record a complaint that weirs still existed on the Grant (Cam) River at Wicken, which were impediments to navigation and the passage of flood waters (CRO R59/31/9/8). The minutes of the Commissioners of Sewers for November 1687 state that the drain in Isleham known as Isleham Load, which conveyed water from the fens at Isleham and Soham to the Mildenhall River, was 'defective and grown up', and required ditching and scouring (CRO R59/31/9/12).

In both short and long term, the drainage schemes helped to increase agricultural productivity in the Fens, though clearly the commoners lost much. The new agriculture introduced in the fully drained areas included the cultivation of cole-seed, rape-seed, hemp (for ropes), onions, peas, flax, oats and woad, and improved grasses, introduced to intensify the productivity of animal husbandry. The newly-drained fenlands were the focus of several utopian schemes for model settlement and farm plans, including Cressey Dimmock's theoretical models of crop and livestock zonation (Grove, 1981).

Another aspect of Fenland life which emerges from a study of the documents on drainage at this time is the need to make provision for the poor, who relied on the rights of common over fen and pasture for basic necessities of life. The practice of reserving 'poor's commons' when land was appropriated into individual ownership in the seventeenth and eighteenth centuries is widely evidenced in northeast Cambridgeshire. The poor's commons at Soham, for example, seem to have originated with the end of the major drainage scheme for the Fens in 1663, for in 1664 disputes over common rights were referred to two arbitrators, who reserved 200 acres (80 ha) for the grazing of the cottagers' and other poor commoners' cattle and other animals. Such grazing rights were jealously guarded: a court roll for Isleham for 12 July 1656 contains a complaint that

since the last court . . . the East Fenn of Isleham hath converted from its ancient custom wch formerly was reserved for the feeding of horses and young calves only and not otherwise by some of the inhabitants of the town of Isleham contrary to the custom wch hath been used time out of mind now lately broken . . . (KCC ISL/13)

C. Vancouver (1794: 137) refers to

200 acres of rich pasture ground, belonging to the poor, and affording the possessors of a common right the pasturage of three cows or two horses . . . there are besides about 150 acres of horse common, depastured under a decree from the Court of Exchequer.

Because of the historical anomaly of Soham never having been subject to an Enclosure Act, these commons survive in the twentieth century. A survey of the common lands of Cambridgeshire by the County Planning Department (1956: 27–37) describes seven surviving areas of common, four of which are the original poor's commons: Qua Fen Common, 63 acres (25 ha), East Fen Common, 56 acres (23 ha), Angle Common, 33 acres (14 ha), and Shade Common, 4.90 acres (2 ha), in all a total of 158 acres (64 ha).

A similar allocation was made in the late seventeenth century at Wicken, where the section of Wicken Sedge Fen east of the Drainer's Dyke—an area of 90 acres (36 ha)—was divided and allocated to the commoners (Rowell and Harvey, 1988: 78), as also was an area immediately to the east which became known as Wicken Poor's Fen, 14 acres (5 ha). In 1965 the total area of common land remaining in Wicken was 28 acres (11 ha). The common land in this case was primarily for the provision of sedge, reeds and turf.

The state of the Fens at the end of the seventeenth century has been characterized by Darby (1983: 96):

The immediate consequences of the draining promised more than was fulfilled for many years. Some of the complaints of the time were summarized in the General Drainage Act of 1663: that some lands still remained drowned; that the draining of some localities had only made other areas worse; that there were many discrepancies in the allotments of lands between owners, commoners and townships; and that the maintenance of the Level involved a clash with the interests responsible for navigation.

A major problem that continued to haunt the fen-dwellers was that of the outfall to the sea of the large rivers, especially the Ouse. This is a complex problem, and cannot be analysed in detail here, but the key feature of many publicized complaints from the seventeenth century onwards was the effect of the construction of the Denver Sluice at the point of junction of the Ouse and the New Bedford River in 1652. The quantity of water coming down from the uplands at times of heavy rainfall meant that the sluice or lock could never be left open long enough for the water to be fully discharged, with resulting ponding back of the waters in the South Level effecting great strain on the banks of the drainage channels (Darby, 1983: 98), particularly in winter.

An additional problem for the southern peat fenlands, consequent upon the drainage schemes, was peat shrinkage, which lowered the surface and thus increased the problem of lifting water from the fields to higher drainage channels and outfalls. The problem of raising water to the main rivers and channels was not a new one in the Fens, and windmills (often called 'engines' in descriptions of the region from the sixteenth to the eighteenth centuries) were used for this purpose from at least the sixteenth century (see Figure 4.2). After the drainage of Soham Mere, for example, late-seventeenth century documents refer to four engines which continued to drain water from the mere. This type of engine was an adaptation of the corn-grinding windmill. Although there was opposition to their construction because of their capacity to interfere with navigation and even drainage, windmills increased in number in the Fens during the second half of the seventeenth century. They drove scoop-wheels in a narrow trench, and lifted the water from a lower drainage channel about 5 feet (1.5 m) into a higher channel or river. Scoop wheels could also be driven by horse power.

The eighteenth century

At the beginning of the eighteenth century the activities and problems of this

Figure 4.2   Fenland drainage mill with scoop wheel. Wind-driven drainage mills were the principal means of raising water from lower to higher drainage channels in the seventeenth, eighteenth and early nineteenth centuries, before the general use of the steam engine. Source of illustration: B. Latham, 'On the drainage of the Fens', *Trans. Society of Engineers* (1863), pp. 154–172

region can be gleaned from the records, for example, of the Bedford Level Corporation and the Courts of Sewers. C.N. Cole, the Registrar of the Bedford Level Corporation, produced a map of the Bedford Level in 1789, a revision of a 1706 map by Jonas Moore, which gives some idea of the geography of the Fens (Figure 4.3), though many of the proprietors' names date from the early eighteenth century. The major problems were those of maintaining the existing

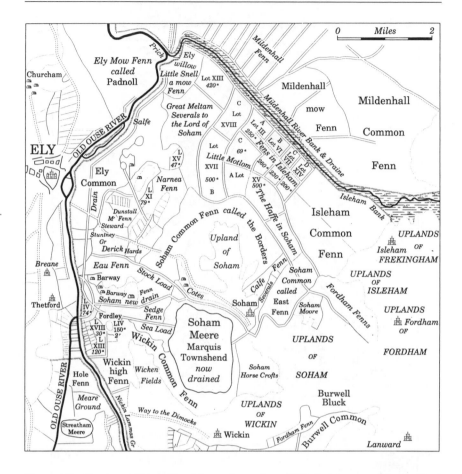

Figure 4.3   Northeast Cambridgeshire: redrawn from C.N. Cole's map of the Bedford Level, 1789 (CRO R59/31/14/17)

system of drainage, the difficulty of co-ordinating a growing number of independent drainage administration units, and of course, continuing natural hazards such as major floods.

Much of the evidence for maintenance problems describes the frequent infilling of drainage channels, including the old 'lodes' such as Wicken Lode, and Isleham Lode, either by natural silting and vegetation growth or by deliberate stoppage. Thus, the minutes of the Bedford Level Corporation for August 1720 report that 'Edward Finch has stopped with earth a water course leading out of Clipsall River into Soham Fen' (CRO R/59/31/9/10). The proceedings of the Corporation for August 1729 reported that the Soham Lode from Soham water mill down to the Cambridge river needed scouring (CRO R31/5/9/11). Conflicts of usage, for example between drainage and the wa:er needs of mills, were not uncommon. The uncertain state of hydrological knowledge and technology is another common feature of the recorded problems. Scouring and banking are frequent costs: in April 1705 the Proceedings of the Bedford Level Conservators record a petition from the inhabitants of Wicken that Wicken Lode is their only drain for carrying water into Burwell Lode, and being grown up to level soil, they have scoured it at cost of £30 (CRO R59/31/10/9). A petition from April 1761 complains that Soham Lode is so overgrown that it is useless for navigation (CRO R59/31/10/27). In April 1770 it was presented that Robert Moody of Isleham had carted turf on the back foreland of Mildenhall south bank and damaged the same, and in 1771 it was ordered that Mr Mayer of Soham be required to make satisfaction for cutting the banks of the River Clipsall to water his quicksets [hedges] (CRO R59/31/10/30).

There was, in addition, the ever-present hazard of catastrophic flooding through North Sea storm surges and the related inability to shift the large quantities of water draining into the southern Fens from the uplands. The destruction of the Denver Sluice in 1713 by a major tidal surge did considerable harm to the drainage system of the southern Fens. The late seventeenth and early eighteenth century was a period of exceptional storminess in the North Sea with major storms recorded for 1680, 1702, 1729 and 1739 (Lamb, 1980). The problem of flooding was worsened by the effects of recent enclosures in the uplands surrounding the Fens:

Instead of the water lying on the open fields until it had evaporated, the great number of new enclosures in the upland counties brought improved drainage to the land so that much of the rain passed straight into the rivers without any hindrance. Therefore water ran down to the Fens more quickly and fenmen complained of the suddenness of the floods as compared with former periods. The fenmen found themselves in a rapidly deteriorating situation, and even while they argued among themselves about what they should do, the outfalls became more and more choked. These external factors, coupled with the gradual sinking of the land, were rapidly making the windmill a completely inadequate machine for drainage. (Hills, 1967: 28–9)

General descriptions of the region in the eighteenth century give differing perspectives on the landscapes and problems involved. William Gilpin, in the later eighteenth century, gave the Fenlands of northeast Cambridgeshire a very bad notice in his *Observations on Several Parts of the Counties of Cambridge, Norfolk and Suffolk and Essex . . . relative chiefly to picturesque beauty, in Two Tours (1769, 1773)*, published in 1809. Speaking of the road from Ely to Mildenhall via Soham, he says that:

The road, through five or six miles, is good turnpike, raised over swampy grounds, cut everywhere across with drains, and ditches, as we found them in our approach to Ely. Rows of pollard with slime hanging from their branches, marked the limits of the hedges which emerged, as the water drained off. In the mean time a circumscribed horizon of fenny surface was our only distance. If it had been remote, it might have lost in obscurity its disgusting form. But its disagreeable features were apparent to the utmost verge of its extent.

We soon however found, that we were in the neighbourhood of a country still more disagreeable, at least for travelling, than a fenny one. This was a vast tract of sand. At Soham, which is a considerable village, we landed, if I may so speak, from the fens; and hoped that we had now gotten upon stable ground. But soon we found our mistake. We had scarce left it, when we entered upon the sands; and only changed the colour of our landscape; both of them being equally wild, open, and dreary. Not a tree was to be seen. (Gilpin, 1809: 28)

A similar pessimistic tone, but from a different perspective, is adopted in C.N. Cole's report on the South Level in 1777, produced for the Board of the Bedford Level Corporation, the general sense of which is that the original major drainage plan had failed, and precipitated such difficulties as serious flooding, breaches in the banks of the drainage channels, costs of maintenance and repair, and natural and artificial obstructions to navigation. An example given is the deposition of sediment at times of flood at the confluence of the Mildenhall and Ouse rivers, on account of the angle of confluence, so that

From this improper point of junction arises this mischief, that when, in times of flood, the two rivers meet partly in contrary directions, charged with particles of earth brought down from the highlands, instead of uniting in one course in their passage, they both, for a time, stagnate at the point of opposition, during which the particles of earth subside, and form banks and shoals at the point of junction, near the mouth of the Mildenhall river, mischievous both to drainage and navigation (Cole, 1777: 6; CRO R59/31/4/8).

The continuing problems of drainage administration in the eighteenth century have been outlined by Darby, who draws attention to the further subdivision of the three levels of the Bedford Level. Thus:

The multiplicity of authorities set up at different times, each responsible for only short lengths of river or embankment, greatly complicated questions of supervision and maintenance . . . in the post-drainage Fenland, as in the pre-drainage Fenland, there was everywhere a chaos of authorities and an absence of authority. (Darby 1983: 118).

Conflicts of interest between individual landowners, and the limited powers of the Bedford Level Corporation (whose jurisdiction included only the main drainage and navigation channels) led to the application by groups of landowners for private Acts of Parliament for the drainage of particular Fenland districts, and the power to levy additional taxes to pay for the costs of drainage initiation and maintenance by bodies of commissioners. The first such body in the South Level was established in 1727 for Haddenham Level. For the district under study, the necessary and relevant Acts to create such a drainage district are those of 1758, 1789 and 1800. These Acts created the Soham or Middle Fen district. The preamble to the 1758 Act states:

Whereas certain Fen Lands and Low Grounds lying and being in the several parishes of Soham, Isleham, and Wicken in the county of Cambridge, and in the parish of Stretham cum Thetford, and township of Ely . . . containing the whole Seventeen Thousand acres, or thereabouts . . . have for divers years past been, and still are, frequently overflowed, and annoyed with waters, through the defect of their outfalls to sea, and thereby rendered of little value . . .

There were to be appointed by the holders of more than 200 acres (81 ha) of land, together with the lords of the manors, commissioners for the purpose of improving drainage and navigation, by means of raising and strengthening the banks of the rivers Cam and Ouse, the Mildenhall River, Soham Drain, Barroway Lode, and of carrying out improvements to bridges and tunnels. In addition the new commissioners were empowered

to erect, work, support, and repair, such and so many mills or engines, not exceeding nine in number . . . and to make and cause to be made, through the said banks, such tunnels or outlets from each of the said mills, for the throwing out and discharging the waters from the said fen lands . . . and also to cleanse, deepen and widen, such other drains . . .

The cost was to be met by an initial acre rate of two shillings, though a reduced half-rate was to be paid in respect of 'common grounds belonging to the poor', such as the fen common called Great Metlam in Soham, and 50 acres (20 ha) in Isleham. The preamble of the following Act of 1789 indicates that the sum of money raised plus a sum of £10,000 borrowed was insufficient for the purpose, and that £5,000 in interest was owned. Further powers were sought for additional fen taxes to be levied. A third Act of 1800 continued this rather sad tale, and sought power to levy additional tax for the meeting of debts incurred and to continue the maintenance of the drainage system.

Darby has indicated that although the second half of the eighteenth century was one in which 'a fresh spirit of improvement came into the region', negative forces such as drainage tax arrears and floods worked against that spirit, and he cites a 1777 observer: 'go but half a mile from Ely, and you come to Middle-Fen, a tract of sixteen thousand acres, given up and abandoned; there you see the ruins of windmills, the last efforts of an industrious people' (Darby, 1983: 123). The more effective drainage of this tract, however, had to await the coming of the steam engine in the nineteenth century.

The system of land use in the southern Fen-edge parishes in the eighteenth century was a continuation of the dual economy which had long been characteristic of the human geography of the region. About 65 per cent of the area of the parishes of Soham, Isleham and Wicken was fen, and Vancouver's *General View* of 1794 provides detailed descriptions of the fenny parts of the parishes in the study area. At Wicken, for example:

One hundred and fifty acres (60 ha) of Laas fen land is annually mown for fodder, and when the fen is not drowned, is rented at five shillings per acre; this has long been in a state of uncertain cultivation, from the frequent drownings of the fens . . . There are three engineer mills occasionally employed in this parish, but are far unequal to its draine, the river Cam is here the only outfalling drain, and should staunches be erected at Upware, the water must be held back, and in addition to the present calamitous state of the country, the whole level would be constantly under water. (Vancouver, 1794: 135)

At Isleham:

The unevenness of the beds of the rivers Lark and Cam, are much complained of, in resisting the descent of the water . . . The working of the bear [a machine that tore out weeds and aquatic plans from the beds of the rivers] has been of much service, but the gravels and hards, forming the obstructions in the beds of these rivers, are only to be removed by hand, which done, the drainage of the fen land in this parish, would be greatly improved. (Vancouver, 1794: 35)

At Soham:

The fen amounts to about eight thousand acres, and in its present condition, is not valued at more than four shillings per acre. The bad state of this fen is not attributed to any want of internal works, or powers of lifting the water, but to the constant pressure and soakage of the Highland waters, through the loose and neglected banks of the rivers Cam and Lark. The most inferior fens, and low grounds, in this parish, effectively drained, and properly cultivated, would on a certainty be improved to the annual value of twenty or twenty-one shillings per acre. (Vancouver, 1794: 136)

Plate 4.2   Wicken and Wicken Fen. A view from the northeast, looking southwestward over Wicken village toward the River Cam. The larger area of uncultivated fen beyond Wicken (right side of photograph) is Wicken Fen Nature Reserve, formerly Wicken Sedge Fen. The smaller uncultivated area to the left is the former Edmund's Fen and Poor Fen. Copyright permission: Cambridge University Collection: Copyright reserved

The principal uses of the peat fens included the digging of turf for fuel and housing material (turbary), the cutting of sedge, fishing, the grazing of animals, notably cattle and sheep, and, when drained, as high-quality arable land. The right of turbary was, of course, long established. Turf bogs or turbaries are referred to in 'Domesday Book', and reference to turf provision for poor houses in Wicken exists for 1321. Details of turbary are given in studies of the fens at Wicken by Rowell and Harvey (1988) and Day (1965). Common turbaries such as Wicken Poor's Fen provided both peat and sedge (Plate 4.2). The peat was used for domestic fires, bakers' ovens and blacksmiths' forges, and turves were also used in the building of Fenland houses and for insulation. Rowell's (1982) short paper on the origins and land-use history of Wicken Poor's Fen shows that its name originated in or after 1666, when the fen remaining after the adventurers' drainage and reallocation was divided among the commoners. 'The inference is that the Poor's Fen was created in 1666 for the use of those without common rights or with rights so small that permanent allotment would not have been worthwhile' (Rowell, 1982: 7). The intensive use of this fen by the poor for fuel, notwithstanding the attempted restrictions and limitations by the Court Leet, meant that it was almost completely dug out by the 1830s. The use, production and value of a particular type of sedge (*Cladium mariscus*) has also been carefully documented by Rowell (1986). He shows that its main uses were for thatching and kindling (the sedge at Wicken was used for thatching), though it was also used as fuel and as a surfacing material for trackways. Wicken Sedge Fen, as it was often called, had been subdivided into small strips or parts in 1666, and the system of management changed accordingly. Thus the

former annual laying out, presumably of large even-aged stands of sedge, gave way to small linear areas under individual management. As the maturity of sedge determines when crops can be cut, the large even-aged stands may have persisted more or less intact for some time. Eventually, individual management preferences and abilities would have prevailed, cropping would have got out of phase . . . (Rowell and Harvey, 1988: 79)

The practice of grazing animals on the Fenlands, especially in drier summers, was old-established, and continued into the eighteenth century, as witnessed by the attempts by manorial courts to restrict and control the extent of common land grazing and the grazing of unhealthy stock. Orders made in the court rolls for Fordham on 16 April 1741, for example, prohibit shepherds taking their sheep beyond 'the Dowles until St. Thomas', and fines were imposed if the sheep 'were thus taken in the West Fenn or the Moore or any other Fenn belonging to the manor' (CRO L1/40,47b). The hazards of grazing sheep on the fen pastures at Fordham are described by Vancouver (1794: 128):

There are eighteen hundred of the Norfolk breed of sheep, amongst which, great losses are often sustained, in consequence of their feeding upon the rotten, boggy, sheepwalks, which however, might be much improved, if not totally avoided, by a better drainage of the lowlands.

The Soham court roll for 26 April 1744 warns of the dangers of allowing unhealthy horses to graze on the fens: the Court Leet orders 'That no Horse or Horse Kine that have either the Mange or Snotty Nose shall feed in either of the Horse Fennes' (CRO L1/141).

The traditional conversion method of the black peat fen soils into land suitable for cultivation is described by Samuel Wells (1830: 440):

The ancient method of management of black fen land, or turf moor, was, to divide the farm into five or six fields. In the first year to pare the land under the plough, place the earth in small heaps, burn those heaps, spread the ashes (which act as a powerful manure), plough the whole over, and sow the land with rape or coleseed, which the cultivator sometimes allows to stand for seed, but more generally feeds off with sheep.

The newer method which Wells describes involved the digging out of clay from beneath the peat surface and its mixture with the peat to give greater body to the soil, and make it more fit for wheat cultivation.

A different but complementary system of land use continued on the upland parts of the fen-edge parishes. The open-field system, described above for the seventeenth century, continued without being subject to Parliamentary enclosure, but with some modification to the crops and rotations. The use of fallows continued into the nineteenth century, and a four-year rotation frequently employed on the open fields, the main crops being wheat, barley, peas and oats. The maintenance of an open-field system in all four parishes until the mid nineteenth century is an indication of the strength of the commoners, the size of the common lands, the history of religious dissent in the region, and the absence of large landowners. That is not to say that land was not being bought or developed at this time. Several of the colleges of Cambridge University, such as Pembroke, St John's and King's, which had held land in this area since the Middle Ages, sought new opportunites for land improvement and investment, but were frustrated in part by the lack of enclosure.

By the end of the eighteenth century, in spite of the many attempts at drainage and improvement over a period of two hundred years, some of the original problems of land drainage and management and some new ones, characterized this region of northeast Cambridgeshire. Low-lying land was still frequently flooded, and the technical and administrative measures available for drainage were still relatively ineffective, insufficient to counter natural hazards and related human conditions such as malaria and poverty. The final mastery of this environment, through more powerful means of pumping and drainage and larger-scale engineering works, was still a long way off.

Acknowledgements

Extracts from college archives referenced in the text are reproduced by kind permission of the Provost and Fellows of King's College, Cambridge and the

Master and Fellows of Pembroke College, Cambridge. Air photogrphs from the collection of the Committee for Aerial Photography, University of Cambridge, are reproduced by kind permission of the Committee. The research was carried out as part of a research project (grant no. D00242009) funded by the ESRC. Much of the research was supported by a visiting professorial fellowship at Wolfson College, Cambridge. The author wishes to acknowledge the considerable assistance afforded by the staff of the Cambridgeshire Record Office, the Map Library of Cambridge University Library, and the Cambridgeshire Collection of the Central Library, Cambridge.

Abbreviations

CRO Cambridgeshire Record Office.
KCC Manuscripts, King's College, Cambridge.
PCC Manuscripts, Pembroke College, Cambridge.

References

Baddeslade, T (1725) *The history of the ancient and present state of the navigation of the port of King's-Lyn, and of Cambridge . . . and . . . of the Bedford Level. Also the history of the ancient and present state of draining in that Level . . . with the method propos'd for draining . . . by J. Armstrong*, London.

Cambridgeshire County Planning Department (1956) *Survey reports. The common lands of Cambridgeshire*, Cambridge.

Camden, J. (1586) *Britannia:* citation is from the Edmund Gibson 1695 ed, from the facsimile edited by S. Piggott, Newton Abbott, 1971.

Cole, C.N. (1777) *Extracts from the report of a view of the South Level. Part of the Great Level of the Fenns, called Bedford Level. Taken in the summer of the year 1777.* CRO R59/31/4/8.

Darby, H.C. (1983) *The Changing Fenland*, Cambridge.

Day, A. (1985) *Turf Village. Peat diggers of Wicken.* Cambridge Libraries and Information Service, Cambridge.

'L.G.' (1906) 'Drainage of the Great Level (No. 12)', *Fenland Notes and Queries*, VI, p. 61.

Gilpin, W. (1809) *Observations on several parts of the counties of Cambridge, Norfolk, Suffolk and Essex . . . relative chiefly to picturesque beauty, in two tours (1769, 1773)*, London.

Gottshalk, M.K.E. (1971–7) *Stormvloeden en rivieroverstromingen in Nederland. 500–700,* 3 vols, Assen.

Grove, R. (1981) Cressey Dimmock and the draining of the fens: an early agricultural model, *Geographical Journal*, 147 (1), 27–37.

Harris, L.E. (1957) Land drainage and reclamation in C. Singer, E.J. Holmyard, A.R. Hall and T.I. Williams, (eds), *A history of technology. Vol.III. From the Renaissance to the Industrial Revolution c. 1500–1750*, Oxford.

Hills, R.L. (1967) *Machines, mills and uncountable costly necessities. A short history of the drainage of the fens*, Norwich.

Holmes, C. (1985) Drainers and fenmen: the problem of popular political consciousness in the seventeenth century in A. Fletcher, and J. Stevenson (eds), *Order and disorder in early modern England*, Cambridge, pp. 166–95.

Lamb, H.H. (1980) 'Climatic fluctuations in historical times and their connections with transgressions of the sea, storm floods and other coastal changes' in A. Verhulst and M.K.E. Gottshalk (eds), *Transgressies en occupatiegeschiedenis in de kustgebieden van Nederland en België*, Gent, pp. 251–84.

Lindley, K. (1982) *Fenland riots and the English revolution*, London.

Owen, A.E.B. (1967) 'Records of Commissions of Sewers', *History*, LII, 35–8.

Owen, A.E.B. (1973) 'Land drainage authorities and their records' in F. Ranger (ed), *Prisea Munimenta: Studies . . . presented to Dr A.E.J. Hollaender*, pp. 274–81

Rowell, T.A. (1982) 'Wicken Poor's Fen: origins and land use history', *Bulletin No. 37*, Cambridgeshire Local History Council, pp. 7–9.

Rowell, T.A. (1986) 'Sedge (*Cladium mariscus*) in Cambridgeshire: its use and production since the 17th century', *Agricultural History Review*, 34, 111–42.

Rowell, T.A. and Harvey, H.J. 1988 'The recent history of Wicken Fen, Cambridgeshire, England: a guide to ecological development', *Journal of Ecology*, 76, 73–90.

Schama, S. (1988) *The embarrassment of riches. An interpretation of Dutch culture in the golden age*, London.

Spufford, M. (1974) *Constrasting communities. English villagers in the sixteenth and seventeenth centuries*, Cambridge.

Spufford, M. (1976) 'Peasant inheritance customs and land distribution in Cambridgeshire from the sixteenth to the eighteenth centuries' in J. Goody, J. Thirsk and E.P. Thompson, (eds), *Family and inheritance. Rural society in western Europe 1200–1800*. Cambridge, 156–76.

Summers, D. (1976) *The great level*, Newton Abbot.

Taylor, C. (1973) *The Cambridgeshire landscape*, London.

Vancouver, C. (1794) *General view of the agriculture in the county of Cambridge: with observations on the means of its improvement*, London.

Wells, S. (1830) *The history of the drainage of the Great Level of the Fens, called Bedford Level*, London.

CHAPTER 5

Ditches and drains: the ecology and conservation of an important wetland refuge

Max Wade

What an inexhaustible store for investigation will be presented by a single ditch, choked with vegetation. (Cook, 1880)

Introduction

Many flat maritime districts of the United Kingdom, the Netherlands and France have been reclaimed from former fens and marshes for productive agricultural land. These feats of drainage engineering began as early as Roman times but were mostly consequent upon seventeenth-century pioneering work by the Dutch (Darby, 1940; Lambert, 1971). Before drainage, these wetlands comprised a mosaic of habitats: reedbeds, meres, saline pools, sedge meadows and willow carr. A diverse flora was the basis for a bewildering variety of insects, birds and fishes, as evidenced by wetland remnants which have been conserved, for example, at Wicken Fen in England (Gardner, 1925) and in the Marais de Grande Brière in France (Bernard and Rolland, 1988). However, today such areas only amount to a tiny percentage of the original wetland area and wildlife is increasingly confined to the networks of channels which drain them. These are known by a variety of different names: the *dikes* and *drains* of the Fenland district, the *rhines* of Somerset and *reens* of south Wales (Marshall *et al.*, 1978). Different names are usually associated with the different sizes of channel. In this chapter, 'ditch' refers to the smaller channels, and 'drain' to the larger.

In Britain, the agricultural development of many fens remained limited until the 1950s by continuing poor drainage; the land was too often liable to inundation, it was bleak and desolate. Names such as the Misson Washlands, Thorne Waste and the Monmouthshire Moors indicate cultural evaluations. Subsequently, the introduction of reliable flood protection, more efficient drainage techniques and, of particular significance, more powerful pumping machines, coupled with post-war food policy, led to their conversion to intensive agriculture.

Cooke (1880) was obviously impressed by the diversity of life supported by drainage channels but it was not until the 1970s that scientists and nature

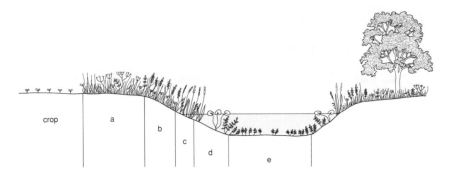

Figure 5.1   The Fen drain ecotone (for explanation of letters, see text)

conservationists came to recognize the significance of the linear habitat they represent. Although the realization of such values is often in direct conflict with agricultural intensification (Scotter *et al.*, 1977), drainage channels make important contributions to the landscape ecology of fenlands. Close examination of a drainage channel reveals that within a width of anything between 2 and 20 m is a series of vegetation strips forming the ecotone between the aquatic and terrestrial communities (Figure 5.1). The fen drain ecotone typically includes five vegetation zones:

(a) the field margin, usually dominated by grasses, which may or may not contain shrubs and trees (Way and Greig-Smith, 1986),
(b) the bank or batter supporting a range of grasses and herbs typically related to the water-table,
(c) the boundary between land and water, that is, the margin of the drainage channel, with a range of amphibious and fringing herbs able to tolerate variations in water level (Haslam and Wolseley, 1981),
(d) the littoral zone of the channel in which emergent vegetation occupies the shallower water, with floating and submerged species being able to extend out into the deeper water,
(e) the deep water zone only found in the larger drainage channels and supporting mainly submerged plant species.

The ecotones of drainage channels are markedly compressed compared to the equivalent marginal and littoral zones of the natural habitat which could have been several tens of metres wide (see Chapter 2). Nevertheless, to a greater or lesser extent they reflect the ecotonal gradient which would have occurred along the edge of a mere or around the pools of the original wetland, and the total length of ecotone along drainage channels represents a significant extent of wetland habitat. This chapter assesses the effectiveness of drainage channel habitat in supporting wetland flora and fauna and its value in intensively cultivated landscapes.

The value of drainage channels

International concern for the loss of lowland aquatic and semi-aquatic habitats (Naiman *et al.*, 1989; Maltby, 1986) has focused attention on drainage networks which are increasingly recognized as a rich resource of flora and fauna and as important refuges for a number of nationally and internationally rare species (de Lange, 1972; Drake *et al.*, 1985; Purseglove, 1988). In the reens of the Gwent Levels, Wales, over 255 flowering plants ferns and mosses have been found growing on the banks and a further 116 in the water (Scotter *et al.*, 1977). Gron (1980) recorded 270 species of aquatic invertebrate along 19 km of ditches in Tønderrmarsken, Denmark, and more than 100 invertebrate species have been found in a single 200 m section of one farm drain in Romney Marsh, England (Southern Water/Nature Conservancy Council, 1989). These examples relate to channels draining pastoral land; in arable land the diversity is commonly less. For example, in the ditches and drains of Hatfield Chase, England, the aquatic macroflora comprised only 93 species (Wade and Wingfield, 1987) and the aquatic invertebrate fauna 144 species (Malard, 1989). The channels draining both arable and pastoral land can, nevertheless, support rare species. Pillwort (*Pilularia globulifera* L.) found in arable field drains of Hatfield Chase (Husak and Wade, 1988), and short-leaved Water-starwort (*Callitriche truncata* Guss.) occuring in pastoral areas of the Belgian polders (Wade *et al.*, 1986) are both internationally rare plants.

Drainage channels are a vital component of the fenland landscape. Trees such as Poplars (*Populus* spp.) and Willows (*Salix* spp.) break the skyline and areas such as the Gwent Levels are characterized by channels hedged by common hawthorn (*Crataegus monogyna* Hacq.) and blackthorn (*Prunus spinosa* L.). The impact of the vegetation can range from minor contributions to visual diversity through to spectacular domination of the scene as with the bright red carpet of water fern (*Azolla filiculoides* Lam.) on the Broadway Reen, Gwent Levels, or the yellow stands of fringed water-lily (*Nymphoides peltata* (S.G. Gmel) Kuntze) in the Royal Military Canal, Romney Marsh. The more obvious animals such as mallard (*Anas platyrhynchos* L.) and heron (*Ardea cinerea* L.) are also important landscape components.

Factors affecting flora and fauna

Conservation depends in large measure upon recognizing and understanding those factors which govern the composition and diversity of flora and fauna. For drainage channels, the three main factors are channel structure, size and extent; community development; and the nature and frequency of management intervention. These factors are considered in turn, in relation to the aquatic biota of the habitat.

The structure, size and extent of the channels

A drainage network is made up of a hierarchy of channels typically with a series of subsidiary channels feeding into a shorter length of arterial or main channels. On the Gwent Levels the ratio of subsidiary channels to main channels is 6:1 (Scotter *et al.*, 1977); in the Marais de Moeze, France, the ratio of primary to secondary to tertiary channels is 10:1:1 (Giraud, 1985). Despite the drainage engineers' standard design for a straight-sided channel with trapezoidal cross-section, a variation of dimensions creates a spectrum of habitat conditions ranging from the small, steep-sided, shallow ditch to the larger, main channel over 4 m wide, with gently sloping banks and up to 2 m deep. The most significant dimension of ditches and drains for the aquatic biota is the depth of water. For subsidiary channels Scotter *et al.* (1977) found the mean depth to be 52 cm but this can be significantly less, especially in arable areas. Winter levels in the rhines of the Somerset Levels, England, can leave some channels without water (Wolseley *et al.*, 1984). The depth of water in main drains can be in excess of 2 m but is more typically 70–90 cm.

Different plant and animal communities develop in these various conditions. Pondweeds (*Potamogeton* spp.), for example, are typically plants of main channels, whereas species such as common reed (*Phragmites australis* Cav. Streud.) and common marsh-bedstraw (*Galium palutre* L.) are usually found in subsidiary channels (Wade, 1977; Wade and Wingfield, 1987). This difference in community composition is particularly relevant to the main channels and the open water communities they can support. As Godwin (1978) pointed out, it is 'the natural components of the early stages of the hydrach vegetational succession ... that have suffered severest restriction and extinction in consequence of Fen drainage'. A balance needs to be achieved between the maintenance necessary to keep a main channel open but able to support submerged plant and animal communities, and the extremes of drainage maintenance such as excessive water lowering and indiscriminate use of aquatic herbicides to control weed growth.

While the total length of main channels for any given area is likely to remain constant, improved drainage engineering has led to a gradual decrease in the length of the subsidiary channels. This loss has been as much as the 40 per cent recorded by Palmer (1986) when permanent pasture of the Pevensey Levels, England was ploughed up for cereal farming. Similar observations have been made for Hatfield Chase: 36 per cent between 1908 and 1986 (Wingfield and Wade, 1988), and for Broadland, 33.5 per cent between 1973 and 1981 (Driscoll, 1983). For the predominantly pastoral Gwent Levels the loss over the period 1882–1975 was only 14 per cent (Wade, 1977).

The development of the plant and animal communities over time

Following the creation of a drainage channel, plants and animals quickly colonize the new habitat (Hingley, 1979). The first plants to arrive are usually submerged and free-floating species such as stoneworts (*Chara* spp.) and duckweeds (*Lemna* spp.). Emergent plants such as branched bur-reed (*Sparganium erectum* L.) will follow, colonizing the littoral zone. In a shallow, usually subsidiary channel these plants will gradually become dominant, one species succeeding another as conditions such as water depth alter (Plate 5.1A). In the deeper channel (Plate 5.2A), the emergent species will remain in the shallower water along the drain side, allowing the submerged and free-floating plants to develop with subsequent changes in the composition of the open water community, typically the colonization of rooted floating species such as broad-leaved pondweed (*Potamogeton natans* L.). In time the smaller shallower channel will fill up with accumulated plant remains and trapped sediment, succeeding to a terrestrial habitat from an aquatic one (Plate 5.1B), as would also occur in the larger deeper channel over a longer time period. This process is accompanied by a succession of animal species.

The successional process may be terminated or altered by management, such as dredging (Plate 5.2B), or weed-cutting and use of herbicides. The ecological effects may persist for a number of years or may be of short duration as the community structure returns to the original pattern of succession within a year or two. However, the species present in a channel prior to management exert a significant effect on the pattern of recovery. The season in which maintenance takes place is also significant (Beltman, 1984).

The different drainage characteristics of main and subsidiary channels necessitate different maintenance strategies. Subsidiary channels are maintained by farmers who recognize varying degrees of importance between one ditch and another. This is reflected in the frequency of maintenance which can vary from once every three years up to once every 20 years. Those ditches which become filled in are usually at the latter end of this spectrum. Ditch maintenance is almost always some form of bank-based mechanical control undertaken either by the farmer (for example, tractor-mounted weed bucket), or by a contractor using purpose-engineered machinery (for example, Bradshaw weed cutting bucket or Priestman dredger) (Wade, 1990).

The maintenance of drains is more frequent than that for ditches. The greater length of these drains is managed by local internal drainage boards, the remainder being the responsibility of the regional water authority. Where mechanical means are used, a drain will be managed once every two to five years. This can be bank-based, as with the ditches, but boat-mounted cutters are an effective means of clearing larger channels. If herbicidal control is used the drain will be treated on an annual basis, with the treatment of emergent and marginal vegetation commonly accompanied by a clearance of dead material using a weed-cutting bucket. The economics of channel maintenance currently favour herbicidal control and this practice has been used widely, though concern about chemicals in the environment has been reflected in both a reduction in the range of chemicals used in water and a decrease in the use of aquatic herbicides in general.

Plate 5.1 Lambsdrain, Romney Marsh in early (a) and late (b) stages of succession

Plate 5.2 Main drain on Hatfield Chase (a) and mechanical clearance of drainage channel Gwent Levels, S. Wales (b)

The ecological effects of different types of mechanical plant are not well understood. It is recognized that dredging is an effective means of pushing the hydroseral succession back to an early stage in community development (Wade, 1978) whereas cutting deflects or disturbs the successional process and, because of its high frequency, tends to maintain the plant community in this deflected or disturbed state. From an ecological viewpoint, the ideal management programme maintains channels at different successional stages. For example, dredging encourages the full cycle of plant and animal succession in a given ditch or drain but it is important not to dredge out large lengths of channel in a given area at one specific time.

Herbicidal treatment also resets the plant community to an earlier hydrosere, or some variant of an earlier seral stage in the succession (Murphy and Barrett, 1990). For example, a chemical aimed at submerged vegetation can create a stage very similar to that found after dredging (for example, a channel dominated by filamentous algae). Compared with dredging, however, the channel will be treated regularly with herbicide, typically annually, suspending the channel in this early phase of development. Furthermore, the herbicide may be translocated into the root and rhizome systems of the plant, or may act on plant propagules, severely reducing its potential to recover after treatment or at some favourable period in the future (Johannes, 1974). On the other hand, some species remain virtually unaffected by herbicidal control and achieve a competitive advantage. Herbicides aimed at submerged plants tend to favour filamentous algae not susceptible to the chemical; those aimed at the emergent and marginal vegetation can favour submerged plants in general through removal of shading.

Herbicides should not be regarded *en block* as environmentally unacceptable. As with mechanical control, herbicides are an important tool in drainage channel management. Wade and Edwards (1980) found that treatment of main channels with 2,4–D and dalapon was a significant factor in maintaining the overall diversity of the drainage system of the Gwent Levels. The option of biological control using grass carp (*Ctenopharyngodon idella* Val.) is being explored, but is not yet an accepted alternative to mechanical or chemical control in northwest Europe (de Vries, 1987; van der Zweerde, 1990).

Changes in land use

The transition from poorly-drained grazing land through intensive grazing to arable agriculture, and its ecological implications for the drainage system, has been recognized for a number of areas: Gwent Levels (Scotter *et al.*, 1977), Marais de Moeze (Giraud, 1985), Romney Marsh (Mountford and Sheail, 1982) and the Pevensey Levels (Palmer, 1986). Differences have already been identified between the drains and ditches of grazing land and those draining arable areas: the latter have lower diversity of flora and fauna, and fewer subsidiary channels relative to main channels, and a deterioration of the extent and quality of habitat (Driscoll, 1982; 1985). The transition from pasture to arable causes the channels to experience a three-phase development. First, in pastoral land, drains and ditches serve as field boundaries and are often important for watering stock. Hence the water levels remain high and constant. Stock are brought off the fields in winter, when the drainage system is managed to prevent flooding. During the second phase, with increased stocking density, drainage becomes more critical as farmers strive to maximise grass production. The erection of fencing dispenses with the need for the field boundary role and the installation of troughs removes the poaching effect of cattle coming down to the water to drink. Farmers control water levels using pumps, creating much greater variability in water level with little or no water present in some ditches and drains at certain times of the year. This increased regulation of water levels enables the third phase, the ploughing up of the fields for arable crops. During the winter and spring, pumps are used to keep water levels low in order to prevent flooding. Wade and Wingfield (1987) observed main channels with regular fluctuations (c. 30 cm) in water which could inhibit the development of emergent and marginal plant species. In the summer the water level is allowed to rise in order to maintain the optimum water-table for crop growth and to make water available for irrigation. Water levels over this period, up to early September, are relatively stable (Wade and Wingfield, 1987).

Conservation measures

The 1980s witnessed a rapid growth in awareness of the ecological and landscape value of drains and ditches. In Britain, attention has been focused on the need for sympathetic channel maintenance and management. Advice has been disseminated through leaflets (see, for example, Nature Conservancy Council, 1976; 1986), in booklets and manuals (see Brooks, 1981; Lewis and Williams, 1984; Gair, 1988) and through the Farming and Wildlife Trust and the Agricultural Development and Advisory Service. The national 'Find a drain' initiative highlighted the wildlife interests which exist even in the most intensively drained agricultural areas (Association of Drainage Authorities, 1986). This literature draws attention to:

(a) the need to maintain permanent aquatic habitats;
(b) the successional processes initiated by management and the length of time required for community development;
(c) the value of habitat/niche diversity along the channel—for example, shallow margins, cattle-trampled sections and retention of trees;
(d) the importance of cleaning only short lengths of ditch in any one year, leaving uncleared lengths to recolonize maintained sections;
(e) the generally undesirable nature of herbicides;
(f) the effect which activities on the land can have on the aquatic biota, eg. fertilizers, slurry and pesticides;
(g) the problems associated with introduced aquatic plant and animal species.

However, significant conservation can only be achieved through coordinated action aimed at specific channel networks in relation to agricultural use. The designation of nature reserves and Sites of Special Scientific Interest (SSSIs) offer such opportunities for coordinated management.

The establishment of a nature reserve based on the fields and drainage system of reclaimed marshlands is an obvious option for ensuring the conservation of the flora, fauna and landscape. However, high land prices of lowland agricultural land with good-grade soils and multiple ownership cause problems in acquiring land for conservation purposes. The Royal Society for the Protection of Birds had to negotiate with over 150 owners in acquiring 707 ha (1,747 acres) of the Ouse Washes, Cambridgeshire, and nearly 90 land owners for 299 ha (739 acres) of West Sedgemoor, Somerset.

The powers of the Wildlife and Countryside Act 1981 enable the Nature Conservancy Council to designate areas of reclaimed marshland or specific lengths of ditches or drains as SSSIs thereby conferring a degree of protection on their wildlife (Nature Conservancy Council, 1988). Ideally, such reserves and sites need to be discrete hydrological units in order for the appropriate control to be achieved over water levels in the drainage channels and to ensure that the flora and fauna are not adversely affected by other factors such as agrochemicals applied to adjacent fields. The problem of establishing protected areas and different management strategies are illustrated below in a series of brief case studies.

The West Sedgemoor SSSI

The nature conservation value of the wet meadows of West Sedgemoor, with their intervening droves, rhynes and ditches, lies in the birds and flora of the fields as well as the diversity of aquatic life in the drainage channels. The designation of the SSSI was stimulated by the need to protect the area from continuing drainage improvements, notably pumped drainage (Lowe et al., 1986). The first pump had already been installed in 1944 and the drainage of the area improved thereafter. Because of slow acceptance by long-established farming families of the need for further improvements to the drainage system, there was little replacement by arable farming, although intensification of the pastoral economy followed (Williams, 1970). This is not surprising as the landholding was very fragmented, and conflict existed between landowners on either side of the rhynes, on the one hand wishing to water stock and on the other keen to lower water levels to improve land for arable farming. The same factors also generated intense opposition to proposals for scheduling 1,000 ha of West Sedgemoor as an SSSI (Lowe et al., 1986). The SSSI was designated en bloc in 1982 amidst a storm of controversy.

The Gwent Levels SSSI

Unlike West Sedgemoor, the strategy for designating the Gwent Levels as an SSSI was based on the ecological value of the ditches and reens, not on the pasture. Nevertheless, the Gwent Levels project recognized that the activities on the land could affect the drainage system. In order to conserve the exceptional variety of aquatic and terrestrial invertebrates, and the diverse flora associated with the drainage system, a programme was devised through which it was eventually intended that the whole of the Gwent Levels would achieve SSSI status. A Technical Advisory Group was established in 1985 to advise the Nature Conservancy Council in its appraisal of nature conservation value and the factors affecting it. Shortly after this, notification began, a gradual process phased over a number of years. At the time of writing, two parishes have been notified (c. 1,000 ha).

Broads Grazing Marshes Conservation Scheme

The mixture of pasture, water-filled dikes and woodland fringes known as the Broads grazing marshes is a key landscape within Norfolk. Ploughing up, improved drainage and arable cropping began during the 1960s and 1970s (Countryside Commission, 1988). Recognizing that a lower water-table and more rigorous programme of channel maintenance would have serious implications for the aquatic flora and fauna (Driscoll, 1982), the Countryside Commission and the Nature Conservancy Council took action to conserve the area. The primary focus of attention here was landscape value, with an emphasis on the fields and associated cultural features. Initial efforts were made to maintain a status quo using the provisions of the Wildlife and Countryside Act 1981. However, management agreements between the landowners and the Nature Conservancy Council proved impossibly expensive. It was against this background that the Broads Grazing Marshes Conservation Scheme was introduced in 1984, a scheme led by the Countryside Commission and run in partnership with the Ministry of Agriculture, Fisheres and Food (MAFF) (Countryside Commission, 1988).

The scheme aimed to keep permanent grassland with grazing livestock on the central Broads marshes, to encourage management of the grazing marshes in ways which would support both farming and conservation objectives, and to re-establish permanent grassland in some areas formerly grazed but converted to arable. The only reference to drainage in the guidelines was a requirement to consult with the Broads Grazing Scheme Unit before 'improving any grazing marshes by under-drainage'. The expectation was that the maintenance of traditional grazing regimes would ensure that the ditches and dikes retained their nature conservation value and that those practices which perpetuated this value would also continue. The scheme, based on flat-rate payments designed to attract the participation of all those with grazing marshes rather than on individual 'profits forgone' arrangements, was initiated in an experimental area. All landowners or full agricultural tenants with land within this area who agreed to farm their land according to special grazing guidelines for the following three years were eligible for a payment of £123 per hectare (£50 per acre) per year. Despite one of the most complicated systems of landownership and annual grazing lets in Britain, and at least 18 different types of stock grazing systems including cattle and sheep, 89 per cent of the experimental area eligible within the scheme was protected in 1985, the first year of operations. The experimental area was extended in 1986.

The above conservation strategy formed the basis of what became in 1988 the Broads Environmentally Sensitive Area. In 1984 the Ministry of Agriculture, Fisheries and Foods (MAFF) had introuced a new scheme to protect exceptionally attractive landscapes and valuable wildlife habitats from damage and loss consequent upon agricultural change in response to recommendations of the Nature Conservancy Council and Countryside Commission. Within these Environmentally Sensitive Areas (ESAs) MAFF enters into voluntary agreements with farmers who are offered payments to adopt and sustain the farming methods and drainage system management responsible for the landscape and wildlife values of the ESA. In the Broads ESA, the main requirements are that farmers:

(a) do not install under-drainage or mole drain, do not use a subsoiler (or tunnel-plough), and do not substantially modify their existing drainage system;

(b) maintain existing dikes (field gutters, surface piping, rig and furrow, ditches) by mechanical means, not sprays;

(c) where ditch water levels are within their control,
   (i) maintain water at a suitable level for grazing livestock (between 31 March and 1 November),
   (ii) ensure that there is at least 30 cm of water in the bottom of the dikes between 30 September and 1 April (at no time is the ditch allowed to dry out);

(d) where dike water levels are within their control, ensure that the water is not more than 45 cm below marsh level between 31 March and 1 October;

(e) slub dikes out in rotation over a period of years.

Large areas of the Somerset Levels including West Sedgemoor are now part of another ESA.

Hatfield Chase

The measures taken to conserve the flora and fauna of the drainage channel systems of the Somerset Levels, Gwent Levels and the Broadland grazing marshes were based on an established nature conservation resource to be maintained into the future. For many other channel networks this resource has deteriorated and the challenge here is to re-establish the diversity of wildlife within the context of intensive agricultural practice and the constraints which such land use places on the drainage system. Such a reclamation scheme has been developed for Hatfield Chase, an area of arable land draining via pumps into the lower reaches of the River Trent. A conservation initiative was taken by the Severn-Trent Water Authority, which commissioned an appraisal of the aquatic flora of the drains and ditches (Wade and Wingfield, 1987). These investigations determined that there was still a significant diversity of aquatic species within the drainage system as a whole, despite a decrease in the distribution of a number of species (Wingfield *et al.*, 1989), and that some of these species were rarities (Husak and Wade, 1988). A 36 per cent decrease in the extent of ditch habitat since 1908 was described, and an account given of intensive channel management including the use of dichlobenil and terbutryne for weed control in drains (Wingfield and Wade, 1988).

In 1988 an informal Hatfield Chase Working Group was established, comprising representatives from the Severn-Trent Water Authority, Hatfield Chase Internal Drainage Board, Nature Conservancy Council, Countryside Commission, regional and local authorities and the Farming and Wildlife Advisory Group. The aims of the group were to maximize the wildlife and general countryside amenity benefits attainable within the workings of the pumped drainage system, while accepting the requirements of agriculturalists and others to make a living from the land. The projects initiated by the group focus on the drains and ditches, highlighting the fundamental role of these features and the landscape ecology of these systems. An extensive tree and shrub planting programme was undertaken during 1987–8 along the banks of drains and ditches; more than 19,300 trees and 6,000 shrubs were planted. The aim of this extensive programme was to return the landscape to a form more typically encountered within a fenland. Recommendations were made for diversifying the aquatic flora and a programme of reintroductions was begun in 1989 (Wingfield *et al.*, 1989).

Discussion

Despite the different approaches used to conserve the wildlife and landscape of polder areas, the primary and consistent aim has been to maintain a permanent aquatic habitat in the ditches and drains. The scheduling of SSSIs and the guidelines for ESAs all stress the need to maintain water levels, with depths being prescribed in some instances. Maintaining water depth is vital for most submerged and floating aquatic plants and aquatic invertebrates. However, achieving an optimal water depth can involve wide water level fluctuations especially where levels are controlled by a pump, such as on Hatfield Chase. Fluctuating water levels are known to be one of the main reasons for the decline in amphibians in polder areas (Cooke and Ferguson, 1976), but the effects of such changes in water level on the aquatic biota and the potential management advantages of flow regulation require further research.

The second common aim in conserving the wildlife and landscape features of drainage channel networks is the retention of traditional channel maintenance and the exclusion of chemical treatments. This is a conservative approach which will maintain the extent and broad range of ditch and drain types (for example, the ratio of primary to secondary channels). The assumption is that maintenance procedures will remain exactly the same, but this is not the case. Most maintenance relies on mechanical control. Changes to the nature of the machines, such as the size of weed-cutting bucket or efficiency of reciprocating butter-bar, will alter the ecology of a channel (Wade, 1990). Mechanical treatment drives or interferes with successional processes in the channel and any alteration of the pattern or frequency of maintenance will materially change the nature of a channel. Investigations are needed of the ecological effects of different types of mechanical control and of advances in weed cutting and other mechanical regimes.

Compared to physical methods of aquatic plant management in channels, the effects of chemical methods on channel ecology are well researched (Murphy and Barrett, 1990). Herbicides, however, are not to be used in SSSIs and ESAs despite observations which have demonstrated that some chemicals, such as dalapon, used in certain ways, can be significant in maintaining the diversity of aquatic flora (Wade and Edwards, 1980). A more rational approach to channel maintenance would be to work towards a management programme which uses a range of techniques to achieve a balance between the different stages in succession within ditches and drains of different types. This would maintain and enhance the conservation value of a drainage system within the context of appropriate drainage (Murphy and Pieterse, 1990).

The most important aspect of the nature conservation strategies employed to protect the wildlife of drainage channels is the attempt to maintain agricultural land use. This prevents an intensification or change of land use which invariably puts more demand on the drainage system and hence stresses the aquatic flora and fauna. There are many specialized species which can exploit new conditions created by different land uses but these are invariably macrophytic algae and fly larvae (for example, species of Chironomidae), having little or no wildlife value and sometimes posing further problems to the drainage engineer. In order to be effective, prevention of land use changes needs to be addressed to large areas of land. The success of conservation strategies for the Gwent Levels, Somerset Levels and Moors and the Broadland grazing marshes substantiate this claim.

While the initiatives described herein are essential in preserving the nature conservation potential of fenland systems, there is an increasing need for integrated land use management strategies to be produced for these polder areas. However, agricultural development and nature conservation are only two of a number of factors which need to be considered. Other factors include peat and mineral excavation, housing and industrial development, forestry, angling, and other recreative activities such as cycling, walking and tourism.

References

Association of Drainage Authorities (1986) 'Find a drain', *ADA Gazette*, Summer, 22–3.

Beltmann, B. (1984) 'Management of ditches. The effect of cleaning ditches on the water coenoses', *Proc. 22nd Int. Assoc. Limnology.*

Bernard, J.Y. and Rolland, R. (1988) 'Remis en état du Marais de Grand Brière Mottière', *Proc. 3rd International Wetlands Conference*, Rennes, p. 321.

Brooks, A. (1981) *Waterways and wetlands. A practical conservation handbook*, British Trust for Conservation Volunteers.

Cooke, A.S. and Ferguson, P.F. (1976) 'Changes in the status of the frog (*Rana temporaria*) and the toad (*Bufo bufo*) on part of the East Anglian fenland in Britain', *Biol. Cons.*, 9, 191–8.

Cooke, M.C. (1880) *Ponds and ditches*, London, Society for Promoting Christian Knowledge.

Countryside Commission (1988) *The Broads Grazing Marshes Conservation Scheme 1985–1988.*

Darby, H.C. (1940) *The draining of the fens*, Cambridge, Cambridge University Press.

Drake, C.M., Foster, A.P. and Palmer, M. (1985) *A survey of the invertebrates of the Somerset Levels and Moors*, Peterborough, Nature Conservancy Council.

Driscoll, R.J. (1982) 'Improvements in land management: their effects on aquatic plants in Broadland', *Watsonia*, 14, 276–7.

Driscoll, R.J. (1983) 'Broadland dykes: The loss of an important wildlife habitat'. *Trans. Norfolk Norwich Nat. Soc.*, 26, 170–2.

Driscoll, R.J. (1985) 'The effect of changes in land management on the dyke flora at Somerton and Winterton', *Trans. Norfolk Norwich Nat. Soc.*, 27, 33–41.

Gair, R. (1988) *Farm conservation guide*, Farming and Wildlife Trust/Schering Agriculture.

Gardner, J.S. (ed.) (1925) *The natural history of Wicken Fen*, Cambridge, Bowes and Bowes.

Giraud, F. (1985) *Action concertée de recherche sur les Marais de l'Ouest; Approche du fonctionnement hydraulique du Marais Agricole de Moeze (Charente-Maritime)*, Musée National d'Histoire Naturelle, University of Rennes 1.

Godwin, H. (1978) *Fenland: its ancient past and uncertain future*, Cambridge, Cambridge University Press.

Gron, P.N. (1980) *Ferskvandsbiologiske undersogelser i Tøndermarsken 1979. 1, Ferskvandsfauna*. Naturhistorisk Museum, Århus.

Haslam, S.M. and Wolseley, P.A. (1981) *River vegetation: its identification, assessment and management*, Cambridge, Cambridge University Press.

Hingley, M.R. (1979) 'The colonisation of newly-dredged drainage channels on the Pevensey Levels (East Sussex), with special reference to gastropods', *J. Conch.*, 30, 105–22.

Husak, S. and Wade, P.M. (1988) '*Pilularia globulifera* L. recorded at Hatfield chase, Lincolnshire', *Watsonia*, 17, 92–3.

Johannes, H. (1974) 'Mehrjährige Herbizidanwendung und ihr Einfluss auf das Ökosystem-Eine Gemeinschaftsarbeit', *Proc. EWRC 4th Symposium Aquatic Weeds*, 1974, 7–11.

Lambert, A.M. (1971) *The making of the Dutch landscape*, London, Seminar Press.

Lange, L. de (1972) 'An ecological study of ditch vegetation in the Netherlands', PhD thesis, University of Amsterdam.

Lewis, G. and Williams, G. (1984) *Rivers and wildlife handbook: a guide to practices which further the conservation of wildlife on rivers*, Sandy, Royal Society for the Protection of Birds/Royal Society for Nature Conservation.

Lowe, P., Cox, G., MacEwen, M. O'Riordan, T. and Winter, M. (1986) *Countryside conflicts*, Aldershot, Gower.

Malard, F. (1989) *Étude des invertébrés aquatiques des canaux de drainage dans une région à agriculture intensive: Hatfield Chase, Angleterre*, Quetigmy, École Nationale d'Ingénieurs des Travaux Agricoles.

Malty, E. (1986) *Waterlogged Wealth*, London, Earthscan, IIED.

Marshall, E.J.P., Wade, P.M. and Clare, P. (1978) 'Land drainage channels in England and Wales', *Geog. J.*, 144, 254–63.

Mountford, J.O. and Sheail, J. (1982) 'The impact of land drainage on wildlife in Romney Marsh: the availability of baseline data', Institute of Terrestrial Ecology Project 718, Natural Environment Research Council.

Murphy, K.J. and Barrett, P.R.F. (1990) 'Chemical control of aquatic weeds' in A. Pieterse and K.J. Murphy (eds), *Aquatic weeds. The ecology and management of nuisance aquatic vegetation*, Oxford, Oxford University Press.

Murphy, K.J. and Pieterse, A.H. (1990) 'Present status and prospects of integrated control of aquatic weeds' in A.H. Pieterse and K.J. Murphy (eds), *Aquatic weeds. The ecology and management of nuisance aquatic vegetation*, Oxford, Oxford University Press.

Naiman, R.J., Decamps, H., and Fournier, F. (1989) 'The role of land/inland water ecotones in landscape management and restoration', *MAB Digest 4*, Unesco, Paris.

Nature Conservancy Council (1976) *Ponds and ditches—a leaflet*, Peterborough, Nature Conservancy Council.

Nature Conservancy Council (1986) *The conservation of farm ponds and ditches*, Peterborough, Nature Conservancy Council, Interpretive Branch.

Nature Conservancy Council (1988) *Sites of Special Scientific Interest*, Peterborough, Nature Conservancy Council.

Palmer, M. (1986) 'The impact of a change from permanent pasture to cereal farming on the flora and invertebrate fauna of watercourses in the Pevensey Levels,' *Proc. EWRS/ AAB 7th Symposium Aquatic Weeds*, Loughborough, 1986, 233–8.

Purseglove, J. (1988) *Taming the flood*, Oxford, Oxford University Press.

Scotter, C.N.G., Wade, P.M., Marshall, E.J.P. and Edwards, R.W. (1977) 'The Monmouthshire Levels' drainage system: its ecology and relation to agriculture', *J. Environ, Manage.*, 5, 75–86.

Southern Water/Nature Conservancy Council (1989) *Romney Marsh. An assessment of the environmental impact of selected drainage operations on the flora and fauna of Lambs Farm Dyke of Romney Marsh*, Chatham, Southern Water.

Vries, P.J.R. de (1987) 'Ervaringen met de graskarper bij waterschappen', *Waterschapsbelangen*, 72, 384–9.

Wade, P.M. (1977) 'Dredging of drainage channels—its ecological effects', PhD thesis, UWIST, Cardiff.

Wade, P.M. (1978) 'The effect of mechanical excavators on the drainage channel habitat', *Proc. EWRS Symp. Aquatic Weeds*, 1978, 333–42.

Wade, P.M. (1990) 'Physical control methods': In: Pieterse, A. and Murphy, K.J. (eds), *Aquatic weeds. The ecology and management of nuisance aquatic vegetation*, Oxford, Oxford University Press.

Wade, P.M. and Edwards, R.W. (1980) 'The effect of channel maintenance on the aquatic macrophytes of the drainage channels of the Monmouthshire Levels, South Wales, 1870–1976', *Aquatic Botany*, 8, 307–22.

Wade, P.M., Vanhecke, L. and Barry, R. (1986) 'The importance of habitat creation, weed management and other habitat disturbance to the conservation of the rare aquatic plant, *Callitriche truncata* Guss'. *Proc. EWRS/AA 7th Symposium Aquatic Weeds*, Loughborough, 1986, 389–93.

Wade, P.M. and Wingfield, M. (1987) *The aquatic flora of Hatfield Chase. Recommendations for botanical conservation*, Severn-Trent Water Authority/Nature Conservancy Council.

Way, J.M. and Greig-Smith, P.W. (eds) (1986) *Field margins*, British Crop Protection Council Monograph 35, p. 128.

Williams, M. (1970) *The draining of the Somerset Levels*, Cambridge, Cambridge University Press.

Wingfield, M., Steven, K. and Wade, P.M. (1989) *Recommendations for the conservation of the rare aquatic plants of Hatfield Chase*, Nottingham, Severn-Trent Water Authority, Nottingham.

Wingfield, M. and Wade, P.M. (1988) 'Hatfield Chase: the loss of drainage channel habitat', *The Naturalist*, 113, 21–4.

Wolseley, P.A., Palmer, M.A. and Williams, R. (1984) *The aquatic flora of the Somerset Levels*, Taunton Nature Conservancy Council, S.W. Region.

Zweerde, W. van der (1990) 'Biological control of aquatic weeds by means of phytophagous Fish' in A.H. Pieterse and K.J. Murphy (eds), *Aquatic weeds. The ecology and management of nuisance aquatic vegetation*, Oxford, Oxford University Press.

CHAPTER 6

Bringing the desert to bloom: French ambitions in the Sahara desert during the late nineteenth century—the strange case of 'la mer intérieure'

Michael J. Heffernan

Nineteenth-century Europeans exhibited an extraordinary faith in the power of science to control, manipulate and enhance the natural world. To a large extent, this confidence was entirely justified. Scientific innovation and technical skill were certainly the essential driving forces in the dramatic expansion in European commercial and industrial power during the nineteenth century. It has also been argued that this technological renaissance both enabled and sustained European imperial expansion into Africa and Asia in the same period (Headrick, 1981). From the perspective of the colonial conquerors, these huge continents were underdeveloped, unmanaged and inadequately exploited. Although frequently unjustified, this perception of the 'new' colonial lands was the very basis of European military and commercial expansion. Driven by a supreme self-confidence and an almost limitless ambition, European science found the greatest challenge to its ingenuity and technical expertise in the colonies. Here lay the vast and unexploited forests, the needlessly infertile expanses of marshland and swamp, and most challenging of all, the huge deserts of sunblasted sand and rock.

Of all the great blank zones on the map, none exerted a more hypnotic attraction than the barren wastes of the Sahara. Here was a hostile and desolate wilderness in the midst of a continent of richness and variety, an apparently impenetrable barrier separating the Mediterranean from the treasures of the African interior. Europe had gained a foothold on the northern edge of the desert in the summer of 1830 when an expeditionary force of 30,000 French troops seized the Ottoman city of Algiers (Julien, 1979: 21–63; Hamdani, 1985). Thereafter, the French army gradually expanded its sphere of control in the face of sporadic opposition from local tribes (Danziger, 1977; Sullivan, 1983). The unrest forced many of the native inhabitants into the upland and desert regions of the interior, leaving large areas of the fertile coastal zone underpopulated. This in turn prompted a wave of European colonization to 'develop' this 'vacant' land. By the late 1860s, there were more than 200,000 European settlers in Algeria, only half originating from mainland France (Julien, 1979: 106–63, 210–69; Heffernan, 1989a).

The process of colonization and French expansion into North Africa grew more rapid after the Franco-Prussian war and the humiliating loss of Alsace-Lorraine in 1870–1. For many patriotic Frenchmen, colonial development was the best means of re-establishing France's damaged international reputation and compensating for the territorial loss suffered in Europe. The obvious starting point were the vast French colonial territories beyond the Mediterranean. If the barren wastes of the Algerian interior could be developed and settled then a new and rejuvenated France might be created; an imperial France of '100 million people' stretching from Calais and Dunkerque to Saint-Louis and Lake Chad (Prévost-Paradol, 1868; Ganiage, 1968; Brunschwig, 1966; Girardet, 1972; Ageron, 1979; Andrew and Kanya-Forstner, 1981). One important repercussion of this renewed enthusiasm for colonial expansion in the last decades of the nineteenth century was a dramatic increase in the size and influence of the French geographical movement which was already so closely linked to the colonial lobby as to be virtually synonymous with it (MacKay, 1943; Murphy, 1948; Broc, 1970; 1974; 1976; 1977; 1987; 1988; Berdoulay, 1981).

It was in this context that a remarkable scheme was hatched by a group of military surveyors, engineers and entrepreneurs to increase the commercial and environmental potential of North Africa by creating a vast, inland 'sea' deep within the arid wastes of the Sahara. This ambitious and controversial project was widely publicized and received considerable public and official support. Although ultimately unsuccessful, the scheme represents a revealing episode in the history of Western water engineering and landscape creation and provides, at the same time, an insight into the nature of the European colonial mind in the nineteenth century.

The origins of the project

The principal architect of this scheme was François Élie Roudaire (1836–85), a military topographer and surveyor. After graduating from St Cyr and the École d'État Major, Roudaire worked on the topographic survey of Savoy during the early 1860s and then moved to Algeria in 1864 as part of a special topographic unit established by the Armée d'Afrique to improve French military knowledge of the upland and desert regions of the interior (AN F80 962–6). In the early 1870s, Roudaire began survey work in the region of saline depressions or chotts which lay to the south of the Aurès mountains on the edge of the Sahara itself (Figure 6.1). This desolate lowland plain stretched in a 350 km arc from the oasis of Chegga eastwards into what was then the Regency of Tunis and onwards to within a few kilometres of the Gulf of Gabès. During the eighteenth century, the English traveller, Dr Thomas Shaw, had speculated that the chotts represented the last remnants of the Sea of Triton, so named after the mythical sea god who had directed Jason and his Argonauts through the narrow straits which had once linked this legendary sea with the Mediterranean (Shaw, 1738; Thompson, 1987). This idea was developed further by Major James Rennell, the influential

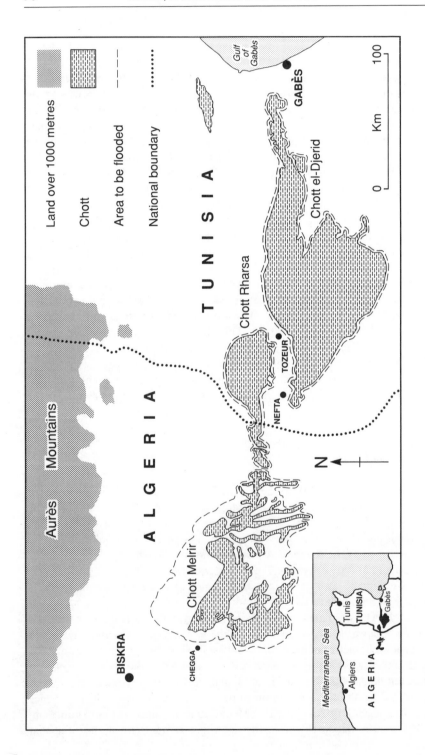

Figure 6.1 The Saharan chotts

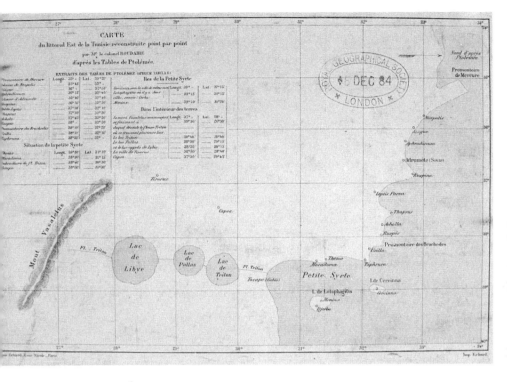

Plate 6.1 François Élie Roudaire: Map of the chotts region based on Ptolemy (*c.* 1877)

English geographer and surveyor. Rennell noted that the changing descriptions of North Africa provided by the classical writers, Herodotus, Scylax, Pomponius Melas and Ptolemy, from the fifth century BC to the secondary century AD, seemed to indicate that a great gulf had once existed in the region but had gradually dried out towards the end of the Roman occupation (Rennell, 1800; Markham, 1895; Downes, 1977) (Figure 6.1). Geological work on the region, carried out in the wake of French military expansion during the 1840s, lent some scientific support to these claims by suggesting that the three major chotts— Melrir, Rharsa and el-Djerid—were below sea level (Virlet d'Aoust, 1844–5). This reawakened interest in the region's environmental history and promoted some geologists to consider the possibility of re-creating this great 'sea' (Duveyrier, 1864; Martins, 1864; Lavigne, 1869).

Roudaire was intrigued by this idea and undertook careful altitudinal measurements throughout his survey work in the region. His figures indicated that Chott Melrir was an average of 27 m below sea level. Roudaire published these results and suggested that, if the other depressions were of similar depth, then the former sea could indeed be re-created by building a series of canals linking the Gulf of Gabès with the chotts. Roudaire was convinced that, if successful, this scheme would bring enormous environmental, commercial and military benefits for France in North Africa. In his view, the project represented one of 'the most important conquests of nature by the intelligence and energy of mankind' (Roudaire, 1874a: 350). Re-creating this former sea would, he felt, confirm France's enlightened and progressive intentions in Algeria and re-establish the climatic and environmental conditions which had been the basis of Roman civilization in the region. This reference to the region's allegedly greater fertility under Roman rule and the historical affinity between modern France and ancient Rome had become a recurring leitmotiv within French colonial discourse on North Africa and was to remain an oft-stated justification for French colonial rule in the region (Bénatou, 1980; Shaw, 1981; Frémaux, 1984; Swearingen, 1985; 1988). According to Roudaire's assessment, North Africa had once been an integral part of the legendary 'granary of Rome'. During centuries of mismanagement and environmental degradation under Arab and Turkish rule, this cradle of Carthaginian civilization and birthplace of Augustinian Christianity had steadily declined (Roudaire, 1874b; Duveyrier, 1874a). Modern France, the self-appointed 'heir' to the moral and intellectual legacy of classical civilization, had a duty to re-establish the 'natural' environmental conditions of North Africa enjoyed by the Romans.

Early controversy

Roudaire's ideas provoked a storm of controversy, particularly within the august salons of the Académie des Sciences. Academicians like Charles Houyvet felt that his project 'would have thê sole outcome of creating, at great cost, an immense salt-marsh'. In Houyvet's (1874) view, history would simply repeat itself and the sea would evaporate under the burning Saharan sun and driving desert winds. The distinguished geologist, Auguste Pomel, was equally hostile. He rejected the idea that the region had ever been linked to the sea (Pomel, 1872) and suggested that the bedrock around the Gulf and Gabès would probably be too hard for the construction of a deep canal 16 km in length (Pomel, 1874; 1875; Delestre, 1874). Another Academician, Ernest Cosson, suggested that the sea would swamp numerous populated and productive oases adjacent to the chotts (Virlet d'Aoust, 1874).

Roudaire offered an impassioned defence of his ideas before the Académie. He argued that the original sea had only dried out after siltation of the Straits of Gabès. An artificial channel could be kept clear and deep enough to allow the highly saline water of the lake to flow out into the Mediterranean beneath an equal inflow of less saline water. As to the evaporation rates, Roudaire was convinced that such a large water body would transform the meso-climate of the region, reducing the potential water loss from the surface. In the absence of detailed geological knowledge of the area, Roudaire made a plea for a full scientific investigation of his ideas (Roudaire, 1874-5).

This oration seems to have convinced several members of the Académie. In particular, Roudaire received enthusiastic support from Ferdinand de Lesseps, the great entrepreneurial opportunist and builder of the Suez Canal (Beatty, 1956; Bonnet, 1959; Pudney, 1960; Marlowe, 1964; Kinross, 1968). The two men began to campaign vigorously for an official expedition and quickly persuaded the Académie to set up a full investigative committee. Following an eloquent speech in support of his project in the Assemblée Nationale by Paul Bert, the prominent scientist and republican politician, Roudaire was given a special government grant of 10,000F to continue his investigations. Further grants followed, including one of 3,000F from the Société de Géographie de Paris. By the autumn, Roudaire had gathered around him a expedition comprising two fellow *capitaines de'État Major*, Parisot and Martin, a young *lieutenant* named Baudot, a military doctor and amateur zoologist named Jacquent, and two special delegates, the explorer, Henri Duveyrier, from the Société de Géographie de Paris (Heffernan, 1989b) and an engineer, Henri Le Chatelier, from the Ministère des Travaux Publics. The mission was to be protected and assisted by 51 men from the Bataillon d'Afrique (Duveyrier, 1875a).

The first mission

On 1 December 1874, the expedition set off from Biskra in the direction of Chegga, on the western edge of Chott Melrir. The objective was to determine the extent of potential flooding around Chott Melrir and Chott Rharsa and to calculate the depth of water which would be produced if the area were inundated. Working non-stop, the expedition moved along the northern edge of Chott Melrir and Chott Rharsa towards the Tunisian frontier, making frequent forays into the heart of the depressions. They returned along the southern edge of the chotts and reached Chegga on 12 April 1875. Some 650 kilometres had been surveyed in 134 days (just under 5 km per day) with two separate readings taken every 120–150 m (A.N. F17 3004A) (Plate 6.1).

This was a remarkable feat. Although it was winter, temperatures often approached 30°C during the day and usually fell below freezing at night. Surveying was hampered by the heat haze and the blinding reflection from the white salt crystals of the chotts. Each man covered at least 20 km on foot each day and was permitted only four hours' sleep a night. By early February, Baudot, Martin and Le Chatelier were suffering from fever and hallucinations brought on by fatigue and the debilitating effect of the local drinking water (Duveyrier, 1875b; Roudaire, 1875).

Despite these difficulties, the expedition produced creditable survey results which suggested that the sea would cover around 6,700 km² of unproductive Algerian desert to a depth of between 21 and 31 m. Only three tiny oases would be inundated—those at Nsira, Dendouga and Sidi Mohammed. The results were warmly commended by the commission of the Académie des Sciences and Roudaire presented his findings to widespread acclaim at the 1875 Congrès International des Sciences Géographiques in Paris. Encouraged by powerful figures like Émile Levasseur, the Congrès proposed a motion supporting a final

Plate 6.2   François Élie Roudaire during the second Tunisian expedition, 1879

expedition into the Regency of Tunis where Roudaire could complete his surveying activities (Levasseur, 1875). De Lesseps and Roudaire set to work once again to raise the necessary funding.

One potential source of financial assistance was the Commission des Missions Scientifiques et Littéraires, which had been established within the Ministère de l'Instruction Publique in 1874 to evaluate and finance scientific missions. On 13

November 1875, Roudaire wrote to the Commission outlining his plans for a new Tunisian expedition. He requested 8,000F to support himself and four assistants—*Capitaine* de Villars, a colleague from the 1872–3 geodetic expedition, *Lieutenants* Nay and Baudot, and an Arab-speaking engineer named Gaselin. The commission unanimously accepted the project and voted through the necessary funding (AN F17 3004A).

However, the diplomatic implications of a French military expedition into an independent country were considerable and the commission duly sought the advice of the Ministère des Affaires Étrangères. As the ultimate objective was the flooding of a large part of an independent state, it is scarcely surprising that the officials in the Quai d'Orsay were less enthusiastic than the scientists of the Ministère de l'Instruction Publique. The Regency of Tunis would need to be persuaded that the scheme was desirable and that the expedition was a purely scientific exercise and not a prelude to invasion. This meant that the Ministère de la Guerre would have to forfeit direct involvement in the expedition and this implied that Roudaire would have to rely on a Tunisian, rather than a French, military escort. The expedition therefore needed an entirely new team of non-military personnel. After advertisements in the press and numerous interviews, three engineers and a surveyor were recruited (AN F17 3004A).

The second mission and the first report

On 13 February 1876, Roudaire and his companions left for Tunis, where they were welcomed by Roustan, the French Consul, and by General Khereddine of the Tunisian army. The expedition was given an escort of ten local men plus an interpreter called Allegro. The plan was to survey around the edge of Chott el-Djerid and make several crossings of the depression itself. It was already warm when operations began in early March. Progress was slow as the chott contained unexpectedly large amounts of saline water. Despite desert storms and plagues of snakes, the task was eventually completed by 2 May. The group had surveyed nearly 440 kilometres in 63 days (about 7 km per day) and had performed 2,072 levellings, one every 211 m (A.N. F17 3004A) (Figure 6.1).

After a few days' rest in Gabès, Roudaire filed a short report to the Ministère de l'Instruction Publique (AN F17 3004A). He was now in a position to construct a very detailed map which would demonstrate conclusively the feasibility of his plan. He filed a preliminary report, and returned to Paris in time to see it published in the *Journal Officiel* on 9 July 1876. He immediately began work on his map and his final report to the Ministère de l'Instruction Publique. Although his critics remained sceptical (Duponchel, 1876; Angot, 1877; Pomel, 1877; Fuchs, 1877), Roudaire's findings were received with general enthusiasm and were widely reported (Girard de Rialle, 1876; le Chatelier, 1876; Ville, 1876; 1877; Gros, 1876; Sainte-Marie, 1876; Abbadie, 1877). The scheme caught the imagination of the politicians, academics and the general public alike and, for a few months, Roudaire was the toast of Parisian society. In December 1876 he was promoted to the rank of *Colonel* and in February 1877, he received the coveted gold medal of the Société de Géographie de Paris. At his very moment of triumph however, the sad news reached him that his trusted Tunisian interpreter, Allegro, had gone blind as a result of his work in the dazzling whiteness of the chotts. Roudaire quickly negotiated a 250F government compensation and returned to his work. The final 114-page report and accompanying map appeared in the official review of French expeditions, the *Archives des Missions*, early in 1877 (Roudaire, 1877). Complimentary copies were sent to prominent intellectuals and politicians including Émile Levasseur, Victor Duruy, Paul Bert, Léon Gambetta, Henri Duveyrier, Élisée Reclus and Jules Verne (AN F17 3004A).

The results indicated that Chott el-Djerid was a complex saline lake covering about 5,000 km². In parts, this depression was 20 m deep. However, the water and thickly-deposited layers of salt crystals often brought the observable surface of the chott above sea level. This easternmost depression was separated from Chott Rharsa by a series of dry sandy dunes. Chott Rharsa covered an area of 1,350 km², contained far less water and had a much thinner layer of salt deposition. In absolute terms, this depression was much deeper being, on average, 24 m below sea level. Chott Rharsa was separated from Chott Melrir by a narrow band of sandy undulations. This westernmost depression was approximately the same depth as Chott Rharsa and covered 6,700 km². Roudaire calculated that Chott Rharsa and Chott Melrir could accommodate 32.4 million and 160.8 million cubic metres of water, respectively. His plan was to drive a short canal across the soft sand between Chott Melrir and Chott Rharsa and then build a much bigger and longer canal linking Chott el-Djerid to the rest of the complex. As Chott el-Djerid contained larger quantities of water, this second canal would drain the contents of Chott el-Djerid into the rest of the system. This would allow the entire complex to be flooded by driving a final deep canal from the eastern tip of Chott el-Djerid across the 16 km of desert to the Gulf of Gabès (Roudaire, 1877).

Roudaire provided details of the most suitable locations for these canals and then turned his attention to the problem of evaporation. Would such a sea survive for long in a desert climate? On this the report was adamant. The sea would transform the climate of the area in ways entirely beneficial to the local economy and society. After all, had not the sea existed in the past when the entire region was much more populated and fertile? Far from interfering with nature, the creation of the inland sea would simply re-establish the original environmental conditions which had so tragically deteriorated. Not only would the climate become more temperate, but the evaporating water vapour would be transported northwards by the prevailing wind over the Aurès mountains. The resulting relief rainfall would generate a whole new fluvial system on the southern side of these mountains, reintroducing water to the new sea as part of a more dynamic hydrological cycle. The sea would thus create a more fertile climate, improving the health of the local population, increasing the area of commercial arable farming and allowing the introduction of new export crops like cotton. In short, 'fertility and life would take the place of sterility and death; the power of civilization would drive back the forces of fatalism'. Indeed, 'The inland sea will be for Algeria what the Mediterranean is for France' (Roudaire, 1877: 238).

To support these claims, Roudaire cited the case of the Bitter Lakes, artificially created in the course of building the Suez Canal. These lakes, tiny by comparison to the proposed sea, were on an almost identical latitude and existed under very similar climatic conditions. According to Roudaire, the construction of these lakes had profoundly altered the meso-climatic conditions of the locality such that only 3 mm of water was lost from their surface each day, an amount easily replenished by the inflow of water (Roudaire, 1877: 258–64). The same point had been made by de Lesseps (1876). His long experience in Egypt led him to observe that 'Twenty years ago one almost never saw rain in the isthmus [of Suez] . . . nowadays, we are obliged to use French roof-tiles to cover our houses. We have had, this year, considerable rains'.

Roudaire also argued that the Saharan sea would provide a new gateway into the African interior. Ports could be built along its southern coastline to facilitate trade between the outside world and central Africa, an area many believed was blessed with incalculable mineral riches. The sea would also have a strategic significance for the pacification of the Sahara. It would provide a second, easily defended front to protect the Mediterranean littoral and allow French forces to cut off supplies to hostile tribes in the Aurès mountains. Finally, the construction of a sea in the midst of the desert would be yet another example of French genius, flair and daring. It would strike awe into the hearts of the water-starved African population and would earn the respect and admiration of rival colonial powers. Pessimistic views about evaporation problems, excessive cost and engineering difficulties were all swept aside as either misinformed or trivial. Faced with the rather bizarre objection that the sea would lead to an increase in the price of ostrich feathers in Europe, Roudaire could scarcely control his fury. 'So what!', he fumed. 'We admit that these luxury plumes will become scarcer and more expensive in Europe, and we will confidently leave it to the committee to decide whether such an argument is reasonable' (Roudaire 1877: 259).

Growing doubts

The document was passed to a new committee from the Académie de Sciences for consideration. Their response praised Roudaire for his dedication and perseverance, but observed:

The enterprise, assuming it is feasible, would not present commercial advantages comparable to those produced by the construction of the Suez Canal. The produce of central Africa, transported as it is on the backs of camels across the desert, does not seem sufficiently abundant to furnish the cargo of a large number of ships.

The committee was also unconvinced by the pronouncements about a major climatic change and was further unnerved about the lack of information provided by Roudaire on the nature of the bedrock, particularly in view of an Italian geological survey, undertaken in June 1875, which had dismissed the possibility of a canal link. Although the committee accepted that the scheme would facilitate the penetration of European civilization 'towards the centre of a still barbarous continent', they insisted that further work should be carried out (Rapport sur les missions des chotts, 1877).

Roudaire was devastated by this unexpectedly cool reception. Although he had hoped to raise private capital to begin work on the canals, he knew that, in view of the scale and international nature of the project, state backing would be crucial. He immediately wrote to the Ministère de l'Instruction Publique to demand a final chance to prove his point. In particular he wanted to undertake the necessary geological sampling of the bedrock around Chott el-Djerid. He requested the enormous sum of 70,000F to support himself, three geologists, a doctor, an interpreter and 40 Arab guides and escorts for a total of six months. Observing the growing international publicity his scheme had attracted (Paladini, 1874; Rohlfs, 1874; Duveyrier, 1874b), Roudaire insisted that France should not allow a foreign power to take over the funding and development of the project (AN F17 3004A).

The Ministry prevaricated but could hardly refuse the request in light of its earlier investment and the previous recommendations of the Acadèmie des Sciences. However, it was not until 26 July 1878 that an initial sum of 40,000F was granted, with an assurance that the remainder would be made available from a special grant being negotiated through the Chambre des Députés. Having received leave of absence from the Ministère de la Guerre and permission from the authorities in Tunis, Roudaire set off from Marseille on 13 November. Within weeks, he was reporting encouraging results to his friend and supporter, Baron de Watteville. By the middle of January 1879, however, Roudaire was complaining to de Watteville about the failure of the government to provide him with the promised extra funds. 'When will I have my money?' he wrote. 'In about a month, I will be absolutely at the end of my first forty thousand francs' (AN F17 3004A). He sent numerous letters inquiring about his missing cash but by the middle of February 1879 it was clear that the extra money would not be forthcoming. Although he was forced to abort this final mission, Roudaire's team completed surveys at 22 different sites and produced over 500 deep-core geological samples (Plate 6.2).

Armed with this new information and encouraged by a new wave of supportive articles (Tissot, 1879; Hébet, 1878; Parquet, 1878), Roudaire set about writing another, definitive report for the Archives des Missions. The document ran to 182 pages and included a revised version of his earlier map, six plates of newly-discovered zoological species, tables of meteorological data and full details on the new geological samples. According to his calculations, the whole project would take eight years to complete and would cost a maximum of 75 million francs. He concluded with a quote from his most famous supporter, Victor Hugo, who had spoken of his scheme in a speech in Paris on 3 August 1879.

The people [of North Africa] are disinherited, their world is a desert . . . Must we conquer this world by force of arms? No! Let us astonish the universe by great achievements which do not involve warfare. It is up to us, it is the duty of civilization. Algeria requires a sea: let us create it there. A sea brings with it ships, ships create towns, and towns create civilization (Roudaire, 1881: 413).

Yet even these stirring words from the most respected Frenchman of his day could not convince a government which had become cautious and wary. No commission was established to review Roudaire's finding and his report drew no official response.

Collapse and defeat

Dismayed and disillusioned, Roudaire withdrew from the scene. The indefatigable de Lesseps valiantly continued to support the project and drew new inspiration from the French occupation of Tunisia in 1881. As there was no longer an independent foreign power involved, de Lesseps wrote numerous letters to scientists and politicians pleading for a re-examination of Roudaire's ideas. De Lesseps's energetic advocacy of Roudaire's idea generated some international interest (Brunialti, 1882; Dumergue, 1882; Zittel, 1883; Krebs, 1885), and after a visit to the area late in 1882 (AN F17 3004A), he arranged for Roudaire's two long reports to be published together as a single volume (Roudaire, 1883). De Lesseps then championed the scheme in a speech before the Académie des Sciences on 17 April 1883. Abandoning his enthusiasm for the Saharan sea as a gateway to the riches of Africa, de Lesseps stressed instead the strategic military significance of an artificial sea, arguing:

We would possess an admirable frontier which . . . would permit us to establish our authority in the southern regions of both Algeria and Tunisia as firmly as on the Mediterranean coast. [The sea] would represent at the same time a military boundary and a point of departure to penetrate into the interior of the Sahara . . . The accomplishment of this work . . . would give to the indigenous population a clear impression of our power and our grandeur (Lesseps, 1883: 496).

De Lesseps managed to convince *Général* Philbert, a senior colonial army officer with over 30 years' experience in Algeria and Tunisia, that the inland sea would have a major strategic role. Philbert produced a long report which was sent to Jules Ferry, the new *Ministre de l'Instruction Publique* and President of the Conseil des Ministres. According to this, 'The inland sea would help us considerably in the pacification and colonisation of Algeria and Tunisia . . . if such an inland sea had existed . . . the current Tunisian insurrection would not have been possible' (AN F17 3004A). A sea would allow the French forces in North Africa to be reduced by 3,000 men and 1,800 horses and mules. Not only would this produce a considerable saving but it would also release soldiers to defend mainland France from a European attack. In a polite reply, Ferry merely thanked de Lesseps and Philbert for their efforts (AN F17 3004A). From that moment it was clear, even to de Lesseps, that the desert sea would never be a reality.

His dream shattered, Roudaire found it increasingly difficult to readjust to life as a peacetime *Colonel* in Paris. Feeling betrayed and humiliated, he took extended leave in early 1883 on grounds of ill health. His illness was partly the result of overwork but was exacerbated by his increasing reliance on alcohol. Back in his family home in Guéret, Roudaire continued to deteriorate and on 14 January 1885, at the age of 49, he died from a liver infection (Carriat, 1970: 474–5).

The reasons why Roudaire's scheme was passed over are in one sense straightforward. Many people doubted the feasibility of the project from the beginning. Prior to 1881, the necessary involvement of an independent Regency of Tunis was a source of unease, and there were still influential anti-colonial voices who believed that French military and commercial investment should be concentrated in Europe rather than squandered on speculative ventures overseas. The scientific doubts were reinforced by new palaeoecological evidence which emerged in 1879 to challenge the assumption that the region had once been linked to the sea. By the mid-1880s, the new orthodoxy was that the chotts represented the remnants of an ancient inland lake. According to this thesis, any attempt to establish a Saharan sea would end in environmental disaster and financial ruin (Martins and Désor, 1879; Désor and Letourneux, 1880; Coumet-Adamson, 1884; Rouire, 1884; Rolland, 1884a and 1884b; Letourneux, 1884). In the caustic words of one critic: 'Rather than flooding these chotts, we should perhaps consider draining them to reduce the prevalence of disease in the region' (Cosson, 1884: 70).

The withdrawal of official support for Roudaire was obviously related to these doubts, but it is unlikely that they provide a complete explanation. Other factors were also important. First, the new Third Republic was notoriously unstable. The elections of 1876 and 1877 had secured the Republic from the threat of monarchism but the forces of conservatism and radicalism resurfaced to play out their ideological battles on the new political terrain of republicanism. Governments and ministers came and went with bewildering frequency and this political environment was scarcely conducive to the formulation of consistent, long-term colonial policies. In a climate of assertive republicanism, Roudaire's case cannot have been helped by his well-known monarchist sympathies (Roudaire, 1872). To an extent, therefore, Roudaire's scheme was the victim of an uncertain and ever-changing political climate.

Second, although many prominent politicians were committed to colonial expansion, there was still a lingering hostility to grand schemes and large-scale projects which brought back the bitter memories of Louis Napoleon's Second Empire. Although the imperial regime before 1870 had undeniably achieved a great deal—most conspicuously through the transformation of Paris into a glittering European capital and the construction of a new, extensive railway network—many republican observers still felt that these ambitious and eye-catching projects of economic development and civic reconstruction were designed primarily to divert attention from the shortcomings of Napoleon III's domestic and foreign policies. This seemed particularly true of French ventures overseas during the 1850s and 1860s. The Suez Canal was an obvious example. When opened in 1869, the last year of the Second Empire, the canal had cost twice it original budget and created a major financial crisis which persisted into the early 1870s. The British, who controlled the majority of the world's shipping, obstinately refused to use the new facility. In 1876, only half the predicted 1 million tons of ships were using the canal and it was clear that without British co-operation and joint control, the canal was doomed to be an expensive failure (Pudney, 1960; Marlowe, 1964; Kinross, 1968). Public hostility to prestige engineering projects became even more pronounced after 1881. In April of that year, news reached Paris of the horrific massacre of Flatters' mission which was exploring the route for a proposed trans-Saharan railway designed to link French colonial territories in North and West Africa (Porch, 1984: 83–125; Carrière, 1988). This disaster brought an abrupt halt to the railway project and had a similar effect on other ambitious colonial schemes, including the inland sea.

Third, the French scientific community was becoming professional, university-based and dominated by theoreticians and intellectuals who owed their positions to the educational policies of the Third Republic. These professional scientists were suspicious of men of action and experience like Roudaire and de Lesseps. At best, they were dismissed as well-meaning but crude amateurs. At worst, they were despised as crass opportunists motivated solely by personal financial gain. Roudaire and his colleagues, unconstrained by the emerging disciplinary boundaries erected within the rapidly growing universities of the Third Republic, were representatives of an older science which was both empirical and speculative, romantic and practical. By the 1880s, this form of amateur science was becoming marginal and its remaining practitioners lacked the political influence of the new, university-based professional scientists (Weisz, 1983).

Thus, by the mid-1880s, the intellectual and political climate had become distinctly less favourable to the kind of idealistic and inspired efforts of men like Roudaire, de Lesseps and Duveyrier. Even Jules Verne, the visionary novelist, felt that Roudaire's ambitions were somewhat excessive. Verne used the story of the inland sea as the basis for his last novel, *L'Invasion de la mer*, published posthumously in 1905. In this tale, Roudaire's plans were re-examined by an early twentieth-century scientist and entrepreneur named de Schaller, a character clearly based on de Lesseps. De Schaller persuades the authorities to reconsider Roudaire's evidence and work duly begins on the project despite the fierce and violent opposition of the North African tribes. Before the man-made canals are completed however, an earthquake strikes, re-establishing the ancient sea amidst general carnage and destruction. Although probably a veiled attack on de Lesseps following his disastrous and fraudulent activities during the French attempt to construct the Panama Canal, the moral of Verne's book is clear: although science can enhance the potential of the environment, mankind should remain humble before the awesome power of nature (Verne, 1905).

Despite the failure of his scheme, Roudaire's idea of an inland sea in the desert has exerted a continuing fascination. As late as 1912, the travel writer, Norman Douglas, was still referring to the chotts as, 'dried up oceans . . . where in olden days the fleets of Atlantis rode at anchor' (Douglas, 1912:1). More generally, Roudaire's vision of a 'peaceful' European conquest of the Sahara—a conquest based on the power of science and technology rather than the force of arms—was certainly the dominant theme of the classic early histories and geographies of French rule in North Africa and the Sahara (Vuillot, 1985; Bernard and Lacroix, 1906; Gautier, 1910; Naciri, 1984). Indeed, in the midst of the Algerian war of independence during the late 1950s, Roudaire's idea was seriously re-examined. Spurred on by the discovery of huge natural gas reserves in the Sahara and by the rumours of vast untapped oil fields, a few optimists proclaimed that, with the aid of modern technology, Roudaire's half-forgotten dreams might yet become a reality (Denarie, 1958). More recently still, environmental scientists have reopened the debate about the origins of the chotts and about the likely meso-climatic changes produced by flooding similar desert depressions (Richards and Vita-Finzi, 1982; Segal èt al., 1983).

Conclusion

The sage of *la mer intérieure* represents a classical illustration of European imperial ambition. The ideas which Roudaire promoted were recognizably part of an emerging modernist faith in science and 'progress' which, though originating in the Englightenment (Bury, 1924; Frankel, 1948; Pollard, 1968; Sorel, 1969), was to reach its *apogée* in late nineteenth-century Europe (Kern, 1983; Rabinow, 1989). Yet, this idea of 'progress' ('modernization' in more recent parlance) was transformed in the process of its own development. By the end of the nineteenth century—in an era of high imperialism—the optimistic, eighteenth-century belief that 'the scientific domination of nature promised freedom from scarcity, want, and the arbitrariness of natural calamity' had given way to a 'lust to dominate nature' which had become synonymous with a desire to dominate human beings and whole areas of the world (Harvey, 1989: 12–13). It is difficult to avoid the conclusion that, although Roudaire may have been genuinely inspired by a faith in the power of rational European science to tame the hostile environments of the earth for the good of all humanity, he was motivated in at least equal measure by a fierce and uncompromising patriotism mixed with a reckless personal ambition. These latter characteristics manifested themselves in an arrogant assumption about the power and superiority of European civilization and a complete insensitivity to the people and environment of North Africa. To an extent, this is demonstrated by the gigantism which was a crucial feature of Roudaire's scheme and a central component of the entire modernist programme. Roudaire would doubtless have justified this by arguing that 'big' problems required similarly 'big' solutions but, in a deeper sense, the scale of his project was designed consciously to convey the monolithic power and authority of European rule in Africa. Like most imperialist visionaries, Roudaire justified these ambitious objectives by construcing a powerful image of his chosen colonial domain. Although this was articulated in the language of rational European science, his vision of the North African desert was nevertheless an intensely poetic and evocative representation based on potent combination of myth, legend and science (Said, 1978).

Although it is tempting to dismiss Roudaire's beliefs as long-forgotten dreams, to do so would be to ignore the continuing legacy of his thinking. Certainly, the version of 'modernism' which he promoted has dominated the intellectual landscape of Europe and North America throughout most of the twentieth century. As a result, Eurocentric and technocratic ideas have underpinned development thinking until very recently. The most recent manifestation of these beliefs are to be found in the mammoth African river regulation and hydro-electric power schemes which were promoted by Western developmental theorists in the immediate post-colonial era of the 1960s. Although Roudaire's project failed, it is worth recounting, for it represents a particular European mentality which, though quintessentially imperialist in nature, was rooted in a pattern of belief which is only now being to crumble.

Acknowledgements

The author would like to thank Professor Claudio Vita-Finzi and Dr Neil Roberts for their comments on an earlier draft of this paper.

Unpublished sources

AN F17 3004A, *Service des Missions: dossier Roudaire*, Paris, Archives Nationales.
AN F80 962-6, *Service Topographique: personnel, projets, documents divers*, Aix-en-Provence, Archives Nationales, Dépôt d'Outre-Mer

References

Abbadie, A. d' (1877) 'La Mer intérieure de l'Algérie', *Bulletin de la Société de Géographie de Paris*, 14, 103.
Ageron, C.-R. (1979) *Histoire de l'Algérie contemporaine. II: de l'insurrection de 1871 au déclenchement de la guerre de libération, 1954*, 2nd edn, Paris, Presses Universitaires de France.
Andrew, C.M. and Kanya-Forstner, A.S. (1981) *France Overseas: The Great War and the Climax of French Imperial Expansion*, London, Thames and Hudson.
Angot, A (1877) 'Le Régime des vents et l'évaporation dans la région des chotts algériens', *Comptes rendus des séances de l'Académie des Sciences*, 85(2); 396–9.
Baudot, M. (1880) 'État actuel de la question de la mer intérieure de l'Algérie', *Bulletin de la Société de Géographie de Lyon*, 3, 331.

Beatty, C. (1956), *Ferdinand de Lesseps: A Biographical Study*, London, Eyre & Spottiswoode.

Bénatou, M. (1980) 'L'Impérialism et l'Afrique du Nord: le Modèle romain' in D. Nordman and J.-P. Raison (eds), *Sciences de l'homme et conquête coloniale: constitution et usages des humanités en Afrique (XIXe–XXe siècle)*, Paris, PENS, pp. 15–22.

Berdoulay, V.R.H. (1981) *La Formation de l'École Française de Géographie (1870–1914)*, Paris, Comité des Travaux Historiques et Scientiques, Bibliothèque Nationale.

Bernard, A. and Lacroix, N. (1906) *La Pénétration du Sahara (1830–1906)*, Algiers, Imprimerie Algérienne.

Bonnet, G.-E. (1959) *Ferdinand de Lesseps*, Paris, Plon.

Broc, N. (1970) 'Histoire de la géographie et nationalisme en France sous la IIIe République (1871–1914)', *L'Information historique*, 32, 21–6.

Broc, N., (1974) 'L'Établissement de la géographie en France: diffusion, institutions, projets (1870–1890)', *Annales de Géographie*, 83, 545–68.

Broc, N. (1976) 'La Pensée géographique en France au XIXe siècle: continuité ou rupture', *Revue géographique des Pyrénées et du Sud-Ouest*, 47, 225–47.

Broc, N. (1977) 'La Géographie française face à la science allemande (1870–1914)', *Annales de Géographie* 86, 71–94.

Broc, N. (1987) 'Les Français face à l'inconnue saharienne: géographes, explorateurs, ingéieurs (1880–1881)', *Annales de Géographie*, 535, 302–38.

Broc, N. (1988) *Dictionnaire illustré des explorateurs et grands voyageurs français du XIXe siècle: Tome 1—Afrique*, Paris, Comité des Travaux Historiques et Scientifiques.

Brunialti, M. (1882) 'Il mare del Sahara', *Esploratore*, 6, 6–17.

Brunschwig, H. (1966) *French Colonialism, 1871–1914: Myths and Realities*, London, Pall Mall.

Bury, J.P., (1924) *The idea of progress: an inquiry into its origins and growth*, London, Dover Publications, reprinted 1955.

Carriat, A. (1970) *Dictionnaire bio-bibliographique des auteurs du pays creusais et des écrits le concernant, des origines à nos jours*, Gueret, Presses du Massif Central.

Carrière, B. (1988) 'Le Transsaharien: histoire et géographie d'un projet inahevé', *Acta Geographica*, 74 (2), 23–38.

Cosson, E. (1884) 'Sur le projet de création en Algérie et en Tunisie d'une mer dite intérieure', *Association française pour l'avancement des sciences: compte rendu de la XIIIe session, Blois, 1884*, 57–72.

Coumet-Adamson, A. (1884) 'Sur le régime des eaux qui alimentent les oasis du sud de la Tunisie', *Association française pour l'avancement des sciences: compte rendu de la XIIIe session, Blois, 1884*, 72–5.

Danziger, R. (1977) *Abd-el Qadir and the Algerians: Resistance to the French and Internal Consolidation*, New York, Holmes and Meier.

Delestre, E. (1874) *A propos de la mer intérieure, ou fausse interprétation géographique*, Algiers, P. Ferouillat.

Denarie, P. (1958) 'Une mer intérieure au Sahara', *Sahara de Demain*, 5, 16–19.

Désor, E. and Letourneux, A. (1880) 'Sur les coquilles marines de la région des chotts algériens', *Bulletin de la Société Géologique de la France*, 36, 230–4.

Douglas, N. (1912) *Fountains in the Sand*, Oxford, Oxford University Press, reprinted 1986.

Downes, A. (1977) 'James Rennell, 1742–1830' in T.W. Freeman (ed.), *Geographers: Bio-bibliographical Studies*, I, London, Mansell.

Dumergue, E. (1882) *The Chotts of Tunis: Or, the Great Inland Sea of North Africa in Ancient Times*, London, W.H. Allen.

Duponchel, A. (1876) 'La mer intérieure', *Bulletin de la Société de Géographie de Lyon*, 5, 99–100.

Duveyrier, H. (1864) *Exploration du Sahara: les Touareg du Nord*, Paris, Challamel.

Duveyrier, H. (1874a) 'Une mer intérieure en Algérie', *Bulletin de la Société de Géographie de Paris*, 7, 458–63.

Duveyrier, H. (1874b) 'Spedizione del livellamente degli sciott', *Cosmos di Guido Cora*, 3, 37–45.

Duveyrier, H. (1875a) Untitled letters, *Bulletin de la Société de Géographie de Paris*, 9, 94–100, 203–7 and 303–17.

Duveyrier, H. (1875b) 'Premier rapport sur la mission des chotts du Sahara de Constantine', *Bulletin de la Société de Géographie de Paris*, 9, 482–503.

Frankel, C. (1948) *The Faith in Reason: The Idea of Progress in the French Enlightenment*, New York, King's Crown Press, Columbia University.

Frémaux, J. (1984), 'Souvenirs de Rome et présence française au Maghreb: essai d'investigation' in J.-C. Vatin (ed.), *Connaissances du Maghreb: sciences sociales et colonisation*, Paris, CNRS, pp. 29–46.

Fuchs, E. (1877) 'Notes sur l'isthme de Gabès à l'extremité orientale de la saharienne', *Bulletin de la Société de Géographie de Paris*, 14, 248–76.

Ganiage, J. (1968) *L'Expansion coloniale de la France sous la Troisième République (1871–1914)*, Paris, Payot.

Gautier, E.-F. (1910) *La Conquête du Sahara: essai de pyschologie politique*, Paris, Armand Colin.

Girard de Rialle, B. (1876) 'La Mer intérieure du Sahara', *Revue Scientifique* 18, 409–17.

Girardet, R. (1972) *L'Idée coloniale en France de 1871 à 1962*, La Table Ronde, Paris.

Gros, M. (1876) 'La Mer intérieure du Sahara du capitaine Roudaire', *L'Explorateur*, 282–95.

Hamdani, A. (1985) *La Verité sur l'expédition d'Alger*, Paris, Editions Balland.

Harvey, D. (1989) *The Condition of Postmodernity*, Oxford, Basil Blackwell.

Headrick, D.R. (1981) *The Tools of Empire: Technology and European Imperialism in the Nineteenth Century*, New York and Oxford, Oxford University Press.

Hébet, M. (1878) 'Conséquences économiques de la création d'une mer intérieure en Algérie', *Revue politique et littéraire*, 15, 445–50.

Heffernan, M.J. (1989a) 'The Parisian poor and the colonisation of Algeria during the Second Republic', *French History*, 3 (4), 377–403.

Heffernan, M.J. (1989b) 'The limits of utopia: Henri Duveyrier and the exploration of the Sahara in the nineteenth century', *Geographical Journal*, 156 (3), 342–52.

Houyvet, C. (1874) Untitled comment, *Comptes rendus des séances de l'Académie des Sciences*, 69 (2), 101–2.

Julien, C.-A. (1979) *Histoire de l'Algérie contemporaine. I: la conquête et les débuts de la colonisation, 1827–1871*, 2nd edn, Paris, Presses Universitaires de France.

Kern, S. (1983) *The culture of time and space, 1880–1918*, Cambridge, Mass., Harvard University Press.

Kinross, Lord (Balfour, J.P.D.) (1968) *Between Two Seas: The Creation of the Suez Canal*, London, John Murray.

Krebs, M. (1885) 'Sahara und Saharemeer', *Aus allen Weltheilen*, 18, 77–86.

Lafont, P. (1980) *Histoire de la France en Algérie*, Paris, Plon.

Lavigne, G. (1869) *Percement de l'isthme de Gabès*, Coulommiers, A. Brodard.

Le Chatelier, H. (1876) 'La Mer intérieure. De l'existence aux temps historiques d'une mer intérieure en Algerie', *Revue Scientifique*, 18, 656–60.

Lesseps, F. de, (1876) 'Sur les lacs Amers et autres point de l'isthme de Suez en rapport avec l'inondation des chotts algériens et tunisiens', *Revue Scientifique*, 18, 527–9.

Lesseps, F. de (1883) 'La Mer intérieure de Gabès', *Revue Scientifique*, 3, 495–6.

Letourneux, A. (1884) 'Sur le projet de mer intérieure', *Association Française pour l'Avancement des Sciences: compte rendu de la XIIIe session, Blois, 1884*, 546–9.

Levasseur, E. (1875) Untitled comments, *Comptes rendus des séances de l'Académie des Sciences*, 70 (1), 510–11, and 70 (2), 403.

MacKay, D.V. (1943) 'Colonialism and development in the French geographical movement, 1871–1881', *Geographical Review*, 33, 214–32.

Markham, C.R. (1895) *Major James Rennell and the Rise of Modern English Geography*, London, Cassell.

Marlowe, J. (1964) *The Making of the Suez Canal*, London, Cresset Press.

Martins, C. (1864) 'Le Sahara: souvenirs d'un voyage d'hiver', *Revue des Deux Mondes*, 4, 295–322 and 611–37.

Martins, C. and Désor, E. (1879) 'Observations sur le projet de la création d'une mer intérieure dans le Sahara oriental', *Comptes rendus des séances de l'Académie des Sciences*, 87, 265–9.

Murphy, A. (1948) *The Ideology of French Imperialism, 1871–1881*, New York, Catholic University of America Press.

Naciri, M. (1984) 'La Géographie coloniale: une "science appliquée" à la colonisation. Perceptions et interprétations du fait colonial chez J. Célerier et G. Hardy' in J.-C. Vatin, (ed.), *Connaissances du Maghreb: sciences sociales et colonisation*, Paris, CNRS, pp. 309–43.

Paladini, M. (1874) 'Il nuovo mare del Sahara algerino', *Giornale politica*, 17 July, 24–5.

Parquet, M. (1878) 'La Mer intérieure et ses contradicteurs', *L'Explorateur*, 236–8.

Pollard, S. (1968) *The Idea of Progress: History and Society*, London, Watts.

Pomel, A. (1872) *Le Sahara: observations de géologie et de géographie physique et biologique*, Algiers, Ailland.

Pomel, A. (1874) 'Sur la prétendue mer saharienne', *Comptes rendus des séances de l'Académie des Sciences*, 69 (2), 792–8.

Pomel, A. (1875) 'Il n'y a pas eu de mer intérieure au Sahara', *Comtes rendus des séances de l'Académie des Sciences*, 70 (4), 1342–50.

Pomel, A. (1877) 'La Mer intérieure d'Algérie', *Revue Scientifique*, 19, 433–40.

Porch, D. (1984) *The Conquest of the Sahara*, Oxford, Oxford University Press.

Prévost-Paradol, L.-A. (1868) *La France nouvelle*, Paris, Michel Levy.

Pudney, J. (1960) *Suez: de Lesseps' Canal*, London, J.M. Dent.

Rabinow, P. (1989) *French Modern: Norms and Forms of the Social Environment*, Cambridge, Mass., MIT Press.

Rapport sur les missions des chotts (1877) *Comptes rendus des séances de l'Académie des Sciences*, 85, 457–68.

Renaudot, F. (1979) *L'Histoire des Français en Algérie, 1830–1962*, Paris, R. Laffont.

Rennell, J. (1800) *The Geographical System of Herodotus Examined and Explained by a Comparison with those of Other Ancient Authors, and with Modern Geography*, London, G. and W. Nicol.

Richards, G.W. and Vita-Finzi, C. (1982) 'Marine deposits 35,000–25,000 years old in the Chott el Djerid, southern Tunisia', *Nature*, 295, 54–5.

Rohlfs, G. (1874) 'Ein binnensee in Algerien', *Das Ausland*, 839–42.

Rolland, G. (1884a) 'Terrains de transports et terrains lacustres du bassin du chott Melrir', *Association Française pour l'Avancement des sciences: compte rendu de la XIIIe session, Blois, 1884*, 267–77.

Rolland, G. (1884b) 'Le Mer saharienne', *Revue Scientifique*, 23, 705–18.

Roudaire, E. (1872) *Donnez-nous un roi! Epitre aux conservateurs*, Paris.

Roudaire, E. (1874a) 'Une mer intérieure en Algérie', *Revue des Deux Mondes*, 3, 323–50.

Roudaire, E. (1874b) 'Notes sur les chotts situés au sud de Biskra', *Bulletin de la Société de Géographie de Paris*, 7, 297–300.

Roudaire, E. (1874–5) 'La Mer intérieure de l'Algérie', *Comptes rendus des séances de l'Académie des Sciences*, 69 (2), 289–90, 501–4, and 70 (2), 1593–6.

Roudaire, E. (1875) 'La Mission des chotts du Sahara de Constantine', *Bulletin de la Société de Géographie de Paris*, 10, 113–25 and 574–86.

Roudaire, E. (1877) 'Rapport à M. le Ministre de l'Instruction Publique sur la mission des chotts: études relatives au projet de mer intérieure', *Archives des Missions*, 4, 157–271.

Roudaire, E. (1881) 'Rapport à M. le Ministre de l'Instruction Publique sur la dernière expédition des chotts: complément des études relatives au projet de mer intérieure', *Archives des Missions*, 7, 231–413.

Roudaire, E. (1883) *La Mer intérieure africaine*, Paris, Société Anonyme des Publications Périodiques.

Rouire, F. (1884) 'La Mer intérieure africaine', *Association Française pour l'Avancement des sciences: compte rendu de la XIIIe session, Blois, 1884*, 75–86.

Said, E.W. (1978) *Orientalism*, London, Routledge and Kegan Paul.

Sainte-Marie, E. de (1876) 'La Mission du capitaine Roudaire en Tunisie et la mer intérieure', *L'Explorateur*, 273–5.

Segal, M., Pielke, R.A. and Mahrer, Y. (1983) 'On climatic changes due to a deliberate flooding of the Quattara depression (Egypt)', *Climatic Change*, 5, 73–83.

Shaw, B. (1981) 'Climate, environment, and history: the case of Roman North Africa' in T.M.L. Wigley, M.J. Ingram and G. Farmer (eds), *Climate and History: Studies in Past Climates and their Impact on Man*, Cambridge, Cambridge University Press, pp. 379–403.

Shaw, T. (1738) *Travels or Observations Relating to Several Parts of Barbary and the Levant*, Oxford, At the Theatre.

Sorel, G. (1969) *The Illusions of Progress*, Berkeley and Los Angeles, University of California Press.

Sullivan, A.T. (1983) *Thomas-Robert Bugeaud, France and Algeria, 1784–1849: Politics, Power and the Good Society*, Archon Books, Hamden, Connecticut.

Swearingen, W.D. (1985) In search of the granary of Rome: France's wheat policy in Morocco, 1915–1931, *International Journal of Middle East Studies*, 17, 347–63.

Swearingen, W.D. (1988) *Moroccan Mirages: Agrarian Dreams and Deceptions, 1912–1986*, London, I.B. Tauris.

Thompson, A. (1987) *Barbary and Englightenment: European Attitudes towards the Maghreb in the Eighteenth Century*, Leiden, E.J. Brill.

Tissot, C. (1879) 'Notice sur le chott el Djerid', *Bulletin de la Société de Géographie de Paris*, 8, 5–25.

Verne, J. (1905) *L'Invasion de la mer*, Paris.

Ville, M. (1876) 'La Mer intérieure de l'Afrique septentrionale et la carte de navigation des Argonautes', *L'Explorateur*, 502–5.

Ville, M. (1877) 'La Question de la mer intérieure du Sahara', *L'Explorateur*, 655–8.

Virlet d'Aoust, A. (1844–5), 'Notes sur la géographie ancienne', *Bulletin de la Société*

Géologique de la France, 2, 349–57.

Virlet d'Aoust, A. (1874) Untitled comments, *Comptes rendus des séances de l'Académie des Sciences* 69 (2), 218–19; 794–5.

Vuillot, P. (1895) *L'Exploration du Sahara: étude historique et géographique*, Paris, Challamel.

Weisz, G. (1983) *The Emergence of the Modern Universities in France, 1863–1924*, Princeton, NJ, Princeton University Press.

Zittel, M. (1883) 'Das Saharameer', *Das Ausland*, 524–8.

CHAPTER 7

The mechanical conservation of soil in Rhodesia/Zimbabwe

Jenny Elliott

In 1889, Cecil Rhodes and his British South Africa Company moved north from the Cape across the Limpopo River to occupy the territory to be known as Rhodesia. By the turn of the century, hopes of a 'Second Rand' mining colony had not been realized and agriculture was seen as the economic foundation of the colony. Settlers helped themselves liberally to land. Before long, Rhodesians had recreated the situation further south where,

As a result of the conditions created by the white civilization in South Africa, the power of the surface of the land as a whole to hold up and absorb water has been diminished . . . caused by the deterioration of its protecting vegetal cover and by soil erosion. (Haviland, 1927: 332)

By the end of the 1930s, 'it had become universal wisdom that the reserves [African farming areas] were in full blown ecological crisis' (Ranger, 1985: 69). Subsequently, soil conservation, particularly in the African areas, was to become the cutting edge of justification for many colonial policies (Beinart, 1984). On independence, crisis again seemed to loom. In 1983 imminent large-scale malnutrition and starvation were predicted in African areas if existing rates of soil erosion continued (Elwell, 1983).

This chapter explores the historical and cultural contexts of colonial conservation policies in Rhodesia. While not underestimating the challenges presented by the physical environment to agricultural development, it is argued that many 'conservation' programmes implemented in the name of resource trusteeship during the colonial period did more for the position of European settlers than for the environment. This is not a novel assertion; authors such as Beinart (1984) and Phimister (1986) have debated the process. The analysis presented below, however, illustrates that the particular model for erosion control which was selected, promoted and eventually enforced in the African farming areas, reinforced the political and cultural hegemony of Europeans, subordinated African knowledge and removed local control of the environment.

Various climatic and physiographic factors combine to render Zimbabwe naturally susceptible to erosion of soil particles by rainsplash, runoff or wind.

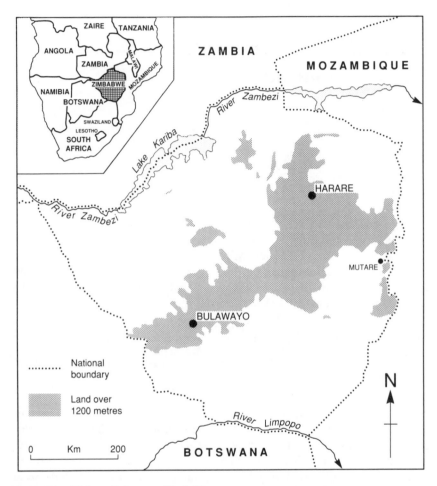

Figure 7.1   Major relief zones, Zimbabwe

Although mean annual rainfall ranges from less than 400 mm in the extreme south of the country to over 1000 mm in the Eastern Highlands, rainfall erosivity is high, with much of the rainfall occuring during infrequent tropical storms. Soils are mainly granite-derived or originate from the Karoo sands, both exhibiting low resistance to detachment and transportation. The country is divided by a plateau running southwest–northeast known as the 'highveld' (1200–1500 m) (Figure 7.1). The Zambezi River drains the area north of this axis, and the Limpopo the area south. The valleys of these rivers constitute the 'lowveld', with the 'middleveld' consisting of the wider plateau 600–1200 m above sea level. Slopes in the middleveld are commonly above 10° and highly susceptible to soil erosion.

The country may also be divided into 'agro-ecological' zones (Vincent and Thomas, 1960) or 'Natural Regions' on the basis of rainfall amount and

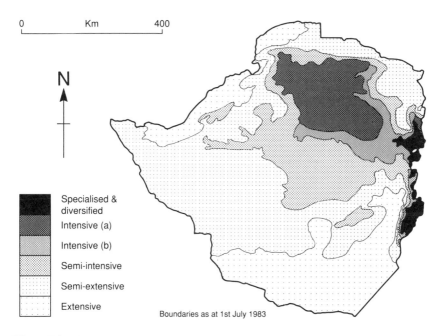

0   Km   400

N

Specialised &
diversified

Intensive (a)

Intensive (b)

Semi-intensive

Semi-extensive

Extensive

Boundaries as at 1st July 1983

Figure 7.2 'Natural regions' based on rainfall characteristics, Zimbabwe

variability (Figure 7.2). Only 2 per cent of the country enjoys annual rainfall over 900 mm and is suitable for the intensive production of most crops (Region 1). A further 15 per cent receives reliable rainfall of over 750 mm, although intensive production may be disrupted in some seasons by dry spells (Region 2). Sixty five per cent of the country receives low, erratic rainfall with often severe drought periods (Regions 3–5); 27 per cent of this area is suited only to the extensive production of livestock (Region 5).

Techniques for preventing erosion and conserving soil are conventionally divided up into mechanical (designed to control the movement of water over the surface normally via some physical structure) and biological (based on plant cover and soil management). The lead in both soil erosion and conservation research has come from the United States. In 1907, the US Department of Agriculture declared a national policy of land protection via mechanical conservation works. These consisted of stormdrains, contour ridges and grass waterways designed to control the passage of storm water and to redirect runoff safely from cultivated lands at non-erosive velocities. In 1929, the Rhodesian Department of Agriculture recommended the introduction of the same model for erosion control into settler farms in the colony. In 1937, contouring was introduced into the African farming areas.

There is evidence within Zimbabwe to suggest that systems of terracing apparently designed for conservation purposes, and possibly for irrigation, were part of the indigenous landscape: 'We have complete evidence that some early

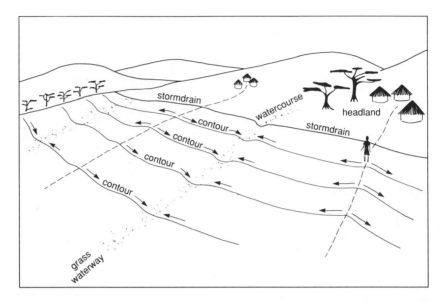

Figure 7.3   The mechanical model of erosion control in Rhodesia/Zimbabwe (after Elwell 1986)

people practised soil conservation with a high degree of efficiency and applied it generally to all their lands' (Aylen, 1941: 148). The widespread introduction of the mechanical model of conservation drawn from America came to dominate the natural and human landscapes in the African areas of Zimbabwe and this forms the focus of this chapter. The impact of the American model is evident today in the ubiquitous patchwork of dryland holdings separated by contour banks and drainage ditches throughout the country (see Figure 7.3). The social impact of this European/American-inspired hydrological engineering scheme on the cultural landscape was also profound.

Mechanical conservation structures are most effective in controlling gully erosion. They do little to prevent soil loss via sheet wash, the least spectacular but most serious form of erosion. It was gully erosion and its control, however, which dominated research in both America and Rhodesia. Rhodesia's research facilities, established in 1934, were unrivalled in Africa and were the primary source of both mechanical and biological erosion control until the end of the Second World War. Colonial conservation within African farming areas, however, remained dominated by a single mechanical control model until independence in 1980.

Land apportionment

The concept of native or 'reserve' areas was transferred with the settlers from the Cape. The first reserves in Rhodesia were established in Matabeleland in 1894 in compensation for land lost to the settlers by the indigenous population. By 1920, there were 83 reserves accommodating 800,000 Africans on 21 million acres (Kay, 1970: 49). The 1931 Land Apportionment Act (LAA) legally formalized the racial division of land in the country. Fifty-one per cent of the country was set aside for exclusive private ownership by Europeans, in areas separate from the Native Reserves (23 per cent) in which land would be held under customary tenure and the Native Purchase Areas (7 per cent) in which individual Africans could acquire land. Despite many subsequent changes to the LAA, reclassification of African and European land was minimal. It was not until 1969 that a kind of parity was introduced into the land law. At independence, successive apportionments had left land divided more or less evenly between blacks and whites although the latter had at no time constituted more than 6 per cent of the population (Kinsey, 1983: 165).

In addition to this disparity in the amount of land available to each population group, there were marked differences in the quality of land within each category. In the early reserves, large portions of the land allocated for African use were virtually useless for human habitation (Floyd, 1962) and were described as more like graves than places to live (Bannerman, 1982: 102). At independence, 57 per cent of the total population was resident in the African farming areas (now termed Communal Areas) constituting only 40 per cent of the country. Furthermore, 74 per cent of this land lay in Natural Regions 4 or 5, in conditions ideally suited only to extensive livestock production or cultivation of drought-resistent crops.

Traditional agriculture in Rhodesia as practiced by the Shona and Ndebele peoples, was based on shifting cultivation and reciprocal transactions. These inevitably became severely constrained within the segregationist land policies of the colonial government and in conditions of rising population densities. The mainly sandy soils of the reserve areas very quickly lost fertility under permanent cultivation and soil structures were degraded in areas naturally susceptible to high rates of erosion. Clearly, while serious soil erosion currently exists in the Communal Areas, it cannot be understood outside the historical context of land subdivision along racial lines.

Colonial conservation 1900–1930

The evils of soil erosion and the potential threat to Rhodesia's agricultural base were first voiced by Cripps (1909) in the *Rhodesia Agricultural Journal* (*RAJ*). Torrential rains were presented as the primary cause of soil erosion but the potentially destructive impact of overstocking, herding, kraaling and improper tillage by settlers was also referenced. By 1913, nearly all settler farmers were experiencing the evils of gully formation and soil loss (Watt, 1913). Agricultural yields were reported to be suffering accordingly, with maize yields falling from 20 bags per acre to four over the 20-year period of colonization (Haviland, 1928: 1220).

The conservation solutions advocated by government officers at this time were to be echoed frequently in the future. Cripps (1909: 670) referred to a practice 'customary on some farms' of cutting a trench on the upper side of cultivated lands to carry off storm water and the cultivation of narrow strips separated by six-foot widths of virgin veld to slow the movement of water. Watt recommended timber preservation within ten yards of the margins of public streams, control of grass burning, provision of bores and wells, control of stocking levels, contour ploughing and minimization of cattle tracking as essential measures in controlling future erosion. However, the advice of such 'informed experts' was largely ignored by the government. Ordinances covering water use and herbage preservation were passed in 1913, but were rarely enforced.

It was not until 1929 that the mechanical control of erosion via large-scale construction of contours was introduced. Stimulated by severe drought and maize crop failures, the government offered various incentives to the European farmers to improve their methods. Tractor units became available for soil conservation projects and a bonus of two shillings per bag of maize grown in accordance with sound farming practices was awarded. In later years, loans also became available in the European sector 'to enable farmers to maintain standards of living during times when it was essential to cease cultivation to restore fertility' (Natural Resources Board of Rhodesia (NRB), 1948: 11).

Colonial conservation 1930–1950

In the early 1930s there was a marked shift of concern over the careless and dangerous use of the environment from settler to indigenous farmers. Subsequently articles about soil erosion and conservation issues burgeoned and every criticism concerning settler malpractices was now repealed with respect to native methods. Whereas problems in the European areas were framed as a result of shortages of extension staff able to give advice rather than any wilful neglect on the part of the farmers (NRB, 1947), problems in the reserves were regarded as the consequence of ignorance and apathy on the part of the Africans.

Before the 1930s, state interventions in African agriculture had been limited and reports of soil erosion were scarce. Native policy had centred on the demonstration of 'improved' methods of agriculture to Africans in order to effect their transition from shifting to permanent agriculture. The primary objective of the policy was not to stimulate the viable production of cash crops by Africans, but to raise labour productivity. In this way, indigenous agriculture would become the supplier of labour for the capitalist economy. In the event, uptake of the new methods was slow. The demonstration programme remained voluntary and in the light of already discriminatory marketing arrangements few farmers had the motivation to invest in the extra inputs required. Staff shortages and problems of organization further restricted the effects of the programme.

The economic depression of the 1930s shook the confidence of settler communities throughout Africa. In many areas of Rhodesia, indigenous production came through this period better than settler agriculture and an African entrepreneurial class began to emerge (Ranger, 1985). By the mid-1930s, however, the administration was concerned about the danger of a few expanding their farms at the expense of others in the reserves. Entrepreneurs who had been admired and encouraged within the demonstration policy now became the central culprits in the increasingly popular portrayal of a black crisis of conservation.

During the 1930s Native Commissioners were instrumental in purveying the image of heightening problems in the reserves through their frequent references to soil erosion. A Commission established to inquire into the preservation of the resources of the colony in 1939 concluded that, 'as was to be expected, rarely is the native alive to the importance of conserving the soil' (Southern Rhodesia, 1939: 12). Some Native Commissioners, however, were critical of native policy from the outset. In his annual report of 1929, the Chief Native Commissioner (CNC) referenced a comparison of the standard of husbandry on two adjacent plots in Mrewa district, one cultivated by the plough and the other by traditional hoe cultivation:

In the one done with the hoe, the contour of the ground has been studied, and the ridges made with a view to draining the lands from heavy flood, but *still more to prevent soil erosion*; the crop stands high and dry in the heaviest of rains, and gets all the benefits of the humus turned under between the sods which form the ridge. (CNC, 1929: 4, emphasis added)

The Agriculturalist for the Instruction of Natives (E.D. Alvord), who had initiated the demonstration programme, was also forced to acknowledge that the 'improved' methods being demonstrated were in fact having harmful effects on the soil;

Soil erosion is also showing a decided effect on our demonstration plots and we have decided that a change in demonstration methods must be made. The usual square or rectangular plot must be changed to plots laid out on contours with terracing, strip cropping and vegetative control. (Agriculturalist for the Instruction of Natives, 1935: 30)

Despite the reservations expressed by key officers within the colonial administration, the principles of the demonstration programme were consolidated in the subsequent centralization policy implemented in the reserves from 1929 and the imported mechanical model for erosion control remained the central tenet of colonial conservation in the reserves.

The final blow to the entrepreneurial African was dealt by the LAA. Under the 1894 Order-in-Council, Africans were theoretically able to hold land on the same terms as Europeans. The confinement of Africans within totally inadequate portions of the country under the LAA was a direct response to the perceived threat posed to European farming by African production given equal access to good soils and markets. In addition, by continually emphasizing the destructive use of resources by African farmers, the colonial administration felt justified in restricting native access to resources and, in later years, for refusing demands for more land.

With the implementation of the LAA, colonial policy in the reserves became directed by the need to accommodate an increasing African population on a static resource base. The policy of centralization was forwarded as the means to achieve this: 'For the regeneration of the reserves there are two essentials— organisation and control: organisation to ensure the best use being made of the natural resources; and control to prevent abuses by the individual' (Southern Rhodesia, 1939: 57). Under the centralization policy arable and pastoral areas were consolidated to produce a more 'rational' use of resources. Settlement patterns were also reorganized along straight lines to enable the most 'efficient' provision of services. Although originally a voluntary policy, persuasion soon became replaced by compulsion. The urgency of raising carrying capacities in the African areas was compounded by the implementation of the LAA and as 'squatters' from European and unoccupied lands were forced into the reserves. The report of the 1939 Commission epitomized the way emphasis on native malpractices was used to justify refusals for more land:

It may be that with the present rate of increase of the native population, difficulty will be experienced in finding enough suitable land for their requirement, but as it would not only be futile but also highly undesirable to attempt to meet these needs by allocating further areas for uncontrolled exploitation, the obvious course is to adopt measures designed for making the best use of land already assigned to them. (Southern Rhodesia, 1939: 14)

The numerous reports of environmental degradation in the reserve areas of Rhodesia in the 1930s cannot be linked to any objective assessment of the state of resources at either the national or district level at this time. Indeed, air photographs and oral evidence at the local level suggest that there was no sudden worsening of the erosion status during the 1930s (Elliott, 1989). The Native Commissioner (1945) for Marandellas District, 20 km southeast of Salisbury, reported gullies in Svosve reserve which were big enough to hide trains. Local level analysis, however, has shown that these gully systems were already stabilized, were spatially very limited and had non-anthropogenic origins (Elliott, 1989).

While localized problems of erosion undoubtedly existed, the switch of blame from settler to African farmer during the 1930s and 1940s was a reflection of events external to the African sector and indeed external to the colony itself. It had the effect of both diverting attention away from settler malpractices and also increasing control over indigenous production and the African way of life: 'The logic of white survival in the countryside . . . compelled the state to implement land management and conservation policies which would underwrite the racial division of land' (Phimister, 1986: 270).

Events external to the colony, particularly in the United States, added fuel to the colonial administrator's fire in justifying increasingly interventionist and centralized agricultural policies. The destruction in the dust bowl of North America peaked in the mid-1930s and was well publicized in Africa. Undoubtedly, there was deep concern in the colonial offices at Whitehall that the North American experience should not be repeated in Africa. Despite the lack of information about the problem in the colonies, from 1938, all colonies were required to submit an annual account of conservation work undertaken by their departments. In Rhodesia, the administration lost no time in publicizing the plight of North Americans and the need to take rapid action to save the colony's soil resources.

The 1940s in Rhodesia was a period of increased intervention in African agriculture, mounting tension between black and white, new legislation and increased compulsion. As a direct product of the 1939 Commission of Enquiry, the Natural Resources Act (NRA) was promulgated in 1941. This Act legalized procedures for ensuring reasonable standards of husbandry and for protecting natural resources. In addition, an inspectorate was established to 'police' the use of resources and a Natural Resources Board to oversee all activities. The NRA remained the primary legislation concerning resource use until independence.

In 1944 a further commission urged the need for even more authoritarian action in the reserves. The report of the Native Production and Trade Commission recommended compulsory planned production, the control of markets and the enforcement of good husbandry measures in the reserves, prioritizing contour construction and contour ploughing (Southern Rhodesia, 1944). In response to the report, centralization was speeded up and legal control over peasant production effected through the NRA. Overstocking also became framed as part of the soil erosion problem in these areas and in 1944 compulsory destocking became operative in 49 reserves. In some reserves localized relocation of kraals were enforced in the name of resource trusteeship.

Until 1944, soil and water conservation in both European and African areas was the responsibility of the Rhodesia Ministry of Agriculture's Department of Water Irrigation. In that year, the Department of Native Agriculture was formed and soil conservation in the reserves became its responsibility. The Agriculturalist for the Instruction of Natives (1944) expressed concern over the content of conservation programmes in the reserves:

The methods of soil conservation at present being used in these reserves are those evolved by the Department of Water Irrigation . . . a more or less standard technique has been applied whether the soil is a heavy clay loam or a loose coarse sand, whether the land is nearly flat or steeply sloping; in high or low rainfall areas.

The geographical specificity of the conservation advantages of the American-inspired model was also recognized by the Natural Resources Board: 'Much information on conservation of "European" farmland has been obtained from American printed matter, correspondence and visits, but the conditions peculiar to the Native Reserves pertain only to Africa' (NRB, 1945: 13).

Despite such concern and the known benefits of combining mechanical and biological measures, conservation in both European and African areas in the

1940s continued to be dominated heavily by mechanical control measures. The persistence of American mechanical conservation layouts had immediate spatial and racial biases. Mechanical conservation measures focus on the *control* of water rather than its retention. Their adoption favoured the highveld areas where the problem was indeed only of periodic excess of water. Since European farmland was concentrated on the deeper, more fertile soils of the highveld, these farmers were favoured by the decision. For the majority of African farmers the problem was one of water shortage and moisture *retention*.

Promotion of mechanical protection for arable lands in the European sector represented a policy of 'least resistance'. Biological conservation, because it relied on the integration of pastoral and arable sectors and a cessation of mono-cropping, would have 'raised precisely those questions about the relationship between tobacco planting and other branches of agriculture which the state was in no hurry to resolve' (Phimister, 1986: 267). Once again, conservation farming was smoothed into European agriculture through loans and, from 1946, the inclusion of a conservation element in all commodity prices. Government policy with respect to settler agriculture during the 1940s was strictly non-interventionist. Post-war problems in maize and cattle production were overlooked in preference to supporting tobacco farmers who represented the majority of the electorate.

In the African areas, the implementation of mechanical conservation measures was far from politically neutral and was increasingly enforced. In conditions of land shortage, contour banks and storm drains took valuable land out of cultivation. Although government conservation gangs constructed the top contour in the conservation layout for individual farmers, further construction and maintenance required substantial labour input often at critical periods in the farming calendar.

Just as colonial conservation programmes ignored cultural or environmental specificity, so the socio-economic appropriateness of the erosion control model was not addressed. Establishing either the suitable content of conservation programmes or the root cause of degradation in the reserves were not prioritized; the politics of African land use was more important than the problem of soil erosion. Concern for the indigenous population or the environment was secondary to the cultural and political concerns of the white settler economy. For the colonial administration, the issue of conservation in the reserves was resolved by a technical solution. For Africans, decreasing returns from agriculture were perceived as a function of increased diversion of labour into conservation works, government intervention into markets, low prices and land shortage. Such antagonism was fertile ground for the emerging nationalism in the reserves.

Colonial conservation 1950-1980

The 1950s represented a phase of 'second colonial occupation' in many parts of Africa. This was characterized by increased enforcement of agricultural change in native sectors and a heightened political consciousness on the part of Africans. Although the precise content of policy varied, colonial administrations in Tanganyika, Kenya and the Rhodesian Federation all embarked on large-scale reforms aimed at developing and intensifying native agriculture. Policy in Rhodesia took the form of the Native Land Husbandry Act (NLHA) of 1951. Environmental degradation in the reserves was now blamed on more than merely overstocking or overpopulation. Its solution required a change in the very structure of African society: 'The other provisions . . . are little better than holding action, preventing catastrophic deterioration, but making little headway against a mass of inertia and ignorance rooted in tribal custom and systems' (Southern Rhodesia, 1955: 5).

Under the NLHA, the traditional African concept of land as a collective resource was removed and replaced with an alien one of individual tenure. Land as well as labour were now commodities; Africans were to become either settled farmers, practising proper agriculture, or industrialized workers with no roots in the reserve areas. Only those actively cultivating in the reserve on the day of implementation of the NLHA qualified for arable rights. In consequence, by 1959, 102,000 families had been rendered landless under the allocation process (Kay, 1970). Furthermore, those who did have ownership found their holdings too small to support anything other than a subsistence level of production.

The original aims of the NLHA included both mechanical and biological conservation. All arable holdings were to be protected before cultivation through the standard layout of mechanical barriers and stormdrains. A set of 'good farming practices' was also outlined, covering the prevention of soil erosion, the protection of natural resources, livestock control and cultivation practices generally. With individual landownership under the NLHA, penalties for non-compliance with any aspect of these could be enforced under the NRA, if so required. Mechanical conservation, however, was still given priority; it was not intended to enforce the 'good farming practices' until conditions were restored in the reserves in which education of Africans could occur. Mechanical conservation soon absorbed the majority of extension staff and funds, the success of the Act being measured in terms of yards of contour banks and storm drains constructed. By 1959, 231,5000 ha of arable land in the native areas alone had been fully protected by contour ridges (Director of Native Agriculture, 1959: 67). Clearly, it was easier to apply legislation than it was to educate people to better standards of agronomy.

Individual tenure was heralded as the key not only to successful conservation, but also to re-establishing control over the indigenous population, while simultaneously serving the needs of an expanding industrial sector:

A settled and thriving agricultural population is probably one of the best sheet-anchors of political stability . . . By discontinuing a system which allows the Native to vacillate between spells of work in the European area and spells of semi-loafing in the reserves, it will do much to stabilize also the industrial working population (Southern Rhodesia, 1955, 14).

The large numbers of people rendered landless by the NLHA were not absorbed into urban or industrial areas and, as a group, became a source of political instability. Elsewhere the process of decolonization was starting and in Rhodesia, the activities of the nationalist movements were increasing. In an attempt to stem resistance in the reserves, amendments were made to the NLHA relaxing controls over the allocation of lands and enhancing the role of traditional authorities in resource decisions. After the Unilateral Declaration of Independence (UDI) in 1965, pacifying the native population had to be balanced with the need to instil white farmers' confidence in the regime and attain self-sufficiency in food production. In fact, problems for European agriculture and the settler community mounted over the last five years of UDI. The world economic recession compounded the effects of the political and economic isolation of Rhodesia and the liberation war intensified during the 1970s. In such conditions, the maintenance of existing conservation works became difficult and the construction of new ones slowed. At independence, the 'crisis' of conservation in the African areas was heralded once more.

Discussion

The causes of soil erosion lie in the specificities of both the physical and social-economic environments. In turn, soil conservation 'is as much about social processes as physical ones, and the major constraints are not technical but social' (Blaikie, 1985: 50). On independence, the new government of Zimbabwe inherited a compounded problem of soil erosion precisely because such unity of natural and cultural processes in shaping the environment had not been acknowledged or responded to during the colonial period. Despite the long history of conservation in the country, success had been limited because of a restricted conception of the problem which failed to address the underlying causes of environmental degradation.

Promoting, and responding to, a conception of soil erosion as an environmental problem for which a technical solution was available, enabled the colonial government to tinker with the issue while pursuing its own protectionist and sectional ends. By excluding the political economy as a causal element in soil erosion, any failure in the programme could by attributed directly to the land manager and used to justify increasing intervention and compulsion. The optimism and arrogance of the colonial administrators stemmed from, and was reinforced by, the characteristics of Western science. It was assumed that the repeated application of rational Western management techniques to a neutral environment would solve the problem of soil erosion. Even when this supposition was questioned by informed experts within the administration, their advice was ignored. The environment *per se* was not its primary concern. Agricultural development in the reserves during the colonial period occurred to the extent of releasing labour to European industrial and agricultural sectors, but not so far as to threaten European markets. The mechanical conservation model fitted this requirement; it demanded the establishment of permanent agriculture and this paved the way for imposing further Western-inspired husbandry methods and means of 'rationalizing' resource use. By preventing the emergence of an entrepreneurial class it also stifled competition and forced Africans to take up opportunities for off-farm income.

The standard broad-brush approach to soil erosion subordinated indigenous cultures and institutions generally and was insensitive to the social differentiation within the reserves. Throughout the entire colonial period, 'there is the theme of rejection, a general denial that there was anything good in the former system of native cultivation and resultant ways of life' (Floyd, 1959: 290). The American model of soil erosion control replaced earlier indigenous methods of turning the soil into mounds. Within the land reforms of the centralization programme, Western conceptions of efficient allocation and use of resources were introduced; and within the NLHA, Western management institutions and individual landownership were added to the conservation requirements in the Communal Areas. In consequence, indigenous knowledge was gradually subsumed, local institutions replaced by new, centrally determined legislation, and African control over the environment removed. Again, the colonial policy was questioned:

Is it necessary that the whole of native institutions and all cultures be destroyed to make room for the implanting of ideas, our learning and our civilization? Surely the stock could remain and some twig be grafted on which would bring forth good fruit in due season (Native Commissioner for Marandellas, 1929: 6–7).

However, as policies in the reserves became increasingly centralized and interventionist, dialogue between parties or the opportunities for local determination became very limited. Technocentric conceptions of soil erosion and the associated conservation solution helped to reinforce a 'West-is-best' ideology within Rhodesia. With increased compulsion and widening of the conservation programmes from the 1940s, more and more people in the reserves were brought under the influence of Western technological culture.

The challenge for the independent government of Zimbabwe is to overcome the legacies in both the physical and human landscapes of a fifty-year conservation programme. The environment needs to be placed back in local hands, new models for erosion control developed on the basis of indigenous and imported knowledge, and multiple conservation solutions devised to accommodate the ecological diversity which exists locally.

Bibliography

Agriculturalist for the Instruction of Natives (1935) Annual Report, Salisbury, Government Printer.

Agriculturalist for the Instruction of Natives (1944) Memo to Chief Native Commissioner, National Archives of Zimbabwe, S160 sc.

Aylen, D. (1941) 'Who built the first contour ridges?', *Rhodesia Agricultural Journal*, 38, 144–8.

Bannerman, J.H. (1982) 'The Land Apportionment Act: a paper tiger?', *Zimbabwe Agricultural Journal*, 79 (3), 101–6.

Beinart, W. (1984) 'Soil erosion, conservationism and ideas about development: a Southern African exploration, 1900–1960, *Journal of Southern African Studies*, 11 (1), 52–83.

Blaikie, P. (1985) *The Political Economy of Soil Erosion in Developing Countries*, London, Longman.

Chief Native Commissioner (1929) Annual Report, Salisbury, Government Printer.

Cripps, L. (1909) 'The erosion of the soil', *Rhodesia Agricultural Journal*, 6, 669–70.

Director of Native Agriculture (1959) Annual Report, Salisbury, Government Printer.

Elliott, J.A. (1989) 'Soil erosion and conservation in Zimbabwe: Political economy and the environment', unpublished PhD thesis, Loughborough University of Technology.

Elwell, H.A. (1983) 'The degrading soil and water resources of the Communal Areas', *Zimbabwe Science News*, 17 (9–10), 145–7.

Elwell, H.A. (1986) *Soil Conservation*, Harare, The College Press.

Floyd, B. (1959) 'Changing patterns of African Land use in Southern Rhodesia', unpublished PhD thesis, Graduate School, Syracuse, NY.

Floyd, B. (1962) 'Land apportionment in Rhodesia', *Geographical Review*, 52, 566–82.

Haviland, P.H. (1927) 'Soil erosion', *Rhodesia Agricultural Journal*, 24, 328–33.

Haviland, P.H. (1928) 'Soil erosion', *Rhodesia Agricultural Journal*, 25, 1217–24.

Kay, G. (1970) *Rhodesia: A Human Geography*, London, University of London Press.

Kinsey, B.H. (1983) 'Emerging issues in Zimbabwe's resettlement programmes', *Development Policy Review*, 1, 163–96.

Native Commissioner for Marandellas District (1929–45), Annual Reports, Salisbury, Government Printer.

Natural Resources Board (1945–8), Annual Reports, Salisbury, Government Printer.

Phimister, I. (1986) 'Discourse and the discipline of historical context: conservationism and ideas about development in Southern Rhodesia 1930–1950', *Journal of Southern African Studies*, 12 (2), 263–75.

Ranger, T. (1985) *Peasant Consciousness and Guerrilla War in Zimbabwe*, London, James Curry.

Southern Rhodesia (1939) *Report of the Commission to Enquire into the Preservation etc. of the Natural Resources of the Country*, Salisbury, Government Printer.

Southern Rhodesia (1944) *Report of the Native production and Trade Commission*, Salisbury, Government Printer.

Southern Rhodesia (1955) *What the Native Land Husbandry Act Means to the Rural African of Southern Rhodesia*, Salisbury, Government Printer.

Vincent, V. and Thomas, R.G. (1960) *An Agricultural Survey of Southern Rhodesia. Part 1: Agro-Ecological Survey*, Salisbury, Government Printer.

Watt, W.M. (1913) 'The dangers and prevention of soil erosion', *Rhodesia Agricultural Journal*, 10, 667–75.

Wilson, K.B. (1986) 'History ecology and conservation in Southern Zimbabwe', seminar paper delivered at the Department of Sociology, University of Manchester, 12 February.

CHAPTER 8

The politics and culture of dambo irrigation in Zimbabwe
Morag Bell and Neil Roberts

Introduction

Since the mid-twentieth century a dramatic transformation in Africa's hydro-landscape has resulted from the imposition of Western engineering technology, manifest in impressive structures like the Kariba and Aswan dams. Widespread faith in the modernizing and progressive influence of Western science and technology has often produced naive and simplistic images of African environments. Thus, the Nile Valley excepted, Africa's pre-modern landscape is thought to have remained relatively little changed from a 'primeval' state, such human transformations as have occurred resulting from human use of fire rather than water. In recent years, and on social, economic and environmental grounds, disillusionment has increased with large-scale, Western-style hydraulic schemes, such as the Bakalori dam in Nigeria and the Tana basin scheme in Kenya (Adams and Grove, 1984). The search for smaller-scale alternatives reveals that before European colonial rule there already existed a significant African tradition of water management (Adams and Anderson, 1988). It was small in scale, often informal in organization, and lacked the impressive engineering structures of ancient or modern hydraulic civilizations. Precisely for these reasons it was overlooked by Europeans, for whom manifestations of traditional African water use in the landscape were largely invisible. Indigenous African achievements were by no means unimpressive, however, and they continue to be important today despite decades of neglect or even discouragement by governments and other agencies.

Indigenous African traditions of water resource use have employed a diverse array of technologies, related primarily to local environmental conditions. Thus on the steeply sloping ground of the East African rift, there are extensive pre-colonial agricultural terraces and gravity-fed furrow irrigation systems (Adams and Anderson, 1988). On major river floodplains, such as the inland delta of the River Niger, very different hydro-ecological conditions prevail. Here the seasonal rise and fall of flood waters have been employed in the cultivation of African rice (McIntosh, 1983; Adams and Carter, 1987). As elsewhere in Africa, specific crops are planted and grown in a catenary sequence at the floodplain edge according to the known local hydrological regime. In these circumstances, detailed indigenous knowledge of the soil-water requirements for individual crops has provided an effective alternative to technological control of water. Other resources traditionally utilized for agriculture in sub-Saharan Africa are inland valley swamps (*bas fonds*), such as the *bolilands* and *fadamas* of West Africa and the *marais* of Rwanda, where manual lifting technologies such as the *shaduf* raise the shallow ground water for micro-scale irrigation (Turner, 1984; Kay *et al.*, 1985).

Traditional forms of water and land use have not required centralized planning and coordination, nor the collection of hydrological or agricultural statistics, and, as a result, their spatial extent and contribution to agricultural output have consistently been under-recorded. The same is true of informal cultivation systems in other continents and cultures. The unofficial smallholder plots of the Soviet Union, for example, occupy only 4 per cent of the area farmed collectively, but are estimated to produce half of all Soviet vegetables (Cole, 1984). Similarly, the humble allotment probably accounted for 10 per cent of Britain's total food production during and after the Second World War, with over 1 million plots occupying a mere 40,000 hectares of land (Thorp, 1975; Crouch and Ward, 1988). Yet, because allotments are part of the informal agricultural sector, they have been largely ignored by government statistics.

In most of sub-Saharan Africa food security is now a permanent priority producing considerable debate on how small water sources may be identified and harnessed in the search for future African food self-sufficiency (Underhill, 1984; Adams and Carter, 1987). The particular water sources discussed here are *dambos*, or *vleis* in Afrikaans. These are small valley wetlands found throughout the plateau savannas of sub-Saharan Africa, which retain moisture to within 2–3 m of the ground surface during the dry season (see Thomas and Goudie, 1985, for a discussion of physical characteristics). In Zimbabwe's Communal farming areas, there are at present an estimated 15,000–20,000 hectares under informal garden irrigation on dambos (Bell *et al.*, 1987). This is significantly more than the approximately 3,000 hectares of land brought under smallholder irrigation via formal, government-sponsored schemes since independence in 1980. What is more, dambo irrigation has been successful despite rather than because of state intervention. Peasant farmers receive neither agricultural advice, nor financial credit to support their gardens, for dambo cultivation is deemed illegal as a result of colonial legislation which remains in force today. In order to explain and understand this contradiction between policy and reality it is necessary to investigate the historical struggle for control of dambo water resources in colonial Rhodesia, the legacy of which persists in independent Zimbabwe.

The nature and origins of dambo irrigation in Zimbabwe

Studies from many parts of Africa, including Zimbabwe, indicate the wides-

Plate 8.1   Rope-washer handpump being used to lift shallow ground wate for dambo
irrigation

pread use of dambos, not just for garden plot irrigation agriculture, but also for
domestic water consumption, cattle watering and grazing (Russell, 1971;
Whitlow, 1983; Turner, 1986). As the water table is typically within 2 m of the
ground surface, water can be extracted by bucket, hosepipe or simple
handpump, without the need for complex mechanical systems of storage or
lifting (Plate 8.1). Crops irrigated in this way can be depended upon even when
rain-fed crops fail. Thus garden produce acts as an important buffer during dry
seasons and in drought years. While contemporary patterns of use are not wholly
indigenous, nevertheless garden cultivation is recorded in local oral traditions
and was widely observed by early explorers of the region (Selous, 1920; Jollie,
1924; Wilson, 1986). The missionary T.M. Thomas, for example, reported in the
1860s 'valleys converted into the most fruitful gardens full of ripe maize, other
indigenous grains, cotton and tobacco' (cited in Palmer, 1977: 225).

Dambo wetlands are not a homogenous resource. They exhibit a range of
types, varying in size, shape and soil type (Acres *et al.*, 1985). Broad headwater
dambos are found on the older erosion surface plateau of Zimbabwe's highveld,
whereas in the more steeply sloping middleveld most are narrow and linear.
Figure 8.1 shows a schematic cross-section through the sandy type of dambo
commonly found on the granitic rock of the highveld. Rainfall is transmitted to
the dambo from the upper dryland catchment via runoff and, more importantly,
by infiltration and throughflow. The undulating subsurface impermeable
horizon leads to a perched water-table, whose level varies both seasonally and
spatially within the dambo. Several internal dambo zones can be identified

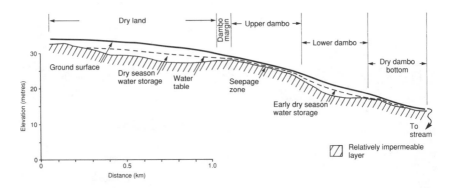

Figure 8.1 Hydrological model of a dambo, based on Chizengeni catchment (from Bell *et al.*, 1987)

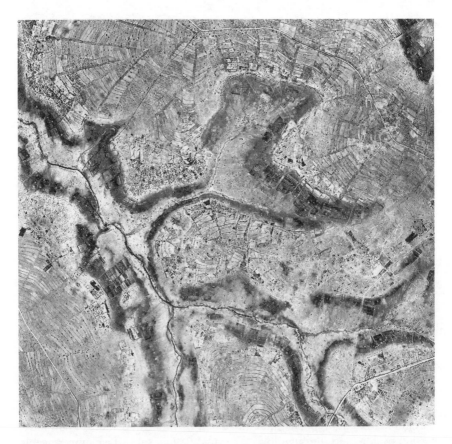

Plate 8.2 Air photograph of part of Chihota CA (September 1984). Dark-toned areas show 'wet' dambo. Chizengeni dambo is located top centre (area shown approx. 5 × 5 km)

according to depth of the water-table and position in the soil catena. At any one time there is likely to be a part of the dambo which is wet and another which is dry. Within the upper dambo zone, or 'wet' dambo, the water-table is sufficiently close to the surface to permit growth of grass or crops. The lower dambo and dambo bottom tend to dry out during the dry season, and stream flow at the outlet may cease. Here the cover of grasses and sedges is thinner, but generally suitable for livestock grazing (Roberts, 1988).

In the wet upper zone the water-table is normally at less than 2 m depth throughout the year, and typically less than 0.5 m during the wet season. These waterlogged conditions create an anoxic environment in which grasses and sedges decompose *in situ* to form a hydromorphic upper soil horizon, rich in organic matter (Roberts, 1988). Soil organic matter has long been held to be the key to successful horticulture (Waksman, 1936) and it is no surprise that many of the world's vegetable gardens are located on reclaimed wetlands where decaying plant matter has created humus-rich soils.

Visible on the air photograph shown in Plate 8.2, a band of darker-toned grass on the upper part of dambos is conspicuous by the end of the dry season. Soil moisture is still available for plant growth when the rest of the area is dry and it is here that soil organic matter values are highest and where cultivated gardens have been established. The close correspondence between the area under gardens and the upper 'wet' zone at Chizengeni dambo can be seen by comparing Plate 8.2 with Figure 8.4. It is clear here and elsewhere that farmers have correctly identified the most suitable agro-ecological zone for garden cultivation.

In Zimbabwe's Communal Areas, land suitable for agriculture is formerly allocated to male household heads for two main purposes: dryfields where rain-fed crops like maize are grown; and gardens on dambos where crops can be grown throughout the year. Once permission for a dambo garden has been granted, only a minimum of physical and infrastructure is needed to transform the land. The plot must be defined on the ground, a fence constructed, a well dug and the land ploughed. The key to successful cultivation lies in the farmer's ability to adapt to and manage the varying soil moisture requirements. Raised beds running along the contour are frequently constructed in order to reduce soil erosion, encourage wet-season drainage and help distribute irrigation water during the dry season. In some cases more complex engineering structures such as bunds, distribution channels and small storage dams may be created. These are almost never built for initial cultivation, however, but are added later by successful and experienced farmers who wish to invest more money and effort into their garden, usually for cash sale of their produce. Irrigation water is obtained from wells inside the gardens by simple technology such as watering cans and buckets, oil drums and hosepipes. By careful adaptation to changing environmental conditions during the agricultural year, households can grow a sufficient and continuous supply of vegetables to feed themselves and to sell. They may also grow the staple crop of maize together with rice under irrigation, to supplement dryfield production and to secure a harvest during the 'hungry' wet season when nutritional levels are at their lowest.

Colonial state interventions in dambo use

The economic and social benefits to be gained from utilizing water resources such as dambos are determined not merely by physical accessibility but also by national government policy and its implementation at local level. This is starkly illustrated by the occupation of Zimbabwe's better-watered highveld by European farmers during the early colonial years between 1890 and 1930, and the restriction or relocation of the African population to native reserves in the drier middleveld (Figure 8.2). The spatial segregation of African and European populations into areas of contrasting land and water resource endowment was formalized in a series of legislation including Orders-in-Council of 1898 and 1920 and the Land Apportionment Act in 1930. Under this legislation the racial division of all land in Southern Rhodesia was institutionalized, severely restricting both the quantity and quality available to African peasant households (Bannerman, 1982; Roder, 1964). The reserves, later known as Tribal Trust Lands or Communal Areas, to which Africans were confined, supported population densities several times greater than in the European farming areas. Furthermore, from the early 1960s, as a consequence of growing population pressure, households in the tribal areas became increasingly dependent on European commercial agriculture for their basic food requirements (Riddell, n.d.).

Segregation of land on racial lines was not the only impact of colonialism on environmental resource use in Rhodesia/Zimbabwe. Europeans also attempted to intervene, directly or indirectly, in the internal workings of indigenous socio-ecological systems. One form of state intervention in the use of water resources in colonial Rhodesia was restriction on customary use of wetland environments carried out in the name of environmental conservation. For much of Zimbabwe's colonial history land degradation in general, and soil erosion in particular, have been important political issues (see Chapter 7). The conservation measures adopted by the colonial state to deal with this included legal restrictions on access to and use of apparently fragile environments.

From the 1920s, official concern over soil erosion and the human interference with river flow led to successive measures severely restricting the use of wetland resources (Bell and Hotchkiss, 1989). The Water Acts of 1927 and 1976 sought to preserve downstream river flow by restricting the extraction of 'public water' in stream source areas, including water from dambos. In addition, the Streambank Protection Regulation of 1952 aimed to conserve both the commercial farming areas and communal lands from erosion by prohibiting cultivation within 30 m of a stream and on wetlands such as dambos.

This protectionist legislation was initiated by problems of soil erosion on European commercial farmland (Whitlow, 1990). Beinart (1984) refers to official discussions as early as 1913 over the careless degradation of dambos by settler farmers. It was also introduced to control requests by commercial firms, notably asbestos mines, to extract water from public streams. However, the impact of the legislation was felt most severely in the already densely populated communal

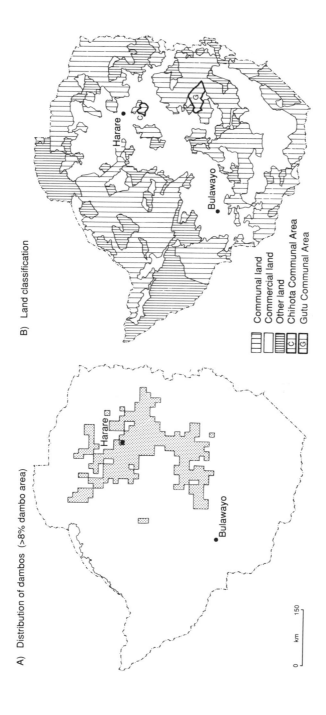

Figure 8.2 Distribution of dambos (modified from Whitlow, 1984) and landholding in Zimbabwe

lands where households were further restricted in their access to valuable land and water resources. Wilson (1986) contends that legislation of this type was also enacted as a means of controlling African farmers and reducing competition for agricultural markets. Many peasant households were indeed forced to seek alternative ways of meeting their nutritional needs.

A primary concern of technical departments in the Rhodesian administration, including the Department of Water Development, was the design and purchase of appropriate machinery for agriculture. This included drilling equipment for the extraction of ground water for irrigation and domestic supply, and anti-erosion implements like ditchers. Official correspondence indicates frequent requests for the sharing of technical knowledge between colonial territories. During the late 1920s and 1930s, Basutoland, Kenya, Katanga, Northern Rhodesia, Nyasaland and Tanganyika sought advice from Southern Rhodesia on appropriate agricultural technologies (ZNA, 1927–36). Irrigation expertise was further diffused from Australia and New Zealand to Rhodesia during visits by technical staff from the Union of South Africa to Salisbury. This pool of sophisticated technical knowledge was applied in both the Rhodesian commercial lands and the native reserves in the form of borehole drilling programmes, conservation works and formal irrigation schemes (ZNA, 1923–39).

However, these technical interventions in the African lands were rarely coupled with detailed studies of local practices. In the case of fragile environments such as dambos, the legalistic approach adopted towards conservation was restrictive in nature in that it placed measurable limits on the area of cultivation and technical restrictions on the opportunities for rural households to practise irrigated · agriculture. It was an authoritarian and technocratic solution to a perceived environmental problem requiring little training on the part of the implementers. White colonial government officials were largely blind to the ability of African farmers to cope with seasonal variations in water supply through technologically simple but environmentally effective water management. In the absence of large engineering structures or neatly contoured slopes, the African agricultural landscape appeared to be haphazard, disorganized and inefficient.

Dambo irrigation in two Communal Areas

Neither the procedures for implementing conservation legislation within the Communal Areas (CAs) nor peasant responses to government interference was uniform. The range of intra-regional variations in dambo utilization can be illustrated by two CAs with different natural resource endowments and contrasting histories of garden cultivation: Gutu and Chihota. Gutu CA lies some 200 km south of Harare in the middleveld, and receives an average of 700 mm rainfall per year. The western half of the CA contains a significant proportion of dambo wetland (Table 8.1). Given the relatively low and unreliable rainfall in Gutu, it might be expected that dambo irrigation would be

Table 8.1 Contrasts in dambo utilization between two Communal Areas of Zimbabwe

Communal Area	Western Gutu	Chihota
Mean annual rainfall (mm)	700	850
Dambo area (km²)	125	195
Dambo area/total area (%)	12.2	29.6
Dambo garden area (km²)	1.7	24.5
Average dambo garden size (ha)	0.06	0.50
Study village Households with access to dambo garden (%)	Shumbairerwa 56	Chizengeni 96
Households gaining income from garden (%)	46	95

Sources: Bell *et al.*, 1987; O'Sullivan, 1988

widely used as a buffer against failure of rain-fed crops. However, air photograph mapping shows that only 1.7 per cent of cultivable dambo land in western Gutu is in fact used for garden cultivation. The reasons for this under-use of a potentially valuable environmental resource are complex, but a survey of households in Shumbairerwa village, western Gutu, indicates that only some 56 per cent of all families have access to a dambo garden, a much lower figure than in some other parts of Zimbabwe.

Households in Shumbairerwa report that a major constraint on dambo cultivation is the restrictive colonial legislation which remains in place today. Gutu's dambos are narrow and linear, and cultivable dambo land often lies closer to water courses than the 30 m permitted by the Streambank Protection Regulation (Figure 8.3). This Regulation continues to be strictly implemented in Gutu, with households being fined or prohibited from using their gardens. In some cases, households have voluntarily abandoned their gardens for fear of prosecution. It appears that in communities such as Gutu, where colonial legislation was effectively implemented, this essential productive use of wetland environments was disrupted and household food production declined.

Equally, it is apparent that legislation failed to destroy indigenous practices in all regions where dambo wetlands occurred. Strict implementation was not practically feasible throughout the country. For example, in Chihota CA legal controls were much less rigorously enforced, and wetland cultivation appears to have continued and even intensified despite the actions of land inspectors and agricultural extension officers. Chihota lies only 100 km from Harare and receives a higher annual rainfall than Gutu (Table 8.1). In Chihota most dambos

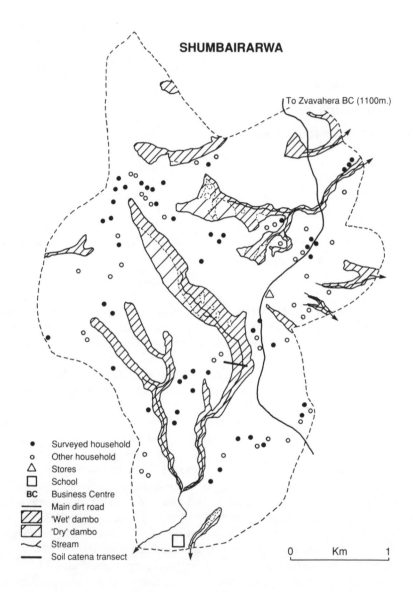

SHUMBAIRARWA

To Zvavahera BC (1100m.)

- • Surveyed household
- ○ Other household
- △ Stores
- ☐ School
- **BC** Business Centre
- ▬ Main dirt road
- ▨ 'Wet' dambo
- ▨ 'Dry' dambo
- ⤙ Stream
- ▬ Soil catena transect

0   Km   1

Figure 8.3   Shumbairerwa study site, Gutu CA

are of broad headwater type and the cultivable dambo zone is normally situated well away from water courses. As a result there is usually no conflict with the 30 metre rule. In contrast to Shumbairerwa, almost all households at Chizengeni village in Chihota have access to a dambo garden, and this has become crucial to the nutritional status of households and to the provision of cash incomes within the peasant economy. Altogether there are some 2,500 ha of cultivated dambo gardens in this CA, representing 30 per cent of total cultivable dambo land within Chihota.

During white colonial rule the rural economy in Rhodesia, as elsewhere in the developing world, came to be integrally linked to urban and world markets. In the case of the African CAs, particularly those located close to major markets such as Harare, rural communities became increasingly orientated to monetary exchange. Here the attraction of wetland environments for cash crops as well as household food production, placed access to a dambo plot at a premium. The consequent expansion in the area under dambo gardens is graphically illustrated by a series of land-use maps at Chizengeni based on old air photographs (Figure

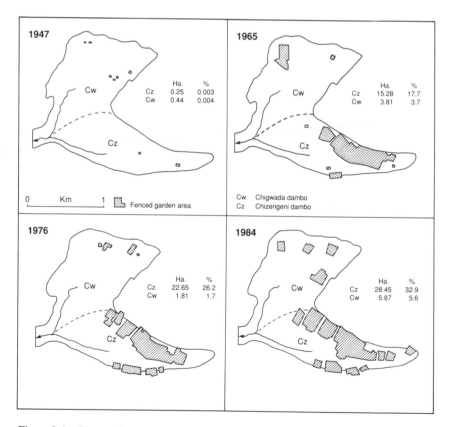

Figure 8.4 Changes in garden area, Chizengeni–Chigwada dambo, Chihota CA, based on sequential air photograph analysis

8.4). As these show, cultivation was minimal in 1947, but increased dramatically between then and 1965, by which time much of Chizengeni's cultivable dambo area was in use as arable land. The cultivated area expanded more gradually during the 1960s and 1970s and saturation point was reached during the 1980s. Oral evidence reinforced by aerial photographs indicates that in many other areas dambo gardens were acquired in the 1970s during Zimbabwe's war of independence. There was a deliberate flouting of colonial authority in many of the CAs immediately prior to independence in 1980, and with it came an indiscriminate land grab as the traditional system of land allocation broke down. Thus, land and water resources have been put under increasing pressure as a result of external political-economic influences.

Since independence the official approach to environmental conservation and irrigation development adopted by the national government of Robert Mugabe has been shaped by new political priorities, namely, a vision of Zimbabwean society based on socialist principles and involving active support for rural development in the CAs. In consequence, the restrictive colonial legislation has been re-examined. The approach currently adopted places less emphasis than before upon enforced implementation and more upon educating the responsible farmer in appropriate conservation practices. While this shift in emphasis reflects changes in what is politically enforceable within the newly independent state, it also symbolizes a broader change in attitude to the irrigated African landscape. It indicates a willingness to accept that rural communities employ diverse social, economic and agronomic strategies by which to cope with recurrent and unpredictable food scarcity (Zinyama *et al.*, 1988). In addition, the technology on which these strategies are based does not necessarily involve grandiose concrete structures or complex water lifting devises.

Despite the disruption of white colonial rule, the impact of external pressures on patterns of land and water use has been mediated through local circumstances. At Chizengeni, the response of the local community to pressures on finite dambo resources has been to encourage newly formed households requiring a dambo plot to seek land in the resettlement areas outside Chihota CA. For existing farmers at Chizengeni, the solution to the shortage of dambo land has been to intensify cultivation by cropping more frequently on existing gardens rather than to expand the cultivated area. Gardens are now cropped not only in the dry season for vegetables, as at Shumbairerwa, but also during the wet season for the staple crop, maize. During this period of the year, labour, fertilizer and other agricultural inputs are diverted, at least in part, from rain-fed croplands to dambo gardens. This strategy has helped ensure food security, especially in drought years such as 1986–7 when the only maize harvested in Chizengeni came from dambo gardens.

Conclusion

Landscape transformation involving water management is not always a large-scale, formally planned affair. Behind the drama of grand technological engineering there have been and remain less formal traditions of using water and land resources. These have been by no means insignificant spatially or socio-economically, but they have been largely neglected in studies of resource use. The landscape resulting from the French *culture maraîchère* or from African dambo cultivation can present a seemingly haphazard patchwork of small plots. It is a product of cumulative communal and individual decisions over the use of land and water resources for agriculture. As Figure 8.4 shows for Chizengeni, farmers using dambos have created their own cultural landscape, as the area under gardens has grown through accretion. But these culturally-accepted patterns of resource utilization have not escaped the external pressures of Western capitalist penetration and state intervention. Colonial political economy played a vital role in the developing competition between alternative uses of dambo environments and the strains imposed on the valuable land and water resources they represented. Perversely, colonial impacts both encouraged dambo gardens via economic pressure towards commodification, while simultaneously imposing legislative restrictions on wetland cultivation.

There were, however, important variations between areas in response to the measures imposed by the colonial state which are reflected today in different intensities of resource use. Thus, extensive cultivation in the form of an intensively cultivated landscape (Plate 8.3) may be juxtaposed with scattered and isolated garden plots, while in yet other areas there is no cultivation at all. The diverse dambo landscape is neither planned nor imposed from outside. It is,

Plate 8.3   Intensively-managed and -cultivated dambo landscape, Chinamora CA.

none the less, carefully organized and managed in response to the priorities, needs and resources of individual communities and households. Future interventions by the state affecting water resource use, which are introduced without reference to these existing systems, may unwittingly exacerbate environmental degradation, social inequality, or both.

Acknowledgements

This research was supported by ODA project R3869. We thank project team members Patricia Hotchkiss, Richard Faulkner, Robert Lambert and Alan Windram, and Anne Tarver for cartographic assistance.

References

Acres, B.D., Blair Rains, A., King, R.B., Lawton, R.M., Mitchell, A.J.B. and Rackham, L.J. (1985) 'African dambos: their distribution, characteristics and use', *Zeitschrift für Geomorphologie*, N.F. Supplementband, 52, 63–86.
Adams, W.M. and Anderson, D.M. (1988) 'Irrigation before development: indigenous and induced change in agricultural water management in East Africa', *African Affairs*, 87, 519–35.
Adams, W.M. and Carter, R.C. (1987) 'Small-scale irrigation in sub-Saharan Africa', *Progress in Physical Geography*, 11, 1–27.
Adams, W.M. and Grove, A.T. (eds) (1984) *Irrigation in tropical Africa: problems and problem-solving*. Cambridge African Monographs no. 3, Cambridge.
Bannerman, J.H. (1982) 'The Land Apportionment Act: a paper tiger?', *Zimbabwe Agricultural Journal*, 79(3), 101–106.
Beinart, W. (1984) 'Soil erosion, conservationism and ideas about development: a Southern African exploration, 1900–1960', *Journal of Southern African Studies*, 11(1), 52–83.
Bell, M., Faulkner, R., Hotchkiss, P., Lambert, R., Roberts, N. and Windram, A. (1987) *The Use of Dambos in Rural Development, with Reference to Zimbabwe*. Final report to ODA of Loughborough University/University of Zimbabwe project.
Bell, M. and Hotchkiss, P. (1989) 'Political interventions in environmental resource use. Dambos in Zimbabwe', *Land Use Policy*, 6, 313–23.
Cole, J.P. (1984) *Geography of the U.S.S.R.*, London, Butterworth.
Crouch, D. and Ward, C. (1988) *The Allotment. Its Landscape and Culture*, London, Faber and Faber.
Jollie, E.T. (1924) *The Real Rhodesia*, London, Hutchinson & Co.
Kay, M.G., Stephens, W. and Carr, M.K.V. (1985) 'The prospects for small-scale irrigation in sub-Saharan Africa', *Outlook on Agriculture*, 14, 115–21.
McIntosh, R.J. (1983) 'Floodplain geomorphology and human occupation of the upper inland Niger delta', *Geographical Journal*, 149, 182–201.
O'Sullivan, M. (1988) 'The use of remote sensing methods to examine dambo cultivation in Communal Areas of Zimbabwe on an inter- and intra-regional scale' unpublished BSc dissertation, Loughborough University, Department of Geography.

Palmer, R. (1977) 'Agricultural history of Rhodesia' in R. Palmer, and Q.N. Parsons (eds), *The Roots of Rural Poverty in Central and Southern Africa*, London, Heinemann, pp. 221–54.

Riddell, R. (n.d.) *The Land Question*, London Catholic Institute of International Relations.

Roberts, N. (1988) 'Dambos in development: management of a fragile ecological resource', *Journal of Biogeography*, 15, 141–8.

Roder, W. (1964) 'The division of land resources in Southern Rhodesia', *Annals, Association of American Geographers*, 54, 41–52.

Russell, R.G. (1971) *Dambo Utilisation Survey*. Bunda College of Agriculture, Lilongwe, Malawi.

Selous, F.C. (1920) *A Hunter's Wanderings in Africa*, London, Macmillan.

Thomas, M.F. and Goudie, A.S. (eds) (1985) 'Dambos: small channelless valleys in the tropics', *Zeitschrift für Geomorphologie*, Supplementband, 52.

Thorp, H. (1975) 'The homely allotment: from rural dole to urban amenity: a neglected aspect of urban land use', *Geography*, 268, 169–83.

Turner, B. (1984) 'Changing land-use patterns in fadamas of northern Nigeria in E. Scott (ed.), *Life before the Drought*, London: Allen & Unwin, pp. 149–70.

Turner, B. (1986) 'The importance of dambos in African agriculture', *Land Use Policy*, 3, 343–7.

Underhill, H.W. (1984) *Small-scale Irrigation in Africa in the Context of Rural Development*, Rome, FAO.

Waksman, S.A. (1936) *Humus: Origin, Chemical Composition, and Importance in Nature*, London, Bailliere, Tindall and Cox.

Whitlow, J.R. (1983) 'Vlei cultivation in Zimbabwe', *Zimbabwe Agricultural Journal*, 80, 123–36.

Whitlow, J.R. (1984) 'A survey of dambos in Zimbabwe', *Zimbabwe Agricultural Journal*, 81, 129–38.

Whitlow, J.R. (1990) 'Conservation status of wetlands in Zimbabwe: past and present', *Geo Journal*, 20, 191–202.

Wilson, K. (1986) 'Aspects of the history of vlei (dambo) cultivation in Southern Zimbabwe', unpublished paper submitted to Workshop on the Use of Dambos in Zimbabwe's Communal Areas, University of Zimbabwe.

ZNA (1923–39) Government of Rhodesia, Official Correspondence, Water Development in NRS, S138/7 and S1542/W5, Zimbabwe National Archives.

ZNA (1927–36) Government of Rhodesia, Official Correspondence, File on Advice to Other Countries, Zimbabwe National Archives.

Zinyama, L.M., Campbell, D.J. and Matiza, T. (1988) 'Traditional household strategies to cope with food insecurity in the SADCC region' in M. Rukuni and R.H. Bernstein, (eds), *Southern Africa: Food Security Options*, Harare, Department of Agricultural Economics and Extension.

CHAPTER 9

Hydrotechnology, wilderness and culture in Quebec

Will Hamley

Northern Quebec was released to the province by the federal government in 1912. Until the preliminary surveys revealed its hydro-electric power (HEP) potential in the early 1960s Quebec City showed little interest in developing its abundant water resources. This sub-Arctic wilderness on the Canadian Shield, sparsely settled by Cree indians and Inuit, was contributing little to Quebec's economy. Recognition of the massive potential for electricity generation from the James Bay rivers prompted the provincial government in 1971 to form the Société d'Énergie de la Baie James (SEBJ), soon to become a subsidiary of Hydro-Quebec, the province's nationalized power company. SEBJ was to undertake the programme of environmental engineering necessary to transform northern Quebec into one of the world's major producers of HEP. The complex, centred on the River La Grande, was planned for completion in two phases, the first by 1985 and the second by 1990, ultimately generating over 150×10^9 kWh annually.

Within a decade the province had sunk billions of dollars into a landscape engineering project of herioc proportions. French Canadians saw the scheme as a demonstration of technological enterprise on the part of a society in danger of becoming an industrial backwater. Both the landscape and the provincial economy were to be transformed on the grandiose scale of the New Deal and Stalinist projects of earlier decades, and Quebec would join the 'high-tech' culture by developing its indigenous resources. Yet the scheme was begun in a decade when many countries were questioning the value of such projects on social, economic and environmental grounds.

This chapter reviews the implementation of the James Bay project and sets it in its physical, economic, environmental and cultural contexts. It is perhaps still too early to draw up the final balance sheet but implicit in the study is the fear that such large projects bring more problems than benefits. Differing epistemologies and diverse methods of assessment among water engineers, planners, economists, politicians and environmentalists can lead to different conclusions. A geographical overview may facilitate a more objective assessment of the consequences of large-scale landscape engineering.

The James Bay Region

Situated on the East side of James Bay between latitudes 49°N and 56°N, the region experiences a sub-Arctic climate with short mild summers and long severe winters. July temperatures average between 12°C and 18°C and those in January between -23°C and -21°C. Precipitation averages 580 mm per year with a summer maximum, while snow lies for 200 days or more (Hydro-Quebec, 1985: 9–10). Away from the morainic deposits soil cover is thin and over large areas is vitually non-existent. The forest cover becomes progressively sparser northwards as taiga is replaced by tundra. Except in the more favoured southern areas, the main species of black spruce, jack pine and larch are too sparse for commercial exploitation (Hamley, 1983a: 110). Lichen, mosses and wild flowers bring brief summer colour and variety to an otherwise dull and desolate landscape, though they are accompanied by ubiquitous mosquito and blackfly. Apart from the coastal migratory habitats, the region lacks a populous and varied bird life, unlike the abundance of fish species, dominated by pike, whitefish, trout and salmon. Though animal numbers are unexceptional, beaver, elk, caribou and rabbit have traditionally provided the staple for the Cree hunters (Hamley, 1987: 252).

As part of the Candian Shield, relief is not pronounced and the region can be divided into three morphological units (SEBJ, 1979: 10). To the west is a 150 km wide coastal plain—a poorly drained lowland with a substantial number of depressions occupied by peat bogs and marshes. To the east are the quartzite and conglomerate Otish mountains reaching an altitude of some 1000 m. The bulk of the region, however, consists of a central plateau tilting up from west to east. A *roches moutonnées* landscape, interspersed with countless lakes, offers undulating but monotonous scenery. The Precambrian metamorphic and igneous bedrock has a generally thin and scattered overburden and over 20 per cent of the plateau consists of bare rock. Isostatic uplift is continuing at a rate of 0.5–1.5 cm yr^{-100} (Roy and Messier, 1989: 301). Major rivers drain the plateau (Figure 9.1), in particular, the La Grande and Eastmain rivers which drain westwards into James Bay and the Caniapiscau which flows northwards into Ungava Bay. The total catchment area of the rivers included in the project totals over 176,000 km^2—equivalent to an area larger than the three maritime provinces of Canada, or twice the size of Ireland.

Prior to the scheme's inception, less than 8,000 Cree Indians and a scattering of Inuit inhabited the James Bay wilderness. Semi-nomadic fishing, hunting and trapping was the basis of the traditional native economy, with beaver furs the main source of income (Kohl, 1983: 414–16). In 1976 the permanent population of the James Bay territory as a whole was some 30,000, with most of the non-native people living in the south (SEBJ, 1988: 5). What lumbering is profitable is found here, as well as limited copper and zinc mining with only localized environmental impact. Although the region as a whole contains a variety of mineral deposits, especially iron ore and uranium, they remain virtually unexploited. By contrast with former land uses, the size and nature of the HEP

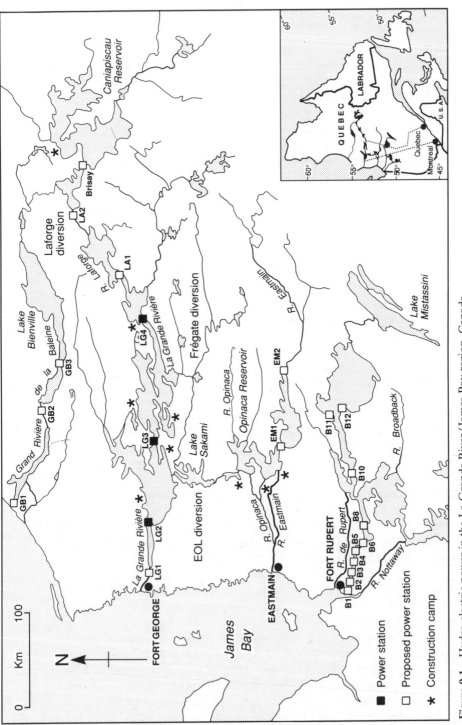

Figure 9.1 Hydro-electric power in the La Grande River/James Bay region, Canada

project has wide-ranging environmental consequences and poses particular threats to the indigenous people and their lifestyle.

The Scheme

Politicians, planners and engineers in Quebec City pictured this barren environment as a gargantuan powerhouse. Initial surveys in the late 1950s and early 1960s led to Hydro-Quebec's 1965 proposal for the development of the three most southerly rivers flowing into James Bay—the Nottaway, Broadbeck and Rupert. Termed the NBR complex, this initial project, when complete, would have an installed capacity of about 5,500 MW. But more extensive studies led to projects of increasing magnitude, culminating in 1971 with the proposal to harness the complete eastern James Bay River network (Bolduc *et al.*, 1979: 353–5). With an initial installed capacity of nearly 23,000 MW the scheme would be capable of generating over 140×10^9 kWh annually, ultimately rising to nearly

Table 9.1 James Bay hydro-electric projects

	Plant	Installed Capacity (Mw)	Generation (kWH per year)	Completion
Phase 1	LG 2 LG 3 LG 4	10,269	60 billion +	1985
	LG 2A	1,900	10 billion +	1992
Phase 2	EM 1 EM 2 LA 1 LA 2 Brisay	3,266	20 billion +	originally 1991–93
NBR	7 plants on Broadback 2 plants on Rupert	6,200	45 billion +	originally 1998
Baleine	3 plants on La Grande Baleine	2,900	15 billion +	originally 1991
Totals		24,535	150 billion +	

Table 9.2   Comparison of James Bay complex with selected major hydro-electric power schemes

Dam	Location	Power Capacity (MW)
Itaipú (1983)	R. Paraná, Brazil–Paraguay	12,600
Guri (1968)	R. Caroní, Venezuela	10,000
Tucuruí (1982)	R. Tocantins, Brazil	8,000
Sayano-Shushensk (1980)	R. Yenisei, USSR	6,400
Krasnoyarsk (1972)	R. Yenisei, USSR	6,000
Corpus Posadas (1990)	R. Paraná, Argentina–Paraguay	6,000
Grande Dixence	Interbasin Transfer, Switzerland	680
La Grande Complex	Phase 1	10,282
Largest Dam (La Grande 2)		5,328
Total planned capacity		24,496

25,000 MW and over 150×10^9 kWh respectively (Table 9.1). Great Britain's current installed capacity of 55,000 MW offers a measure of the scale of the proposed work. Its place among the world's major HEP schemes is illustrated in Table 9.2.

The 1971 draft specified the La Grande as the initial and primary source of power. The river flowed some 800 km east to west, entering James Bay just over 1,000 km north of Montreal. With a drainage basin over 51,000 km², larger than Denmark, it has many tributaries, the Sakami and Laforge being among the largest. The surveys had indicated a high kinetic energy potential. With an overall drop of nearly 550 m along its course and with several suitable damming sites, the system seemed the most appropriate for HEP generation. Apart from some localized sites, the adjacent Eastmain, Opinaca and Caniapiscau systems apparently lacked sufficient gradient for large-scale generation. Yet all experience heavy seasonal flows, and after considering more than a hundred alternatives SEBJ's engineers recommended that 87 per cent of the water in the Eastmain/Opinaca basins and 27 per cent of that in the Caniapiscau basin be diverted into the La Grande (Hamley, 1989: 1–2). The region has an annual specific discharge of 19.2 1s⁻¹ km⁻², which corresponds to a mean annual surface runoff of about 600 mm. The specific discharge follows the patterns of the precipitation, gradually decreasing from southeast to northwest (Roy and Messier, 1989: 302). Table 9.3 summarises the main hydrological characteristics of the three main rivers in the scheme, though mean values mask the daily, seasonal and interannual variations and today the lower than average precipitation of recent years is beginning to cause anxiety within Hydro-Quebec. The large-scale construction works necessary for the diversions were started in 1972 and completed within a decade, virtually doubling La Grande's energy potential.

The development of the La Grande system represents Phase 1 of the James

Table 9.3   Predevelopment characteristics of some of the James Bay rivers

	Means discharge		Minimum discharge	Maximum discharge
River	At mouth (m^3s^{-1})	Specific $(1s^{-1}km^{-2})$	(m^3s^{-1})	(m^3s^{-1})
La Grande	1,760	16	320	6,707
Eastmain	927	20	114	3,537
Caniapiscau	1,804	18	202	9,226

Based on Roy and Messier (1989: Table 1)

Bay project. Four suitable sites were identified for power plants along the river course. LG2, by far the biggest, with an installed capacity of 5,300 MW, was completed in 1979. This was followed by the impounding of the Opinaca and Caniapiscau reservoirs in 1980 and 1981, and the construction of LG3 (2,300 MW) and LG4 (2,650 MW). LG1 downstream was eventually omitted, but an additional 1,900 MW plant is being constructed at LG2, known as LG2A. Apart from this last, the La Grande system was completed in 1985 and so Phase 1 is now capable of generating 60×10^9 kWh annually (Table 9.1). Phase 2 was to have been started in 1983 with powerhouses at LA1, LA2 and Brisay on the Laforge River and EM1 and EM2 on the Eastmain River. With an installed capacity of 3,260 MW, this second phase would have been generating 20×10^9 kWh annually by the early 1990s.

The NBR scheme should, in the revised scheme, have been started in 1987. Seven powerhouses were to have been built on the Broadback, whose flow would have been increased by the diversion of water from the Nottaway and Rupert rivers. Two powerhouses were planned for the upper course of the Rupert. The NBR phase, with an installed capacity of 6,200 MW, would have generated approximately 44×10^9 kWh annually by completion in 1998.

North of the La Grande was the final part in the James Bay project. This would have involved the diversion of part of the Petite Baleine into the Grande Rivière de la Baleine, the creation of an immense reservoir at Lac Bienville and the construction of three powerhouses on the Grande Baleine. With a 2,900 MW capacity this phase would have generated 15×10^9 kWh annually by 1991.

Although only half of the James Bay HEP project has been finished the entire infrastructure has been virtually completed or is capable of easy extension. The wilderness, formerly accessible only by helicopter and light aircraft, now has 1,500 km of all-weather road and five airports linking the HEP sites with the provincial networks. High-voltage transmission lines of 735 kV are used to carry the output in two corridors to load centres at Montreal and Quebec City. Five of these lines were completed by 1984. A sixth is planned to transmit increased volume to the north eastern United States if these markets are developed sufficiently. Very high-voltage lines were pioneered by Hydro-Quebec to minimize energy losses over long distances so that only 5 per cent of energy is lost between LG2 and Montreal.

This second largest HEP scheme in the world after the Itaipú scheme in Brazil occupied 18,000 workers at peak construction. The speed of progress and the immensity of the construction represent a considerable technical and organizational achievement: hydro-landscape engineering in the heroic mode. The resulting reservoir lakes, including the recently-completed Caniapiscau and Eastmain lakes, have inundated some 11,430 km², an area two-thirds the size of Wales. Nine dams up to 160 m high and over 200 dikes have been constructed to retain their waters. Locally available morainic sands and gravels with broken rock have been used in construction. Altogether some 262,400,000 m³ of material has been excavated. Placed end to end, the dikes would form an earthwork 125 km long (SEBJ, 1983): 35). In addition to the enterprise, ingenuity and technical skill involved, the work demands vast capital inputs.

Financial Aspects

For its early advocates the James Bay scheme was to secure the province's economic future and would make Quebeckers 'the permanent Arabs of electricity' (*Globe and Mail* (Toronto), 18 October 1978: 11). The energy crisis of the early 1970s, along with the problems associated with nuclear technology, had helped ensure a climate of opinion favourable to the schemes acceptance, and cautious optimism was justified.

In 1971 Quebec's electricity requirements were expected to rise by 7–8 per cent per annum in a period of escalating oil prices. Even in 1979, when the first electricity from James Bay came into the grid, Quebec had surplus electricity only during the summer. With rates lower than most in North America and a growing trans-border transmission system, any surplus production by the province should have found a ready market, especially in the high-cost energy area of neighbouring New England and New York. But a combination of reduced internal demand consequent upon the provincial government's energy conservation programme, an industrial recession and a slump in demand from outside markets brought a crisis in 1982 (Hamley, 1987: 255). That year Quebec's installed capacity of 23,000 MW had to meet a peak demand of less than 20,000 MW. With Phase 1 of the James Bay project completed ahead of schedule in 1985, this surplus capacity increased again. The original plans for a boost to Quebec's industrial structure by cheap power and a growing export market, so plausible in 1971, have been blown off course by changing economic winds and the violently fluctuating squalls of energy pricing and demand. A technological triumph was being undermined by market forces.

Lacking relevant guidelines for funding such a massive undertaking and subjected to considerable political pressure, SEBJ originally estimated that the whole scheme would cost C$4 billion—a figure greeted with scepticism by many at the time (*Financial Times*, 11 October 1982: 35). Completion of Phase 1 alone has cost over C$15 billion (Hamley, 1983b: 125). Hydro-Quebec's debts have tripled in the last decade, standing at over C$22 million in 1987 and continuing to rise. As the president of the corporation recently admitted, Hydro-Quebec has been through a crisis and has now become capable of making sustained losses (Coulombe and Carpentier, 1988, 22–7). Growth had always been the projected course for this public corporation because of a virtual monopoly over the province's electricity supplies, but with its electricity deliveries suddenly showing a net decline by 1982 Hydro-Quebec is having to reassess its future commitments. Critics argue that the crisis is far from over. Not the least of Hydro-Quebec's financial problems can be traced to the sheer scale of the James Bay project, which now accounts for 40 per cent of the province's total HEP production. It is the main cause of Hydro-Quebec's mounting debts and, with the completion of Phase 1, the enterprise has a current surplus capacity of over 5,000 MW. Critics of mega-projects and gigantism in civil engineering can now point to James Bay in support of their forebodings. Environmentalists argue that there has been an unnecessary sacrifice of a landscape and way of life for an utopian and uneconomic goal.

The responses to these crises have been both negative and positive. In 1982 a decision was made not to proceed beyond Phase 1 of the development. The James Bay scheme was to be reduced to less than half its planned size. The image of Hyrdo-Quebec as a brugeoning enterprise, constantly needing to plan and build ever bigger projects for a constantly increasing demand, collapsed as suddenly as the feasibility of other mega-projects elsewhere in the world. The economic recession of the early 1980s invalidated Hydro-Quebec's forecasts and from 1982 its spending programme plummeted from C$65 billion to C$18 billion annually. But it was still left with a considerable surplus capacity. If that could be used its severe and growing financial problems could be eased.

The response has been to pursue the initial proposals of selling more power to Quebec's industries and outside the province ((Hydro-Quebec, 1987: 41–56). Some spin-off has occurred from Hydro-Quebec's efforts in the research and development field, with several nascent industries appearing in the energy-related production field. Some energy-intensive industries have been attracted into the province, notably aluminium and magnesium production. High-tech industries attracted by the cheap electrical power are slowly beginning to change the image of Quebec, both inside and outside the province, as a manufacturing backwater heavily dependent on a few basic industries, notably paper and pulp, ore processing and chemical production staples. These latter are also being encourged by financial inducements from Hydro-Quebec to change, where appropriate, to cheaper and more versatile HEP. The corporation itself is a major employer in the province, with a total workforce of some 60,000. However, Quebec has some way to go yet before it can claim a strong base of leading contemporary industries. The expected spin-offs from its giant power source are proving slow to appear.

Currently Quebec exports some 15 per cent of its total production of electricity—four times the 1971 level. In the past this was largely to other Canadian provinces but coincident with James Bay power coming into the grid in the late 1970s there have been major marketing thrusts in the United States (Ministère de l'Énergie et des Resources, 1986: 76–90). Several New England and New York power companies have recently concluded agreements with Hydro-Quebec, and Ontario remains a major market. Yet, as with the province's industrial development, so with its energy exports, much potential remains unfulfilled. Nevertheless, for many, earlier visions of Quebec as a major energy producer and a leader in the new high-tech industries remain. The positive image of an expanding economy and an increased self-regard have not been abandoned by the province's politicians. Economic fluctuations have meant unavoidable alterations and curtailments to the James Bay project but a cheap source of energy in a province virtually devoid of oil, coal and gas must remain a key to its future, especially when HEP still provides only 40 per cent of its energy and 45 per cent still comes from oil.

Environmental Impacts

Almost inevitably the scale of the James Bay project gave rise to protests from the environmental lobby. A scheme which would affect the native way of life, transform large areas of landscape and upset what was believed to be a fragile ecosystem, particularly in the environmentally conscious Canada of the 1970s, was bound to generate protests from many quarters, most of which rapidly coalesced into the Committee for the Defence of James Bay. Apart from the emotive issues of native rights, the scheme's opponents also perceived dire threats to the natural environment (McCutcheon, 1984: 35). Obviously changes could be expected at the local and micro level, but wider-scale consequences were also predicted by some environmentalists. For example, it was suggested that the great weight of the newly impounded, massive bodies of water could trigger off local earth movements. This could cause dam breaches, leading to catastropic flooding. Another argument was that through the sheer size of the reservoirs, micro-climatic changes, inevitable around water bodies, would become major ones. Regional climates in the Maritimes and even as far afield as New York would become colder and wetter, to the detriment of Maritime farming in particular (McCutcheon, 1984: 35).

So far there have been no indications that such ominous predictions are ever likely to be fulfilled. Data on major and sudden changes to ecosystems in high latitudes are necessarily for the most part of recent origin (Brunskill, 1986: 435–71) although changes have been monitored on the James Bay from its inception. Warnings of major catastrophies seem a hyperbolic detraction from the innumerable and often equally detrimental changes likely to occur more locally.

Hydro-Quebec, very conscious of a sceptical, not to say hostile, environmental lobby ever since the preliminary stages of the scheme, has always emphasized its concern for the physical environment of the James Bay region (SEBJ, 1982: 17–19). Detailed environmental inventories and impact studies were made from the early 1960s as part of the initial planning processes. To date, over C$250 million has been spent by SEBJ on easing the environmental impact on the project area and environmental protection and beneficial reorganization is accepted by the corporation as a continuing commitment. Protecting—or, better still, improving—the environment is a constant theme in SEBJ literature. For example, reafforestation schemes have led to the planting of over 10 million trees in the region, while studies of fish and marine life have resulted in considerable restocking and replenishing of the enlarged aquatic habitat (SEBJ, 1981: 13–15). Natural habitats have been replanted and regenerated though nothing, as yet, can be done about the disruptions in the caribou migration routes. Particular efforts are being made in planting grasses and bushes around the margins of the reservoirs to emulate existing environments around the region's natural lakes. The major but unavoidable scars of the construction sites themselves have been subject to much replanting, though the severity of the climate means that it will take some time for these scars to heal. The ecosystems do seem to be responding and the sub-Arctic landscape, it is claimed, 'seems to be coping with ease [with] human tinkering' (McCutcheon, 1984: 41). But not all assessments are as favourable and to many environmentalists the future is fraught with trouble as major problems begin to emerge.

While some of the negative consequences to the natural environment could be foreseen, others are only now becoming apparent. Because of the scale of the damming, thousands of kilometres of existing shorelines will be subject to water-level fluctuations. This will adversely affect wildlife, especially waterfowl, otter, beaver and mink. Large areas are now drowned forests, leaving the prospect of decades of slow-rotting for submerged trees in the sub-Arctic conditions. Apart from being affected by water-level fluctuations, fish life will have to adjust to changes in water temperature and increased decomposition of organic matter changing the chemical and aerobic properties of the water (Bodaly et al., 1989: 5). Far-reaching alterations are thus already afoot whose long-term effects on the aquatic ecosystem may be detrimental. Already the local Cree are complaining of high mercury levels in local fish (Hydro-Quebec, 1988: 44). Sedimentation behind dams is creating new wetland sites for vegetation establishment. Reduction in river flow will mean an increase in salt water intrusion into the estuaries, altering the balance between fresh water and marine environments (Simpson-Lewis et al., 1979: 224–6). Infrastructural development, especially of roads and transmission lines, has obvious implications for migration routes, while alterations to local wind speeds and directions could have unpredictable effects on local birdlife. The effects of changes in drainage patterns and soil stability are likewise unknown. Over a wide area the extension of surface water could lead to an increase in black fly and mosquito populations. At best, the environment will gradually adapt by evolving a new ecological balance. At worst, such disruptions could be so widespread and protracted that both flora and fauna could be severely reduced.

Aboriginal Claims and Responses

Changes to the economy and culture of the local Indians brought about by the scheme have been sudden and of questionable benefit. The Cree were first informed about the scheme through press reports (McCutcheon, 1984: 35). Their clear aboriginal land rights over their homeland, with which they had evolved a finely balanced partnership, seemed to pale into insignificance when compared with the potential benefits promised by modern technology. Sales of beaver pelts, the principal export of the Cree, were generating an annual income of some C$0.25 million prior to the scheme. The annual income from the electricity generated at LE2 alone would be in the order of C$500 million. In response, the Cree organized to bring the promoters of the project before the courts and in November 1973 succeeded in obtaining an injunction which stopped all work on the scheme for a few days. Eventually the matter was settled out of court (Gourdeau and Gagnon, 1979: 67) with the signing of the James Bay and Northern Quebec Agreement, ratified on 24 November 1975. In return for surrendering their aboriginal title, the native peoples retained hunting and trapping rights throughout the project area, obtaining legal ownership of only 1.3 per cent of what they regarded as their traditional land. However, they did receive a sum of C$231 million, to be paid in instalments until 1997. The formation of a Cree Regional Authority has given the Cree increasing political clout, evidenced by the further C$148 million granted in 1986 for community, economic and mitigation measures (Anon. 1986). The 1975 agreement was regarded by other native peoples elsewhere in Canada as a serious blow, constituting a precedent for future such settlements based on cash rather than land (Page, 1986: 219–20). The majority of the Cree would have preferred to keep their land, but the settlement reached seems to be regarded by them as acceptable (Wallace, 1982: 394).

Indigenous cultures and lifestyles as well as the natural environment cannot remain unaffected by major technological projects engineering change in the physical and human landscape. The change in the case of the James Bay Cree has been very rapid. According to Salisbury (1986: 8), between 1971 and 1981 Cree society changed from a fragmented society of seven district village bands integrated at a regional level only through non-Cree agencies and non-Cree officials, into a regional society where the villages (now numbering eight) have close ties with each other and administer their own affairs through a Cree governmental structure, staffed largely by Cree. Seven 'home villages' have become one 'homeland'. Increased Cree income has brought a noticeable increase in the consumption of consumer goods and more cosmopolitan styles in clothing and leisure activities. Thus the traditional native Indian culture has become more fully assimilated into a more homogeneous North American culture.

Yet the number of hunting groups nearly doubled between 1971 and 1977, though the increased use of trucks and snowmobiles somewhat changed the manner of hunting. In 1981, 41 per cent of the total Cree population was economically dependent on hunting and government transfer payments (Salis-bury, 1986: 85–105). A further 10 per cent or more of the Cree were engaged in white-collar managerial jobs mainly in the Indian agencies, while just under 10 per cent were in full-time manual work in the villages, in forestry or in mining. Over 11 per cent were classed as part-time wage-earners or hunters. Cree remains the home language, though 80 per cent of the population in 1981 speak and read English while 10 per cent speak French. Cree schools are attempting to maintain Cree cultural traditions while at the same time trying to prepare the young for the changes occurring to their society. Materially, the Cree have benefited by the changes of the 1970s and 1980s, their per capita income approaching that of Canadians as a whole.

How much of this change in traditional Cree society can be attributed to the James Bay project is difficult to estimate, although few Cree were employed on the actual construction. Indigenous societies are having to adapt to change throughout the Canadian North, and such changes, occurring so rapidly in the case of the James Bay Cree, seem inevitable. Some observers regard the changes as beneficial (Salisbury, 1986: 3–12; Coolican, 1987), others see the Cree as losers, with the James Bay Agreement only adding to their historic sense of grievance (Page, 1986: 220). Certainly the large cash awards have been noticeably eroded by inflation. On balance, it would seem that with such economic, political and technological power ranged against them the Cree have made the best of the opportunities available to them and, although changed, their culture remains distinctive.

Provincial Attitudes

In terms of power capacity, the James Bay project is one of the largest HEP schemes in the world (Table 9.3). Projects of this size are always beset by controversy and doubt and inevitably become politicized (Joron, 1979: 20–1). When Premièr Bourassa announced 'the project of the century' in April 1971 (Hamovitch, 1979) it immediately became a partisan issue. The Liberals were anxious to make some spectacular gesture to stimulate a virtually stagnant economy, release some of the province's untapped wealth and stem the strong tide of separatist sentiment. They saw it as the corner-stone of the province's industrial regeneration, claiming that it would create over 100,000 new jobs. It would be both profitable and demonstrate to both nationalist opinion and to the world the ability and independence of the people of Quebec. But the Parti Québecois was unimpressed. To the nationalists it was a white elephant with an outdated technology, the projected costings of which make it a gross extrava-gance. The province would be landed with mounting debts. Far better, they claimed, to spend considerably less on technologically more advanced nuclear power generators (Rodger, 1979). Hindsight has proved the nationalists right about the debt even if their alternative proposals can be challenged, nuclear power generation has become highly controversial and Hydro-Quebec has only one small nuclear generator.

Nearly two decades after its inception, attitudes towards the scheme within the province remain divided, though not necessarily on partisan grounds as the nationalists have come to accept the scheme as an alternative to the nuclear commitment. A 1979 poll of Quebeckers in Montreal (Stanton, 1979: 92–6) indicated an overwhelming desire to develop Quebec's northern resources but a certain unease as to the way the Indian land claims had been handled. The benefits of the James Bay developments are proving slow to emerge from an investment by the provincial corporation equivalent to C$2,300 per head of the province's population. Quebec can hardly be regarded today as a technology-conscious region in the vanguard of scientific developments. With only one thousand permanent jobs resulting directly from the scheme, questions arise as to whether this is a late twentieth-century technological variation on an old Canadian theme of exploiting the North as a mere resource base for the benefit of other regions—drinking Canada, or in this case Quebec, dry.

Although the scheme still has its advocates in the province and Hydro-Quebec continues to plan for its remaining phases, the current financial debt and power surplus must throw doubts across Quebec's foray into the field of the mega-project. James Bay as pristine wilderness or boundless energy source may have seemed the choices in the early 1970s, but now the province has to cope with the consequences of scale in such a grandiose undertaking.

Conclusion

To assess the James Bay project in simple terms of success or failure is naive. The modernist vision of a technological utopia is no more applicable to the James Bay region than the gloomy predictions of environmental disaster. No landscape is permanent and, whether engineered by human hands or nature, change is inevitable and constant. But change is also endemic to human societies, and the altered values of a post-industrial and environmentally conscious age view such mega-constructions sceptically not only in terms of the technology involved, the market demand and capital costs, but also in terms of the moral justification of such intervention. Perhaps the only impressive giganticism involved at James Bay remains the logistics of the scheme. Yet despite altered attitudes, Quebec and its electricity catchment area in northeast North America seem to have an insatiable appetite for energy. Pollution from acid rain caused by burning fossil fuels is regarded in crisis terms in Canada today and, if completed, the James Bay project could produce the equivalent output of 30 nuclear power-stations. Of course, ecological losses from HEP could well outweigh the possible environmental impact of nuclear power, while further technological advances and better management of both physical and human environments could reduce the impact of HEP schemes in the future. Once the initial capital costs have been absorbed, power such as that generated at James Bay is quite cheap. It is also inexhaustible and it does not pollute the atmosphere. Rather than being regarded as an example of dated gigantism, the project may come fully into its own during the twenty-first century. Alternatively, mega-technology and a wilderness landscape transformed within a decade may prove to be Quebec's monument to a faded vision of modernism.

References

Anon. (1986) 'Baie James: trois ententes'. *Recontre* 7 (2), 17.

Bodaly, R.A., Reist, J.D., Rosenburg, D.M., McCart, P.J. and Hecky, R.E. (1989) 'Fish and fisheries of the Mackenzie and Churchill river basins, northern Canada' in D.P. Dodge (ed.), *Proceedings of the International Large River Symposium*, Ottowa, Department of Fisheries and Oceans.

Bolduc, A., Hogue, C. and Larouche, D. (1979) *Quebec: un siècle d'électricité*. Montreal, Editions Libre Expressions.

Brunskill, G.J. (1986) 'Environmental features of the Mackenzie system' in B.R. Davies and K.F. Walker, (eds), *The Ecology of River Systems*, Dordrecht, W. Junk.

Coolican, M. (1987) 'The James Bay Cree: a society changed', *Northern Perspectives* 15 (3), 13.

Coulombe, G. and Carpentier, J.M. (1988) 'Hydro-Quebec plus que jamais un instrument de dévelopment éonomique', *Forces*, 80, 22–7.

Gourdeau, E. and Gagnon, R./M. (1979) 'Les Indiens Cris et le développement du territoire de la Baie-James'. *Forces*, 48 (3), 67–75.

Hamley, W. (1983a) 'Hydroelectrical developments in the James Bay region, Quebec', *Geographical Review*, 71, (1), 109–12.

Hamley, W. (1983b) 'The James Bay HEP complex: the development of a major energy source', *Exploration and Exploitation*, 2 (3), 123–31.

Hamley, W. (1987) 'Some aspects and consequences of the development of the James Bay Hydro-Electric Complex', *British Journal of Canadian Studies*, 2, (2), 250–262.

Hamley, W. (1989) 'Power in the wilderness', *Geographical Magazine*, 61 (2), 1–4.

Hamovitch, E. (1979) 'James Bay opening means the end of a village, beginning of an end', *Globe and Mail*, Toronto, 18 October, 11.

Hydro-Quebec (1985) *James Bay: Taming the La Grande River*. Montreal.

Hydro-Quebec (1987) *Hydro-Quebec Development Plan 1987–1989. Horizon, 1996.* Montreal.

Hydro-Quebec (1988) *Hydro-Quebec and the Environment. Horizon 1997.* Montreal.

Joron, G. (1979) 'Une priorité: le respect de nos ressources énergétiques'. *Forces*, 48 (3), 18–31.

Kohl, L. (1983) 'Quebec's Northern Dynamo'. *National Geographic Magazine*, 161 (3), 406–18.

McCutcheon, S. (1984) 'The Flooding of James Bay'. *New Scientist*, 22 March, 35–41.

Ministère de l'Energie et des Ressources (1986) *Rapport Annuel 1985–1986*, Quebec.

Page, R. (1986) *Northern Development: the Canadian Dilemma.* Toronto.

Rodger, J. (1979) 'James Bay project to start sending its power south six months early'. *Globe and Mail*, Toronto, 17 September, 138.

Roy, D. and Messier, D. (1989) 'A review of the effects of water transfers in the La Grande Hydroelectric complex (Quebec, Canada)', *Regulated Rivers: Research and Management*, 4, 299–316.

Salisbury, R.F. (1986) *A Homeland for the Cree*, Montreal, McGill-Queen's University Press.

Simpson-Lewis, W., Moore, J.E., Pocock, N.J., Taylor M.C. and Swan, H. (1979) *Canada's Special Resource Lands. Map Folio No. 4*, Ottawa, Environment Canada.

Societe d'Énergie de la Baie James (1979) *La Grande Complex*, Montreal.

Societe d'Énergie de la Baie James (1981) *Present Yet Leaving No Trace*, Montreal.

Societe d'Énergie de la Baie James (1982) *Tomorrow's Challenges. S.E.B.J. and its Mandates*, Montreal.

Societe d'Énergie de la Baie James (1983) *From Death to Reality—The La Grande Complex. Phase 1*, Montreal.

Societe d'Énergie de la Baie James (1988) *La Grande Rivière. Un aménagement en harmonie avec le milieu*, Montrel.

Stanton, F. (1979) 'Qu'est-ce que c'est, pour vous, le Nord québecois?', *Forces*, 48 (3), 92–6.

Wallace, I. (1982) 'The Canadian Shield: The Development of a Resource Frontier' in L.D. McCann (ed.), *Heartland and Hinterland*, Scarborough, Ontario, Prentice Hall.

CHAPTER 10

'Uncivil engineering': nature, nationalism and hydro-electrics in north Wales

Pyrs Gruffudd

In the early and mid-twentieth century rural Wales was the scene of conflicts between visions of nature and culture, tradition and modernity, and of the organic and mechanistic. These discourses were complex fusions of aesthetics, sociology and politics. Wales's terrain and landscape were seen by some as resources to be exploited by the mechanics of progress. This progress brought benefits to the rural areas—in improved housing, for instance—but often at the expense of tradition. Though the influence of the old extractive industries was on the wane, the needs of the modern state continued to press in the form of decentralized mobile industries (Ward, 1988); the demands of mass leisure as represented by holiday camps (Ward and Hardy, 1986) and the proposed National Parks (Cherry, 1975); and military training areas (Gruffudd, 1988). But these demands on Welsh land were opposed in two fundamental ways: first, by an environmental movement which had rooted in Wales between the wars; and second, by a growing sense of Welsh nationality which found expression in the formation in 1925 of the Welsh Nationalist Party, Plaid Cymru. The former attempted to reconcile traditional rural aesthetics with 'progress' to ensure that conservation would soften the impact of a technocratic age. The latter sought to shift Wales away from the British state, and towards independent nationhood. The Nationalists claimed Welsh land as the territorial foundation for separatism, and landscapes as symbols of identity. Water became a particular focus of conflict, examined here in the context of proposals for large-scale hydro-electric power (HEP) schemes in mid-century.

Water in the Welsh landscape

Water has been a contested asset in Wales at least since industrialization and the expansion of towns on the Welsh borders. In the late nineteenth century, when the Elan Valley in mid-Wales was drowned for Birmingham and Lake Fyrnwy for Liverpool, unsuccessful opposition was mounted against determined urban modernization. The inter-war period witnessed several proposals for reservoir schemes aimed at supplying the burgeoning towns of northwest England.

Warrington's plans to flood the Ceiriog Valley in northeast Wales were defeated by a protest group led by the educationalist and promoter of patriotism, Alfred T. Davies. In his pamphlet *Evicting a Community*, Davies (1923) pictured an idealized rural society threatened with extinction. His campaign succeeded, but failed to deter other corporations from seeking water in the valleys of Wales.

Hydro-electricity first appeared in Wales to supply small-scale local and industrial needs. Between 1899 and 1910, three HEP schemes were constructed in north Wales—at Blaenau Ffestiniog, Cwm Dyli and Dolgarrog (Thomas, 1989). Small schemes were established elsewhere in Wales; one in Ponterwyd, near Aberystyth, for instance, being installed by an English resident in return for the natives' co-operation in keeping the village 'picturesque' (CPRW 101). Shortly after the turn of the century, the North Wales Power Company was formed to supply electricity to the whole region. The company managed and enlarged the existing schemes, but as demand increased so did the proposed scale of operation. As part of a general assessment of Britain's HEP potential, engineers prepared preliminary large-scale plans for the company in 1944. These involved six new schemes covering much of the mountain country of north and mid-Wales. Existing stations at Dolgarrog and Ffestiniog (Maentwrog) were to be extended, and new schemes established in areas described as Upper Conwy, Mawddach, Rheidol, Snowdon, Ffestiniog and Nant Ffrancon. In all, 650 km² of catchment would be established with up to 90 per cent of all daily stream flow captured. Twenty-two reservoirs would be dammed, fed by 55 km of open leats (concrete channels running around contour lines to catch surface flow) and discharging into 130 km of tunnels. Critically, the Snowdonian massif—long proposed as a National Park (see, for example, Cornish, 1929)—formed the focus of the plans (Figure 10.1). There, a network of reservoirs, pipelines and leats would converge on seven power-stations. The plan was not, in fact, implemented until the electricity generation industry was nationalized by the post-war labour government in 1948. The new British Electricity Authority (BEA)—created to tap potential, harmonize availability and ensure equality of electricity supply—re-examined the proposals and foresaw valuable peak-load contributions to the National Grid.

By the time the BEA published preliminary plans at the end of 1948, alarm was widespread. But the Divisional BEA Controller dismissed opponents' criticism as 'ill-informed and . . . bitterly antagonistic' (Cooper, 1949: 7). He argued that Wales imported 75 per cent of its electricity and thus had a duty to contribute to the Grid. Proffering the carrot though, the Controller argued that electricity distribution in rural Wales would be hastened as a result of the scheme. HEP would also create new employment and promote industrial development. A worker at the Cwm Dyli power-station apparently argued that a queue of unemployed Welshmen outside a Labour Exchange was a far uglier sight than the vast pipelines which supplied his station's turbines. Furthermore, electricity enthusiasts argued that artificial lakes could increase rather than mar beauty and that it would be 'a great credit to all concerned . . . if we can show that beauty and utility can go hand in hand' (Cooper, 1949: 8).

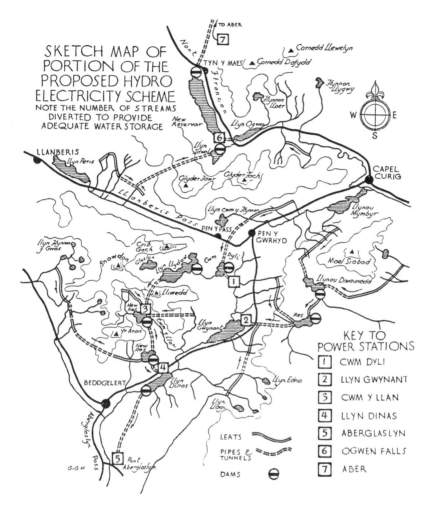

Figure 10.1   The proposed hydro-electric power scheme's impact on Snowdonia. (From NWHEPC, 1950)

'Massacre of the mountains'

The opposition to which the Controller referred had been quick to establish itself. In 1949, a number of groups resolved to co-ordinate opposition in a North Wales (Hydro-Electric) Protection Committee (NWHEPC). Foremost in this movement was the Council for the Preservation of Rural Wales (CPRW), formed in 1928 by an alliance of planning and landowning interests, which argued that 'while it is essential that nothing shall interfere with the legitimate development of the resources of Wales, the wanton destruction of beauty . . . must be stopped' (Abercrombie, 1928). The tension inherent in this statement remained as the CPRW struggled to reconcile the needs of rural development with aesthetic criteria. A largely Anglicized society based in London, the Council was frequently charged with representing alien attitudes to the Welsh landscape, and of failing to understand local concern which revolved around sovereignty, culture and national development. The CPRW found this fusion of often unaesthetic concerns hard to understand, as its pamphlet *Land of my Fathers (and of my Children): Why Only Sing About It?* (CPRW, 1930) made perfectly clear. Confusion was mutual. In response to one piece of measured CPRW criticism, for instance, a north Wales resident argued:

Most, if not all, of the people who are concerned with the C.P.R.W. enjoy electricity facilities, and some of them have electricity even in their garages to heat their cars. And yet these very people object to moves to provide electricity for the rural areas which have no electricity. It does not make sense (*Liverpool Daily Post*, 1953).

The CPRW and NWHEPC's opposition to the schemes followed a carefully calculated line. They argued that little would be done to improve the electrification of rural Wales as all the power was destined for peak-hour use on the Grid, despite the fact that existing north Wales HEP stations supplied an area including the Crewe railway works, and that Wales *could* be made self-sufficient in electricity far more rapidly, if its coalfields were exploited for its own benefit. They questioned the economics of HEP and argued for the use of alternatives to achieve Welsh self-sufficiency (NWHEPC, 1952).

Nationalistic arguments were a relatively recent feature of the Welsh conservationist debate. But here they were not part of a political so much as an aesthetic argument pitched around the issue of scale. The CPRW supported the project of rural electrification but pressed for reductions in scale. A self-sufficient Wales could survive on smaller and less intrusive HEP schemes. The CPRW had evolved a modernist aesthetic which could welcome changes in landscape: 'Order', 'dignity' and 'functionalism' were the keywords. These, however, depended on an appropriate relation between the works of humans and nature. In certain parts of the world, they claimed, large-scale HEP schemes enhanced rather than detracted from fine scenery. Sharing the aesthetic vision which admired the German *Autobahnen*, it was most powerfully articulated by the landscape architect, Sylvia Crowe (1956: 31) who claimed that the huge dams were 'one of the greatest creative achievements of our age'. In the Alps, for instance, the scale of natural scenery allowed human works like great dams to challenge the works of nature. Imaginative landscape design had been combineed with engineering requirements to produce scenes of distinct beauty. Cyril Fox, the archaeologist and Director of the National Museum of Wales, argued that, aesthetically, 'the formation of a big modern water scheme . . . within [Snowdonia] need not be viewed with any apprehension' (CPRW 83i). Other impacts accompanying HEP could also be absorbed by boldness—most notably pylons, which Fox compared to 'the arches of an accqueduct on the Campagna' (CPRW 95). However, most conservationists were agreed that while small, Snowdonia was 'proportionately precious' (NWHEPC, 1950) and that its scenery would be destroyed by large-scale intrusions. Sylvia Crowe (1956: 31) also recognized this threat, which she conceived in terms of a technocratic masculine force subjugating a powerful but benign feminine one: 'Wild mountain scenery is destroyed by a major work of man which, instead of challenging an overpowering dominant nature, achieves domination over her'. The CPRW (1947) then foresaw the massacre of mountain scenery by large-scale, 'uncivil engineering', for British hydro-electricity schemes had none of the grace or sensitivity of their Continental counterparts.

Aesthetic arguments dominated conservationist attacks on the proposed drowning of picturesque valleys and the laying down of pipelines. In truly picturesque manner, the planner Patrick Abercrombie (1951a) noted that the entrance to one valley destined for drowning was so perfectly composed as to be worthy of a painting by Claude. A proposed scheme on the slopes of Cader Idris—described as 'the most vulgar and horrifying' of the proposals (*Montgomery County Times*, 1953)—was rebutted thus in *The Times* by two renowned conservationists:

The great crag faces of Cader Idris, the majestic Llyn at their feet and the lovely quietude of Talyllyn 1,200 ft below, are a superb element in the new North Wales National Park. Richard Wilson's famed picture in the National Gallery of Llyn Cau—a Welshman's great tribute to his own country—is itself argument enough against reservoiring this Llyn by an engineer's dam and filling and emptying it each 24 hours like a bath. It is also an argument against running more than 2,000 yards of exposed overland pipeline down to Talyllyn—the lower reservoir and pump station—far below (Griffin and Symonds, 1953).

Wales's most famous landscape artist had now been invoked by the opposition within a cosmopolitan discourse on aesthetics. The tenor of this picturesque debate was sustained by the arch-polemicist and conservationist Clough Williams-Ellis.

Headlong down the Years

Williams-Ellis had been instrumental in the formation of the CPRW and was its chairman from 1928 to 1947. Best known for two pieces of planning propaganda—the book *England and the Octopus* (1928) and the village of Portmeirion—Williams-Ellis actively tied his native north Wales into broader aesthetic discourses. His main critique of the HEP schemes was the novel, *Headlong down the Years*, written with his wife, Amabel (1951). This took as its model Thomas Love Peacock's *Headlong Hall*, an eighteenth-century attack on landscape 'improvers' who detracted from the morality of wild nature. The Williams-Ellis's version is written in a tone of ironic humour and pastiche, set immediately by its cover (Figure 10.2). Entitled 'Beauties of Snowdonia' in the manner of an eighteenth-century engraving, the first picture shows 'the prospect

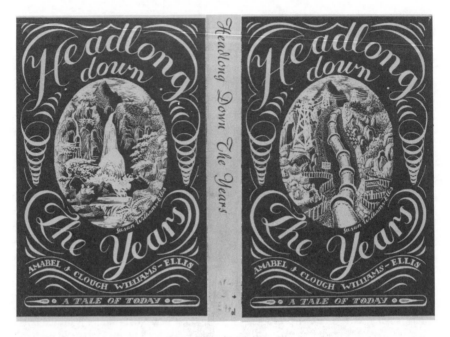

Figure 10.2   'Prospect of a Waterfall'—'The Prospect Improved'. (From Williams-Ellis and Williams-Ellis, 1951)

of a waterfall'. Two tourists sit amidst sheltering trees admiring a foaming cataract as it cascades down a rocky gully. The lines are rounded, the prospect serene. The second picture shows 'the prospect improved'. The scene is now dominated by a massive pipeline which has entrapped the river yet ironically still follows its course. The trees have gone, pylons stride across the mountains, and our tourists are hemmed in by fences, and conducted by signs. Communion with nature has been lost, the irregularity of the picturesque destroyed; and in a witty reference to paintings of the Sublime, the female figure appears about to faint, distressed by that which she sees.

The transforming of nature, and especially of water, is the book's central theme. Exchanges between conservationists and the 'improvers' are translated from Peacock's novel into the context of the HEP scheme. Mrs Headlong expresses delight at lantern slides of wild and picturesque nature, but she is chastised by Mr Galvanic, the BEA's technocratic representative:

here is a stream . . . rushing down through a thick, intricate, wood—here the whole body of water bursts foaming out from among the trees and tumbles wastefully down the cliff. But here is the place corrected! The wood is cleared, the entire stream runs usefully through a pipe, and turns the great wheels of the tremendous Power House that you see below. Note in this close-up . . . what we shall do in case some romantic soul, with a taste for nature, should object to our magnificent pipe-line—we shall plant, in profusion for nearly a mile, the best shrubs that money can buy (Williams-Ellis and Williams-Ellis, 1951: 23).

The novel satirizes the engineer's failure to conceive of co-operation with nature, and of a sense of appropriate scale: the BEA's chairman in the novel is aptly named Sir Hercules Megawatt. His employee, Mr Galvanic, shuns the organic unobtrusiveness of one native's cottage with its small generating plant in a nearby stream. Thus, HEP in Snowdonia is characterized as dangerous because 'the balance between organic and mechanistic in these islands is already tipped so far one way' (Williams-Ellis and Williams-Ellis, 1951: 68). Nature, however, demonstrates its power in a scene in which a storm sets the waters raging. In the face of this adversity, the natives shelter good-humouredly in an inn, enjoying strong tea and a song. By their joviality they implicitly accept their place within nature. Mr Galvanic does not:

If these idiots would only help forward the Hydro-Electric scheme instead of singing nonsense at the tops of their voices, there need be no barbaric scenes of this sort! If I had my way, this disgusting water would soon know its place! The place for water is behind dams and in pipes—all under control. (Williams-Ellis and Williams-Ellis, 1951:87)

Mr Galvanic's error is exposed as he is swept out to sea on a punt by the raging currents.

Water and morality

One outcome of maximum HEP generation for the Grid as opposed to more modest production for local consumption would be the loss of virtually all flow from streams and waterfalls with destructive consequences for scenic beauty. The BEA helpfully suggested that it could ensure sufficient flow during the tourist season, but this proposal was ridiculed (Figure 10.3). A deeper sense of water's place in nature was also advanced, a spiritual opposition to so full a subjugation of nature. The loss of spirit—debasing the recreational attractiveness of north Wales—was a powerful theme in the CPRW's arguments. The careful juxtaposition of images by the NWHEPC added to this perception. In Plate 10.1, the photograph of a hill farmer, at one with his sheepdog, places them very much *in* nature. But this image is paired with the harsh diagonals of a pipeline, viewed from below, as it slices *through* nature, testimony to the NWHEPC's belief that for the HEP engineer 'the water which runs in mountain stream beds is not beauty but x units of electricity pouring to waste' (NWHEPC, 1950: 6).

The 'tidying' and 'channelling' of rivers by engineers signified a taming of nature and in Patrick Abercrombie's opinion held profound dangers. Abercrombie, generally seen as the figurehead of 'rational' planning, was fascinated by the Chinese philosophy of *Feng Shui* (Wind-Water), a belief that the forms assumed by mountains and valleys were the outcome of the moulding influence

'Madame, for 6d. I'll only turn it half on.'

Figure 10.3 '... it would be possible to make suitable arrangements for the water to go over the falls when visitors were about'. (From Welsh Nationalist Party, 1950)

of wind and water (Abercrombie, 1926). *Feng Shui* maintained natural balance by indicating ways in which human additions could 'co-operate and harmonise with the local currents of the cosmic breath' (Abercrombie, 1926: 51). Significantly, Abercrombie illustrated this argument by reference to the Dolgarrog HEP scheme in north Wales where two reservoir bursts caused the deaths of 16 people in the village below. In his opinion, human intrusions had so altered the natural forms as to produce disastrous effects: 'Water, the arch-type of humility, because it always seeks the lowest place, will resent interference with

HILL FARMER IN NANT FFRANCON   THE CWM DYLI "COVERED" PIPE LINE

Plate 10.1   The loss of spirit. (From NWHEPC, 1952)

its natural bent, and as the humble can lose their tempers, it will rage forth from confinement, as happened so disastrously at Dolgarrog' (Abercrombie, 1926: 51–2). He concluded that in confining water to a lake above the village in the valley, the natural harmony of the locality had been altered. *Feng Shui* would suggest that the village be moved out of harm's way, just as it informed Abercrombie's (1951a; 1951b) views on the profound immorality of the technical manipulation of stream flow:

Instead of letting it glide smoothly, rush in spate, lie still or percolate over or through slopes, boggy hillsides, channels, brooks, rivers, tarns, lakes, waterfalls, marshes, saturated subsoil and other acquatic ecentricities, it is to be methodically collected and discharged through pipes into turbines and pelton wheels. Furthermore, its natural falls and watersheds are to be juggled with by leats and tunnels (Abercrombie, (1951: 24).

Elsewhere Abercrombie speaks of the tortured waters of the Mawddach scheme returning from the alien pipes to their natural bed having been entrapped. The landscape had evolved over countless ages, yet through the north Wales HEP schemes 'Nature's ecology cannot fail to be seriously affected' (Abercrombie, 1951b: 24). The evolutionary metaphor, so influential in the early part of the century (Kern 1983), underpinned Abercrombie's theories on planning and on the development of rural Wales. Were small-scale schemes to be instigated, Caernarfon could evolve as a self-sufficient region in harmony with natural laws. The proposed HEP schemes would, however, disrupt the region's 'natural' evolution.

Welsh water

As Mr Galvanic is carried away downstream in *Headlong down the Years*, a Bard shouts defiantly at the 'Rash Saxon', likening the rivers and streams of Snowdonia to the life blood of the Welsh nation. The nationalist argument was expanded in an epilogue by Richard Hughes, who noted that the plans affected 'part of the patrimony of the *Welsh* nation. People distinct from the English in race, history, territory, values, and above all in consciousness of what nation they belong to' (Williams-Ellis and Williams-Ellis, 1951: 116). He argued that coexistence between Wales and England could be endangered by the vast scale of the proposed scheme, experienced alongside poor electricity distribution in rural Wales: 'When we lift our eyes unto our hills we shall see leats, pipe-lines, power-houses, concrete, spoil-heaps, deserted farms: but if we want electricity we shall still have to crank up the old petrol engine as we do today' (Williams-Ellis and Williams-Ellis, 1951: 117). Hughes likened this to 'Imperialist Grab', concluding that through the scheme Parliament would 'be sowing in Wales seeds of hatred where today there is no hatred' (Williams-Ellis and Williams-Ellis, 1951: 118).

The Welsh nationalists themselves, Plaid Cymru, were fully involved in the HEP debate. Their response was a complex, and often contradictory, fusion of aesthetic and cultural criticism. One of their principal philosophical themes was the intimate relationship between a people and its land. But for them, the landscape assumed importance not in any directly aesthetic way, but due to its associations with the national past. A territorial sense of Welshness questioned the right of the British *state* to exploit the resources of the Welsh *nation*. By implicating aesthetics in a political debate, Plaid Cymru attacked the HEP scheme's visual impacts. A Welshness which drew its identity from the rural, mountainous areas could not be sustained in the face of their despoliation:

The incomparable beauty of our country must not be destroyed by this development. This beauty is part of the national heritage of the Welsh people, one of those noble influences which have moulded the distinct national character of the Welsh nation and which still moulds and maintains our national character. (Welsh Nationalist Party, 1950: 12)

This threat was exemplified by the proposal to allow water over the Aber Falls only during the tourist season, highlighting the implied subservience of a tourist economy (Figure 10.3). Plaid Cymru argued for *Electricity without Vandalism* (Welsh Nationalist Party, 1950) and for plans which would protect the integrity of Wales's landscape. They proposed the withdrawal of the Snowdon and Nant Ffrancon schemes, and the amending of the Upper Conwy, Mawddach, Ffestiniog and Rheidol plans.

Though attacking the aesthetic devastation, Plaid Cymru were more concerned with the political injustice which underlay those impacts. They claimed to be alone among the political parties in calling for rural electrification.

In their opinion, this could only be achieved by treating Wales as a national unit with its own administrative powers—a significant step towards devolution. Smaller-scale HEP schemes, together with a rapid build-up in coal power, could electrify the Welsh countryside in five years rather than the 20 proposed by the BEA. Under the current large-scale proposals destined for the National Grid, both Welsh territory and Welsh concerns would be submerged by Britishness. The only answer to this was self-government, for

Under a Welsh government the towns of England will not steal Welsh water with neither payment nor profit to Wales. Under a Welsh government, Welsh rivers will become electricity and wealth to the small villages of the countryside. Under a Welsh government, the Welsh shall not be punished for using the power of their own stream. (Plaid Cymru, 1929)

This was a vision of rural regeneration with HEP as its driving force. Such a model had already been proposed by academics working in Wales between the wars. The Aberystwyth geographer, H.J. Fleure (1919), claimed that the mountainous 'regions of difficulty' were, until the advent of HEP, characterized by poor returns on effort. However, he noted the way in which HEP had transformed the life of Alpine villages and parts of Scandinavia, and specifically suggested that this technology might play a role in the reinvigoration of areas of Cardiganshire. He urged the restoration of the fisheries industry alongside 'a new development of the hill country of Wales through utilisation of water power, if the preliminary afforestation necessary for regularization (*sic*) of streams could be organized' (Fleure 1917: 60). One of Fleure's students, Iorwerth Peate, an early member of both the CPRW and Plaid Cymru, saw the possibilities afforded by technology to arrest the decline of rural Wales. In a vigorous critique of the Scott Report (Ministry of Works and Planning, 1942), Peate (1943) rejected its explicit division of country and city and the implied role of the former as an amenity area for the latter. He argued rather for the reintroduction of industry into rural Wales, thus providing the foundation for revived rural life and cultural flowering. Peate (1943: 14) saw hydro-electric power as 'fundamental to the whole of our life in the future' and as the basis of rural industrial development. No one, he argued, need fear the introduction of clean, HEP-driven industry into the countryside. Many areas had been beautified by reservoir building: 'We must face these facts rather than live in sentimental mists content with the continued stagnation of the countryside. There are dynamic foundations to true beauty.' Less prone than Plaid Cymru colleagues to dismiss industrialism, Peate (1929: 8) saw the old craft traditions and diverse economic life of rural Wales revived by self-sufficiency in HEP:

We cry for the old methods in vain: we attempt to revive the dead in vain, but on the grave of the old methods, we can build new factories and keep, in the sound of this age's machines, the spirit of the rich culture given us as an inheritance by the old craftsmen of Wales.

'The TVA Way'

Plaid Cymru adopted Peate's vision. In 1944, it argued for industrial dispersal to provide an economic stiffening of the rural areas and to stem depopulation. Electricity had an almost transcendent role in the process: 'Properly applied it can make us into a happy, prosperous, self-reliant nation, proud of being something more substantial than *Gwlad y Gân* [the Land of Song]' (Welsh Nationalist Party, 1944: 1). Plaid Cymru proposed its own HEP schemes, deriving inspiration from the Tennessee Valley Authority (TVA) established under the New Deal. Though on a vast scale, the TVA represented a form of regional government which combined central co-ordination with true local democracy, unlike the exploitative way in which Welsh territory was used by the British state. Plaid Cymru (Welsh Nationalist Party, 1946: 9) saw an 'intimate humanity in [the TVA's] relationships' with ordinary folk. The TVA was seen to reconcile democracy and the impact of scientific change, forging a new form of civilization (Matthews, 1949). Here was a way for Wales to achieve electrification and modernity without surrendering sovereignty.

Taking the TVA as its model, and the central role of HEP in that model, Plaid Cymru called for an Act of Parliament establishing a Welsh Economic Authority to control electricity supply. It would use the financial surplus from the sale of power for promotional activities, and research and development. Centralized food-processing plants, demonstration farms and incentives like cheap fertilizers could stimulate agriculture, while light industries could be established in the rural areas. The University of Wales should also play a role in this research process with the finest minds in Wales being brought to bear on the task of reconstruction, arguably forming the bureaucratic machinery of modern nationhood and a basis for separatism.

There was a strong sense of aesthetics to the scheme. Plaid Cymru noted how the TVA dams and reservoirs had opened up new recreational possibilities. By 1942, 11 million people had visited the dams. Throughout his study of the TVA's work, Julian Huxley (1945) stressed the importance of natural beauty in the scheme. Improved access to mountain areas was facilitated by well-designed accommodation, and all aspects of the scheme exhibited aesthetic detail and quality. Plaid Cymru welcomed this potential boost to the tourist trade and the example of how electrification might proceed without vandalism. In Wales, they argued, large-scale coastal and mountain developments could be of vital importance if undertaken by a public body placing emphasis on planned growth and not on exploitation. C.F. Matthews (1949), outlining 'the TVA way', illustrated how four areas of Snowdonia might be developed. Plaid Cymru added that the Authority could issue publications on scenic resources, historical and legendary features, thus making the ethnicity of the land clearly apparent. Planning would reconcile technical advance with a sense of nature, protecting existing scenic beauty but forging new attractions. TVA photographs portray the great dams as noble monuments of a civilization. Lewis Mumford was quoted as saying that their very cast made one think of the pyramids of Egypt. This heroic

Figure 10.4   The TVA Way. (From Welsh Nationalist Party, 1945)

vision also permeated that Welsh perception of progress. The somewhat naive cartoon (Figure 10.4) which closed Plaid Cymru's (Welsh Nationalist Party, 1945) *TVA for Wales*, heralds a country founded on new technologies. A north–south road transcends Wales's geographical difficulties and brings industry to the rural areas alongside a modernized agriculture. Central in this national modernization is the great dam, towards which the figure points, and HEP. Urgency, Plaid Cymru claimed, was the keynote in Tennessee: 'OUR faith shall be as strong, OUR resolve no less determined . . . In this we march with all our countrymen'. (Welsh Nationalist Party, 1945: 16)

Conclusion

Nationalist demands were, predictably, swept aside by the fervour of post-war reconstruction. Acts of Parliament throughout the 1950s authorized enlargements, and the creation of new schemes, including Wales's largest linking Pumlumon and the Rheidol Valley. The BEA placated some of its critics by appointing a landscape consultant who was widely acclaimed for creating a new beauty where the mechanistic and organic were fused through a concern for scenic order and the sensitive use of materials and siting. None the less, the CPRW joined Plaid Cymru in attacking the continued poverty of local electrical supply, despite the exploitation of Welsh streams and valleys. By the end of the 1950s, though, the electrical debate had moved on to nuclear power, bringing new threats to Welsh land. However, water engineering remained central to political debates in Wales with the drowning of the Tryweryn Valley in the late 1950s, for Liverpool's water supply, a particularly emotive focal point. The campaign against the drowning, which spawned acts of sabotage, produced a coalition of territorial defence across Wales and earned Plaid Cymru its first significant electoral showing in 1959 (Keating, 1988).

Hydro-electricity became less controversial as electricity distribution improved in rural Wales and as the schemes mellowed into their environments. However, in the current energy context, HEP seems set to assume a new importance and, potentially to engender new conflict. With reduced confidence in nuclear and coal power, and the possibilities of small contributions to the privatized grid, renewable energy sources are under review (*Guardian*, 1990). Already, plans have been announced for small-scale HEP generation in Wales, including one scheme sponsored by those guardians of scenic beauty, the National Trust. In a changing energy context, the debates of mid-century again become relevant.

References

Abercrombie, Patrick (1926) *The Preservation of Rural England*, Liverpool, Liverpool University Press/London, Hodder & Stoughton.

Abercrombie, Patrick (1928) 'The Preservation of Rural Wales', *Transactions of the Honourable Society of Cymmrodorion*, Session 1926–7, 156–69.

Abercrombie, Patrick (1951a) *Report on Proposed Hydro Electric Schemes, 1951*, Caernarfon, Caernarfon County Council.

Abercrombie, Patrick (1951b) *Report on Proposed Hydro Electric Schemes, 1951*, Meirionydd County Council.

Cherry, Gordon (1975) *Environmental Planning 1939–69: Volume II. National Parks and Recreation in the Countryside*, London, HMSO.

Cooper, A.R. (1949) Statement in *Welsh Land: Three Authoritative Statements* Carmarthen, Druid Press.

Cornish, Vaughan (1929) 'A National Park in Snowdonia', *The Welsh Outlook* 16 (7), 209.

CPRW (1930) *Land of my Fathers (and of my Children): Why Only Sing About It?* London, CPRW.

CPRW (1947) *News and Report* June edn, Aberystwyth, CPRW.

CPRW 83i, 'National Parks', *CPRW Papers*, National Library of Wales.

CPRW 95, 'Memorandum on Policy', *CPRW Papers*, National Library of Wales.

CPRW 101, 'Ponterwyd Village Development Committee', *CPRW Papers*, National Library of Wales.

Crowe, Sylvia (1956) *Tomorrow's Landscape*, London, Architectural Press.

Davies, Alfred (1923) *Evicting a Community: The Case for the Preservation of the Historical and Beautiful Valley of the Ceiriog in North Wales*, London, Honourable Society of Cymmrodorion.

Fleure, H.J. (1917) 'Inshore Fisheries and their Development' in *Welsh Housing and Development Yearbook 1917*, Cardiff, Welsh Housing and Development Association, 60–5.

Fleure, H.J. (1919) 'Human Regions', *Scottish Geographical Magazine*, 35, 94–105.

Griffin, H.G. and Symonds, H.H. (1953) 'A Project in Wales', *The Times* 7 October.

Gruffudd, Pyrs (1988) 'Anthropology and agriculture: rural planning in Wales between the wars' in M. Heffernan, and P. Gruffudd (eds), *A Land Fit for Heroes: Essays in the Human Geography of Inter-War Britain*, Loughborough University, Department of Geography, Occasional Paper 14, 80–109.

The Guardian (1990) 'Powers of Persuasion' and 'Tilting at Wind Bills', 26 January, p. 25.

Huxley, Julian (1945) *T.V.A.: Adventure in Planning*, London, Scientific Book Club.

Keating, Michael (1988) *State and Regional Nationalism: Territorial Politics and the European State*, Hemel Hempstead, Harvester Wheatsheaf.

Kern, Stephen (1983) *The Culture of Time and Space 1880–1918*, Cambridge, Mass., Harvard University Press.

Liverpool Daily Post (1953) 'Dolgelley Critics of the CPRW', 30 November, Welsh edn.

Matthews, C.F. (1949) *Wales Can Prosper the TVA Way*, Caernarfon, Welsh Economic Development Authority.

Ministry of Works and Planning (1942) *Report of the Committee on Land Utilisation in Rural Areas* (the Scott Report) Cmd 6378, London, HMSO.

Montgomery County Times (1953) 'Llyn Cau Electricity Project Protest', 24 October.

NWHEPC (1950) *The Hydro-Electric Schemes of the British Electricity Authority for the North Wales National Park: the Case Against the Scheme*, Liverpool, NWHEPC.

NWHEPC (1952) *Hydro-Electricity in North Wales*, Liverpool, NWHEPC.

Peate, Iorwerth (1929) 'Y Crefftwr yng Nghymru', *Y Ddraig Goch*, 4(1), 4 and 8.

Peate, Iorwerth (1943) 'Yr Ardaloedd Gwledig a'u Dyfodol', *Y Llenor* 22 (1–2), 10–18.

Plaid Cymru (1929) 'Ymreolaeth i Gymru—Paham?', *Y Ddraig Goch* 2(11), 3.

Thomas, Dewi W. (1989) 'Historical Notes on Hydro-Electricity in North Wales', *Caernarfonshire Historical Society Transactions*, 50, 87–110.

Ward, Stephen V. (1988) *The Geography of Inter-War Britain: The State and Uneven Development*, London, Routledge.

Ward, Colin and Hardy, Dennis (1986) *Goodnight Campers: The History of the British Holiday Camp*, London, Mansell.

Welsh Nationalist Party (London Branch) (1944) *Plan Electricity for Wales*, London, Welsh Nationalist Party.

Welsh Nationalist Party (1945) *T.V.A. for Wales*, Caernarfon, Welsh Party Offices.

Welsh Nationalist Party (1946) *T.V.A. Points the Way*, Caernarfon, Welsh Party Offices.

Welsh Nationalist Party (1950) *Electricity without Vandalism*, Cardiff, Welsh Nationalist Party.

Williams-Ellis, Amabel and Williams-Ellis Clough (1951) *Headlong down the Years: A Tale of Today* Liverpool, Liverpool University Press.

CHAPTER 11

Landscape and technology the Gabčikovo–Nagymaros scheme

Keith Boucher

The gentle embrace of Danube's waves
Through past, present and future.
Dissolves the wars of ancestral time
Into a lasting peace.
Our work is to settle our common affairs
And this is no small task!
         (Attila Joseph, *By the Danube*, 1936)

The development of international river basins is a potential source of political, economic and environmental conflict. More than 200 large rivers are shared by more than one country and the longitudinal continuum of fluvial processes mean that downstream water users are dependent upon upstream water and land developments. Dávid (1986) has argued that integrated land and water management within a long-range comprehensive approach to river-basin planning is needed to achieve sustainable water development. International co-operation in the co-ordination of water and land development and nature conservation is needed for such an approach to be successful. This chapter examines the Gabčikovo (Bös)–Nagymaros (GN) scheme on the Danube, Europe's most important international river.

In Roman times the Emperor Augustus had a coin minted with the inscription '*Salus rei publicae—Danubius*' (the Danube, the welfare of the people). Since then, there have been many attempts to link the Danube with the Rhine, the earliest dating back to the time of Charlemagne in 792, but it was not until after the 1950s that improvements in technology allowed serious consideration of a Danube–Main–Rhine canal. The section of the canal in West Germany as far as Nuremberg was completed in 1972 and the linking with the Danube at Kelheim should be completed by 1992 (Nagy, 1988). Improvements to the Danube waterway were required both in the Austrian and in the Czechoslovak–Hungarian sector. Over a hundred different options were considered by Hungary for the latter sector during the period 1952 to 1966. After further discussions the GN scheme was accepted by Hungary and Czechoslovakia as the best solution to navigation problems between Bratislava and Budapest—the most difficult waterway section to manage and control (Lokvenc and Szántó, 1986).

This scheme extends over a 220 km stretch of the Danube downstream from Austria, located mostly within Hungary, with a small but significant section within Czechoslovakia. From 1979 it became the centre of an acrimonious dispute between the riparian states and brought into sharp focus some of the major issues facing Hungary on entering the last decade of the century. These issues possess a technological dimension but there are related environmental and political pressures. This chapter investigates the potential impacts of the GN scheme on aspects of the physical environment and then explores some of the difficulties of project implementation in a period when public concern about the environment has gathered momentum in socialist as well as in Western societies. This momentum was great enough initially to halt the engineering work at Nagymaros and ultimately to force its cancellation.

Gabčikovo-Nagymaros scheme

The CN scheme (Figure 11.1) consists of four main components located on Hungarian and Czechslovakian territory (Nagy, 1988; OVIBER, 1980). The first is the Dunakiliti (Hrušov) Weir and Reservoir extending upstream of the Danube to Bratislava. The second component is the navigation and power canal, with headrace and tailrace, between Dunakiliti and Palkovičovo (Szap). The power canal provides the water to drive the turbines which form the third component—the Gabčikovo (Bös) power-station with installed capacity of 720 MW. The fourth component was to have been a second power-station and barrage at Nagymaros, 123 km downstream within the Danube Bend and 50 km upstream from Budapest. This last component was abandoned in October 1989.

In overall scale, the GN scheme (Figure 11.1a) is not particularly noteworthy. The turbines of the Gabčikovo power plant are reported to be the fifth largest in the world (Karacs, 1989) but if we judge the project by its planned rated capacity, it lies 144th in the notified world listing of hydro-schemes (Mermel, 1988). Its importance for study therefore lies in political, economic and environmental factors. It has become the focus of tensions that developed over the past decade between a burgeoning conservationist-environment pressure group in Hungary and traditional Stalinist-socialist attitudes towards industrial development and energy supplies. The conflict of vision which emerged is not simply to be seen against a backcloth of capitalist entrepreneurial activity or socialist state control. It represents a third force acting to curb the perceived excesses of both these modernist alternatives. Today Hungarians are increasingly free to discuss alternative futures for their environment and have turned, in particular, to the impact that the Nagymaros project might have on the general environment of the Danube Bend. While the GN scheme poses neither a lesser nor greater threat to the environment than many other similar schemes, it has become the *cause célèbre* of the 'Danube Circle', the Hungarian environmental pressure group (Thorpe, 1986).

The overall effect of building dams is to eliminate the natural gradient of a

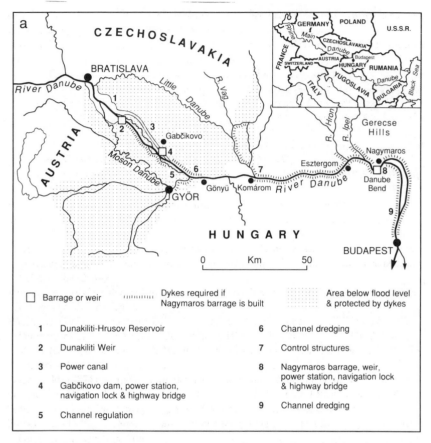

Figure 11.1 (a) The location of the chief components of the Gabčikovo-Nagymaros Barrage System on the Danube in Central Europe. Inset map shows position of the scheme on the Danube–Main–Rhine river system

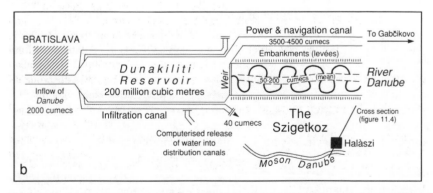

Figure 11.1 (b) Schematic representation of the Dunakiliti section of the Gabčikovo–Nagymaros scheme showing the essential hydrological characteristics. (Based on data from Lokvenc and Szántó, 1986).

river, to regulate the flows and to alter the sediment transport regime (Petts, 1984). Changes are also likely to occur in the alluvial aquifers both upstream and downstream of the dam, particularly where gravels lie close to the surface and adjacent to the river. Water-table variations can increase the duration of soil saturation or magnitude of soil moisture deficit. The effect of such changes on agriculture and ecosystems should not be ignored (see, for example, Dister *et al.*, 1990). In addition, the penetration of polluted fine sediment into the water-bearing strata may contaminate the sub-surface water supplies. Such fears, arising from the GN scheme, led to a fresh appraisal of the Danube project.

Physical characteristics of the Danube

The Danube emerges from the Vienna Basin, flowing through the Deveny Gate to enter the 'small plains' of the Kisalfold region. Immediately downstream from Bratislava, in Czechoslovakia, the Malý Dunaj (Little Danube) branches away east only to return to the main channel of the Danube at Komárom (Figure 11.1a). The Danube Island lying between the two rivers covers an area of 160,000 ha. On the southwest side, the Moson Danube breaks with the main channel to form the island of Szigetköz (33,000 ha). Maintenance of navigation routes between Bratislava and Palkovičovo requires constant and extensive channel regulation through this braided section, but despite these efforts it has been virtually impossible to maintain the necessary channel depths as recommended by the Danube Commission in 1948 (Myers, 1965). At Bratislava, where the gradient is about $30 \, \text{cm} \, \text{km}^{-1}$, the river carries a bedload of $600,000 \, \text{m}^3 \, \text{yr}^{-1}$. In the past this load was transferred downstream through the main braided channel section towards Gönyű where the gradient falls to $20 \, \text{cm} \, \text{km}^{-1}$. It is therefore not surprising that it is the Danube's most difficult waterway section to manage and has only been kept open by dredging some $7 \times 10^6 \, \text{m}^3 \text{yr}^{-1}$ of gravel (Lokvenc and Szántó, 1986).

Below Komárom, the Danube once more flows in a single channel, forming the boundary between Czechoslovakia and Hungary for about 50 km. A few kilometres downstream from Esztergom at the confluence with the Ipel, the river enters Hungarian territory and flows through an open valley in the Gerecse Hills and thence into the 'Danube Bend' section. It is this area which is of great scenic attraction, with potential for tourism and recreational activities (Miczek, 1989). The river then turns south towards Budapest and the Great Hungarian Plain where, for centuries, it meandered unregulated despite attempts to straighten its course (Lessner, (1961).

River Management

The need to improve the waterway between Bratislava in Czechoslovakia and Győr in Hungary has already been indicated. Such improvements are necessary if barge traffic is to pass freely downriver to Budapest. In the past, river traffic was held up for days during times of low flow and was rarely possible at night due to the variable water depth. It is estimated that the potential carrying capacity of the existing fleet will increase by 20 per cent in the Hungarian sector if the greater draught for vessels is realized.

Planning of hydro-power schemes did not begin until 1956 when the Austrians entered the negotiations. This eventually led to the proposal to build a joint hydro-scheme near Bratislava. In the meantime, various alternatives were being considered by Czechoslovakia and Hungary for the section downstream from Bratislava. Over 100 different schemes had been considered by 1966. The oil crises of the mid 1970s led the Hungarian government to change its priorities and to adopt what came to be known as the 'Contract Plan' (Perczel and Libik, 1989). Under this plan, the production of energy became of paramount importance, with lower priorities being given to flood prevention and improved navigation. In fact, the oil crisis made little impact on the Hungarian economy due to the adherence of Hungary to the so-called 'Bucharest Principle', whereby the price of raw materials traded between member Comecon states was based on world market prices over the previous four years. There was also the buffering effect of relatively cheap natural gas from the Soviet Union. Had the Hungarian economy been more sensitive to changing energy patterns, the GN scheme almost certainly would have been completed and in operation before 1990.

In addition to navigation problems, floods have posed a constant threat to villages and farms. Historical records indicate a series of disastrous floods with consequent loss of life, culminating in the great flood of 1838. More recently, significant floods, mostly associated with spring meltwater, have occurred in 1954, 1956, 1965, 1970 and 1988. Floodwaters breached the reinforced levees of the main Danube channel in 1954, inundating half of the Szigetköz area between the main river and the Moson Danube with waters rising to first-floor level in the lower parts of the city of Győr (Dosztányi, 1988). In 1956, two dams collapsed on the Czechoslovak side, leading to the flooding of 100,000 ha of land and the evacuation of 54,000 inhabitants. One of the purposes of the scheme is to protect low-lying areas from flooding. However, flow regulation poses additional problems. For example, the decision to adapt the Dunakiliti navigation canal scheme to provide water for the Gabčikovo power plant is likely to have serious implications for the ecology of the Danube and for farming on the Szigetköz (Gószán and Lóczy, 1986). The debate on the environmental impact of the scheme involves some understanding of the water levels in its constituent parts. The maximum permissible flow in the section between Dunakiliti and Gabčikovo is given as $4,800 \, \text{m}^3 \, \text{s}^{-1}$ at a level 10 m above the existing embankment. The raising of dykes to 133.1 m has therefore been a necessary part of the project (Figure 11.2). Downstream from Gabčikovo, the level of the flow at $2,780 \, \text{m}^3 \, \text{s}^{-1}$ is shown on the assumption that the Nagymaros barrage is built. Without this second barrage, the flow should adjust to the lower level indicated downstream from Nagymaros. The problem then becomes one of planning for the daily release of $4,000 \, \text{m}^3 \, \text{s}^{-1}$ from the Gabčikovo tailrace.

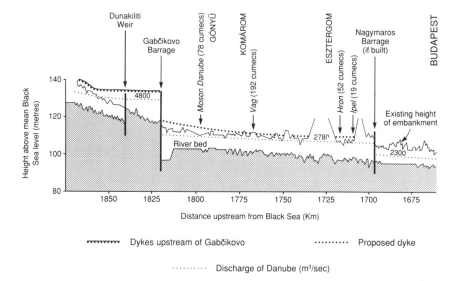

Figure 11.2 Longitudinal profile of the Gabčikovo–Nagymaros Scheme. Average discharges of tributaries into the Danube are indicated in cubic metres/second. Q represents flow at a specified rate in cubic metres/second. (Based on data from the Hungarian Water Authority)

The general characteristics of the Danube régime are laid out in the accompanying tables. Table 11.1 lists the discharge levels at the two main gauging stations of Bratislava (upstream) and Nagymaros (downstream). Table 11.2 indicates the 'normal' water requirements of the Gabčikovo power plant when operating near full capacity. The mean flow at Bratislava at the western

Table 11.1   Danube discharge flows (m^3s^{-1}) (OVIBER)

	Bratislava	Nagymaros
Lowest recorded daily flow	570	590
Mean daily flow exceeds this value for 95% of ave. year	882	1,124
Median flow value	1,810	2,248
Average flow value	2,035	2,390
Mean daily flow exceeds this value for 10% of ave. year	3,300	3,837
Flood return periods:		
Mean daily flow exceeds this value for		
5% of ave. year (Q5)	8,750	7,650
Estimated 100-year return flow (Q1)	10,600	8,700
Estimated 1000-year return flow (Q0.1)	13,000	10,000
Maximum peak flow recorded	10,400	8,180

Table 11.2 Flood discharge rates, Dunakiliti Reservoir

Q value	Bratislava (m³s⁻¹)	Dunakiliti Reservoir (×10⁶m³)	Diversion canal (m³s⁻¹)	Discharge over weir into Danube (m³s⁻¹)
Average	2,035	200	3,500–4,000	50–200
Q1 (100 yr)	10,600	243	4,240	6,360
Q0.1 (1,000 yr)	13,000	243	4,890	8,110
Q0.01 (10,000 yr)	15,000	243	5,270	9,730

end of the Dunakiliti Reservoir is $2,035 \, m^3 s^{-1}$ with a median value of $1810 \, m^3 s^{-1}$. The reservoir has a total capacity of $200 \times 10^6 \, m^3$ under normal operating conditions, of which 30 per cent may be utilized at any one time to maintain the required depth of water in the diversion canal (Figure 11.1b). The power plant at the downstream end of the canal, at Gabčikovo, requires a supply of $4,000 \, m^3 s^{-1}$. If all eight installed turbines were in operation, full power production would be possible for about 10.5 hours per day, excluding start-up and shut-down periods. This would lead to an annual output of 2,980 GWh.

Two problems emerge. The first relates to the power production estimates (Figure 11.3). There will be considerable pressure on the Hungarian authorities to operate the turbines near maximum capacity in order to repay the Austrian loan which helped finance the scheme. This is to be paid off in the form of energy at 1,200 GWh over a 20-year period commencing in 1996 (Dosztányi, 1988). Of this amount, 62 per cent must be delivered in autumn and winter at the very time when Hungary is in most need of supplementing its own energy requirements (Perczel and Libik, 1989). The abandonment of the Nagymaros hydro component means that Hungary will have to export its entire share of generated power from Gabčikovo to Austria.

The second problem emerges from Tables 11.1 and 11.3. Average flow conditions, assumed in the previous paragraph, cannot be relied upon. The mean flow at Bratislava for the months of October to February is only 75 per cent of the mean annual flow. If there had to be similar reductions in electricity

Table 11.3 Monthly flows at Bratislava

	Jan.	Feb.	March	April	May	June	July	Aug.	Sept.	Oct.	Nov.	Dec.
Flow (m³s⁻¹)	1,567	1,585	1,957	2,358	2,700	2,785	2,633	2,271	1,954	1,568	1,480	1,441
Percentage of average flow	77	78	97	116	133	138	130	112	96	77	73	71

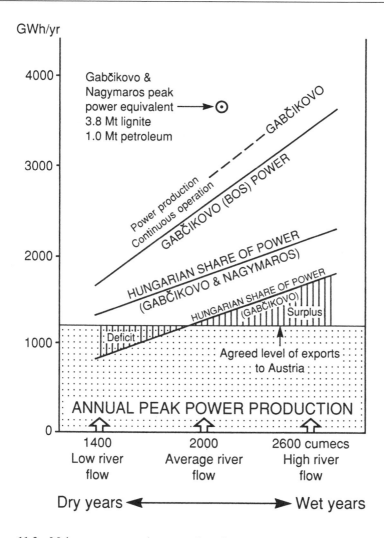

Figure 11.3 Main power generation scenarios of the Gabčikovo–Nagymaros scheme (based on data from Lokvenc and Szántó, 1986; Kozek and Varga, 1986; Perczel and Libik, 1989)

generation in the autumn and winter period then the logical conclusion is that Hungary would have to export power derived from other sources. In addition to the seasonal regime of the Danube, there are significant hydroclimatic fluctuations between humid and dry phases, having a periodicity of 20–30 years (Probst, 1989). Standardized values of mean annual flow $((x_1-\bar{x})/\bar{x})$ for the Danube 600 km downstream at Orsova, Romania, for the period 1871–1975, indicate a range of values from +0.37 to –0.32, although this range is modest when compared with many other European rivers. The situation is exacerbated by the tendency for low winter flows at 56 per cent of the mean monthly discharge to coincide with cold easterly airflows, increasing the demand for power far beyond the capacity to supply (see Gőőz, 1989; Compton, 1989; Kozek and Varga, 1986).

The allocation of water from the Dunakiliti Reservoir

Priority must first be given to the diversion of water from the reservoir into the canal supplying the power-plant. However, the maintenance of an adequate water level in the soils of the farmlands adjacent to the Danube is dependent upon a constant regulated release from the reservoir to maintain a compensation flow of 50–200 m³s⁻¹ in the existing Danube. This will increase sharply during periods of high flow input into the reservoir, rising to 6,360 m³s⁻¹ in the event of a 100-year return period flood (Q1%). In addition, infiltration canals have been constructed alongside the levees of the reservoir making available 40 m³s⁻¹ for distribution through the computer-controlled canal system of the Szigetköz. The possible effect on ground water across the Szigetköz (Figure 11.4) is to reduce the range of fluctuation in the ground water levels. It is clear that the flow of 50 m³s⁻¹ in the Danube system is well below the natural flow but Dosztányi (1988)

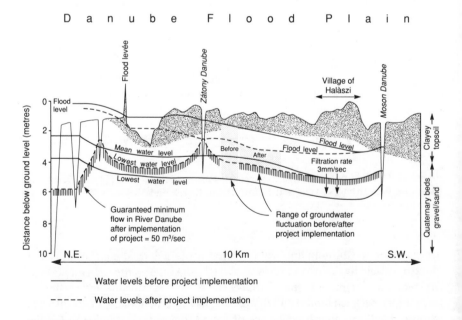

Figure 11.4   Cross-section across the Szigetköz between the main Danube and the Moson Danube, showing ground water levels (mostly after the Hungarian Water Authority and Dosztányi, 1988). For the location, see Figure 11.3

maintains that this 'will be sufficiently large to serve the various interests of the population and economy of the area'. This point is seemingly reinforced by Petrosovits who states (in Dosztányi, 1988: 21) that 'no detrimental impact has been identified to agriculture or to the environment which would occur as a consequence of project implementation'.

However, studies of minimum flows along regulated rivers sufficient to maintain their ecology (see, for example Orth and Leonard, 1990) suggest that 20 per cent of the average daily flow (ADF) provides an appropriate criterion for protecting aquatic habitats, and that a drop to 10 per cent ADF leads to degraded or poor habitat conditions. The scheme would reduce the average flow of $2,035 \, m^3 s^{-1}$, as measured upstream at Bratislava, to between 50 and $200 \, m^3 s^{-1}$ downstream from Dunakiliti, well below the critical environmental level. Even allowing for lower flow-rates in the braided section of the Danube, the reduction in ADF is likely to approach 10 per cent, indicating that instream habitats, especially for fisheries, could be significantly affected.

Kovacs published a report supporting the main aspects of the scheme (Dosztányi, 1988) but expressing reservations about the quality of water in the infiltration canals alongside the Dunakiliti Reservoir. Perczel and Libik (1989) have reported the first signs of eutrophication in the canals which were to be 'a clean and valuable water resource' (Lokvenc and Szántó, 1986). Signs of eutrophication have also been seen in the shallow inlets of the reservoir. The Water Authority maintains that the waters of the reservoir will be renewed every two days under normal flow but other evidence indicates that damming reduces the current velocity through the reservoir, which in turn encourages primary production leading to partial eutrophication (Tóth, 1983). It has recently been suggested that regular dredging of the mud, contaminated by effluent from Bratislava (320,000 pop.) should be carried out and the sediment deposited on the banks of the reservoir (Perczel and Libik, 1989). There is still the fear that polluted water will seep into the substrata and the infiltration canals despite the intention to instal plants to treat sewage and industrial effluent.

There are also fears about the quality of water in the Quaternary gravels which underlie the Szigetköz (Rónai, 1960). The gravels on the Hungarian side of the Danube hold an estimated 6–10 million cubic metres of potable ground water (Dosztányi, 1988) but are under threat from seepage of contaminated water in the main river bed due to accumulation of organic matter (Perczel and Libik, 1989). The filtration rate into the gravels is about $3 \, mm \, s^{-1}$ but the Water Authority gives no indication of horizontal movement (throughflow) so that the rate of contamination is difficult to estimate. The situation could detiorate if the poorly oxygenated waters of the infiltration canals are used to maintain water levels in the small-scale canal system of the Sziketköz.

Water renewal in the cut-off meanders of the Danube will no longer be part of the active river system. Flushout by released floodwaters will periodically occur but the low average flow rates in the main channel will be insufficient to maintain ecological systems in their present form. In particular, concern has been expressed about the future of the woodlands bordering the former active floodplain (Góczán and Lóczy, 1986). The Hungarian National Council for Environmental Protection and Nature Conservation commissioned a detailed survey in 1985 of fauna and flora, protected habitats and endangered species, especially the 'precious grey poplars' which may play an important future role as genetic banks. Such fragmented woodland is all that remains of the mixed stands of sedate ash, black oak, grey and black poplar which formed the most characteristic features of the Szigetköz landscape of the past. There is genuine concern that the fall in the water-table which accompanies the residual river flow will eventually adversely affect the rooting system of the woodland unless it is allowed to adjust to low flow regimes.

Downstream effects of the Gabčikovo Power Plant

Under the provisions of the 'Contract Plan' the periodic release of water from the upstream Gabčikovo power-station would be fed into the downstream Nagymaros Reservoir. The dam in the Danube Bend section was intended to form an integral part of the project. If the effect of the Gabčikovo releases are ignored then the impounded waters of the river would fluctuate by only 0.68 m over the entire section of the projected Nagymaros Reservoir which would stretch from the outflow of the Moson Danube to the proposed Nagymaros dam 100 km downstream. But the daily release of water leading to discharges of 3500–4500 m^{3}s^{-1} from the Gabčikovo dam would cause much greater fluctuations and would require the raising of levees and flood-protection barriers along the Danube and tributaries (Lokvenc and Szántó, 1986). Since the reservoir was to extend to the city of Győr, there were fears that 'backing-up' of waters would occur in the Moson Danube tributary. A high percentage of untreated sewage is usually allowed into the Moson Danube from Győr which has led to fears that periodic halting of the flow would add to the environmental problems (Goszán and Lóczy, 1986). Dosztányi (1988) pointed out in his environmental report that provision would be made for the construction of 95 sewage treatment plants in both the Czechoslovak and Hungarian catchments feeding water into the inter-dam section. Major sewage and wastewater treatment would be provided at the main riparian towns of Győr, Komárom, Esztergom, Tatabánya and Oroszlány. The sewerage network and piped water supply would be extended into the Szigetköz.

The growth of opposition to the GN scheme

Some misgivings had been expressed as soon as the details of the scheme were made known. The Sopron Council, in whose district the Szigetköz lies, expressed opposition, as did the Academy of Science in Budapest (Thorpe, 1986). For its part, the government decided to state the case for the dam in the Communist party daily, *Nepszabadság'*, in January 1984 and to silence opposition. In the same month, a public debate between Janos Vargha, a biologist working with the Academy of Science, and the Water Authority was cancelled. Vargha decided to take every opportunity to speak publicly about the environmental issues. A group called the 'Danube Circle' was formed to arrange more debates and circulate petitions in the regions likely to be affected by the scheme. By early 1985, over 10,000 signatures had been collected and presented to the Hungarian Parliament. At the same time as the Hungarian government had been seeking financial support from the Austrian government, links were being made between the Danube Circle and the Austrian Greens. The latter group had successfully persuaded the Austrian government to abandon the proposed power-station on the Danube at Hainburg and was prepared, in 1985, to extend its campaign of 'saving the Danube' into Hungary with the clear intention of putting pressure on the Hungarian government to abandon the GN scheme. The movement spread to other parts of Europe, culminating in the request by the European Parliament that the Czechoslovak and Austrian governments abandon the project (Perczel and Libik, 1989). Further support came from international environmental organizations such as the World Wide Fund for Nature, Greenpeace and the Sierra Club. In 1987 the Hungarian government requested renegotiation of the project since little construction work had been undertaken during the preceding two years. The Czechoslovaks stated their intention to complete their component on schedule.

With the downfall of the Kadar government in Hungary in 1988 and its replacement with that of the more moderate Grősz, the political will to complete the GN scheme declined. In May 1989, the Hungarian government indicated that it was prepared to abandon the Nagymaros component and this was confirmed in October of the same year.

The cancellation of the Nagymaros project as a result of political and environmental pressure means that a re-evaluation of water management downstream from Gabčikovo will need to be made. Apart from any environmental issue, the fluctuation under average flow conditions will be between the residual flow level in the Danube of $50-200\,\mathrm{m^3s^{-1}}$ and the added daily release flow of about $4,000\,\mathrm{m^3s^{-1}}$. If such large daily fluctuations are permitted, their effect on all aspects of life associated with the Danube will be profound. It may be that evacuation of polluted tributary waters will become less of a problem, but stability of the river banks, navigation and fishing are likely to be severely disrupted over a large section of the Hungarian Danube.

Conclusion

Environmental assessment (EA) forms an important part of large-scale hydro projects. Ideally, EA should be carried out at an early stage in the formulation of the plan. This did not happen with the GN scheme where EA was not a part of the original scheme and was only designed six years later in 1985. As a result, the report by the Water Authority represents a defence of the environmental impacts of the existing scheme rather than modifications made in the light of scientific enquiry. While it is true that the scope of the project in the upper basin of the Danube had been expanded to include regional development plans for recreation and tourism, funding for such extensions is likely to pose a problem, relying as it does on state subsidies, regional taxes and income from tourism itself (Dosztányi, 1988).

Paucity of data on water management in the Szigetköz meant that the Water Authority was unable satisfactorily to model the performance of infiltration into the gravels and thus there remain considerable uncertainties about the nature and effects of pollutants both within the system and in the extended canal system. The effect of the fluctuations in flow rates almost certainly has been underestimated and no provision has been made for modifications should the Nagymaros component not be built. Perczel and Libik (1989) predict that without the Nagymaros barrage in place the northern Hungarian Plain will be flooded when the Gabčikovo power plant is commissioned in 1990. It is therefore ironic that the environmentalists' campaign to 'save the Danube' which has been supported by many environmental organizations in Europe and the United States may have succeeded in halting work on the Nagymaros Barrage but failed to protect the Danube from what may well turn out to be more damaging effects of a half-completed project.

References

Anon. (1989) 'The financial impact of halting Nagymaros', *Water Power and Dam Construction*, 41 (9), 3.

Compton, P.A. (1989) 'Social and economic change in Hungary', *Geography*, 74 (1), 12–19.

Dávid, L. (1986) 'Environmentally sound management of freshwater resources', *Resources Policy*, 12 (4), 290–316.

Dister, E., Gomer, D., Obrdlik, P., Petermann, P. and Schneider, E. (1990) 'Water management and ecological perspectives of the Upper Rhine's floodplains', *Regulated Rivers* 5 (1), 1–16.

Domokos, M. *et al.* (eds) (1976) 'Water management in Hungary' (UN Water Conference), Hydr. Doc. and Info. Centre, Budapest.

Dosztányi, I. (ed) (1988) *Gabčikovo–Nagymaros. Environment and River Dams*. Aqua Kiadó. Budapest, Kossuth Press.

Góczán, L. and Lóczy, D. 1986 'The Slovak–Hungarian Gabčikovo–Nagymaros barrage system and its environmental problems', Geog. Res. Paper. Geog. Res. Institute, Budapest.

Göőz, L. (1989) 'Energy utilization in Hungary between 1970–1986 and its prospects' in P.A. Compton and M. Pesci, (eds), *Theory and Practice in British and Hungarian Geography*, Budapest, Akademiai Kiadó.

Karacs, I. (1989) 'Dam's cancellation makes Hungary "a laughing stock"', *The Independent*, 24 May.

Kozek, M. and Varga, I. (1986) 'An economic analysis of the river barrage system—Gabčikovo–Nagymaros' in Papers presented at the Third International Conference on

Wave, Tidal, OTEC and Small Scale Hydro Energy, Water for Energy (Brighton, 14–16 May). BHRA Paper 26, pp. 347–65.

Lessner, E. (1961) *The Danube*, Westport, Conn., Greenwood Press.

Lokvenc, V. and Szántó, M. (1986) 'The binational Gabčikovo-Nagymaros project', *Water Power and Dam Construction*, 38 (11), 33–40 and 55.

Mermel, T.W. (1988) 'Major Dams of the world—1988', *Water Power and Dam Construction Handbook*.

Miczek, G. (1989) 'An assessment of the tourist potential of the Pilis-Visegrád mountains' in A.P. Compton and M. Pécsi (eds) *Theory and Practice in British and Hungarian Geography*, Budapest, Academiai Kiadó, pp. 213–20.

Myers, T.C. (1965) 'The Danube' in *International Rivers*, Bloomington, Ind., Bloomington Press.

Nagy, L.S. (1988) 'Process for cooperation on international river basin project', *Fourth International Symposium Regulated Rivers*, Loughborough University of Technology.

Orth, D.J. and Leonard, P.M. (1990) 'Comparison of discharge methods and habitat optimization for recommending instream flows to protect fish habitat', *Regulated Rivers* 5 (2).

OVIBER (Orszàgds Vizügyi Beruházási Vállalat) 1980 'The Gabčikovo–Nagymaros River Barrage System', *Nat. Inv. Ent. Hydraulic Proj.*, Budapest.

Perczel, K. and Libik, G. (1989) 'Environmental effects of the dam system on the Danube at Bös-Nagymaros', *Ambio*, 18 (4), 247–9.

Petts, G.E. (1984) *Impounded Rivers*, Chichester, John Wiley & Sons.

Probst, J-L. (1989) 'Hydroclimatic fluctuations of some European rivers since 1800' in G.E. Petts, H. Moller and A.L. Roux, (eds), *Historical Change of Large Alluvial Rivers: Western Europe*, Chichester, John Wiley & Sons.

Rónai, A. (1960) 'Hydrological study of the Little Plain', *Hidrológiai Közlöny* 40, 470–84.

Thorpe, N. (1986) 'The Danube dam and the Hungarian Greens' in E. Goldsmith and N. Hildyard, (eds), *The Social and Environmental Effects of Large Dams*, Vol. 2, Camelford Wadebridge Ecological Centre.

Tóth, J. (1983) 'On the environmental impact and some predictable ecological problems of the Bös-Nagymaros Barrage System'. *Földrajzi Közlemének*, 31 (107), 1–11.

CHAPTER 12

Water, engineering and landscape: development, protection and restoration

Geoffrey Petts

The story of water, engineering and landscape is about the progressive and continuing human ambition to control the spatial and temporal pattern of water availability. Throughout history societies have sought to make wetlands drier and drylands wetter; to make the environment more predictable, reducing the risks of flood and drought. This story is as much a social history as a technological one, and the theme is particularly timely as we are currently witnessing a dramatic change of our fundamental attitudes to both water development and environmental protection.

The previous chapters of this book take a predominantly retrospective view. They demonstrate that in Europe the roots of Modernism lie in the late sixteenth and early seventeenth centuries, a period characterized by commercial expansion, rapid advances in hydraulic engineering, and a change from feudal to early capitalist systems of land evaluation. They emphasize that the subsequent development and expansion of Western modernization was based not only on technological advances but also on improved co-ordination and effective administration of water- and land-management schemes. The drive to control nature was sustained in part by human impacts generated by earlier river works (weirs, bridges, channelization, etc.) and land-use changes, such as deforestation. Faith in the power of technology to control the natural environment spread with colonial expansion to the New World and then to the Third World.

The era of the mega-project opened in the second half of the nineteenth century, as exemplified in this volume by Ellett's proposals for the Missippi and Roudaire's scheme to construct a vast sea in the Sahara. The popular pioneering vision was of Man's struggle to tame natural rivers, large labour forces working long hours in remote areas, often in harsh conditions, and entrepreneurs motivated by the desire for economic growth. Voeikov (1901) wrote that the control of water was one of the main tasks which Man had yet to accomplish. By the end of the 1930s the great multi-purpose dam had come to symbolize social advancement and technological prowess. Complex river developments, first in the Tennessee Valley of the United States, then on the Volga in the Soviet Union and in the Snowy Mountains of Australia (White, 1977), involved the grouping of multi-purpose projects within entire river basins. However, since the mid-

1970s the mega-project has been attacked as destructive and poorly conceived. This chapter examines the issues likely to influence the changing relationship between water, engineering and landscape into the twenty-first century.

Water developments since 1970

By 1971 reservoirs had inundated an area of 800,000 km^2—more than three times the combined area of the five Great Lakes in North America. From data in the *World Register of Dams*, which catalogues all structures more than 15 m in height, Beaumont (1978) identified 1968 as the peak of dam-building activity. However, intensive dam construction continued during the 1970s, and increased in many countries (Petts, 1984). Between 1975 and 1982 new dams were completed at a rate of 258 per year, compared with more than 400 per year during the 1960s, and by 1982 there were 35,000 large dams more than 15 m high (excluding those in China).

The scale of engineering works has increased dramatically since the 1930s. Although the rate of increase in size has slowed since the mid-1960s, the trend since 1970 has been to construct a greater number of large dams and reservoirs. The technological achievements of the 1930s, manifested by the 221 m high Hoover Dam and its 34,852 million cubic metre reservoir Lake Mead on the Colorado River, USA, are dwarfed today by the 300 m high Nurek Dam on the Vakhsh River and the 169,300 million cubic metre Bratsk reservoir on the Angara River in the USSR. Currently, there are 28 large dams over 200 m high and a further 23 are planned or under construction; the number of large reservoirs is 73, including 17 on which work has begun (Mermel, 1989). Since 1970, a rapid growth of large-dam building has taken place throughout Latin America, in India and Nepal, and in Turkey. In 1989, 36 major projects were planned or under construction (Table 12.1). When these are completed, the Hoover Dam and Lake Mead will be relegated to 28th and 35th, respectively, in the world lists!

Water-supply problems

Water is the most manageable resource, being capable of storage, diversion, transport and recycling. On a global basis, agriculture is the largest water user, accounting for nearly 80 per cent of consumption (Biswas, 1983). In many areas, dry climate, intermittent drought, and population growth imply an increasing need for water security in agriculture as well as increasing water needs for domestic and industrial supply. Additional strain on water-supply systems has been generated by rapid urban development in many arid and semi-arid regions, such as the Arabian Gulf. Other important expanding dryland developments include Los Angeles, Tucson and Salt Lake City (see Beaumont, 1989). The developing needs of drylands are being met by more intensive basin development and by inter-basin transfers.

Table 12.1   Major dams and reservoirs under construction or planned. Data from Mermel, 1989

Country	Dam	River basin	Dam height (m)	Reservoir capacity ($\times 10^6 \text{m}^3$)
Argentina	Pati	Paraná	36	38000
	Yacyretá	Paraná	43	21000
	Roncador	Uruguay	78	33580
	Chapeton	Paraná	35	60600
Brazil	Porto Primavera	Paraná	38	20000
	Roncador	Uruguay	78	33580
	Serra de Mesa	Tocantins	144	54000
	Ilha Grande	Paraná	29	30000
Canada	La Grande 2A	La Grande	168	61715
China	Ertan	Yalongjiang	245	5800
	Gaopitan	Wujiang	235	5930
	Laxiwa	Huanghe	250	n/a
	Longtan	Hongshui	216	n/a
Congo	Kouilou	Kouilou	137	35000
Costa Rica	Boruca	Terraba	267	14960
Greece	Kalaritiko	Kalaritikos	210	620
India	Kishau	Tons	253	2400
	Lakhar	Yamuna	204	580
	Tehri	Bhagirathi	261	2600
	Upper Wainganga	Wainganga	43	50700
Indonesia	Cipasang	Cimanuk	200	860
Korea	Kumgang	North Ham	215	9
Malaysia	Bakun	Rajang	210	43800
Nepal	Barakshetra	Sapta Kosi	239	8500
	Burhi Gandaki	Sapta Gandaki	225	3320
	Chisapani	Karnali	260	1500
	Kali Gandaki 1	Sapta Gandaki	260	6900
	Seti	Karnali	227	1560
	Trisuli Ganga	Sapta Gandaki	230	11000
	Pancheswor	Mahakali	262	6800
Philippines	San Roque	Agno	210	990
Turkey	Atatürk	Euphrates	184	48700
USSR	Boguchany	Angara	79	58200
	Sayano-Shushensk	Yenisei	245	31300
	Turukhansk	L. Tunguska	210	45000
	Khudoni	Inguri	201	365

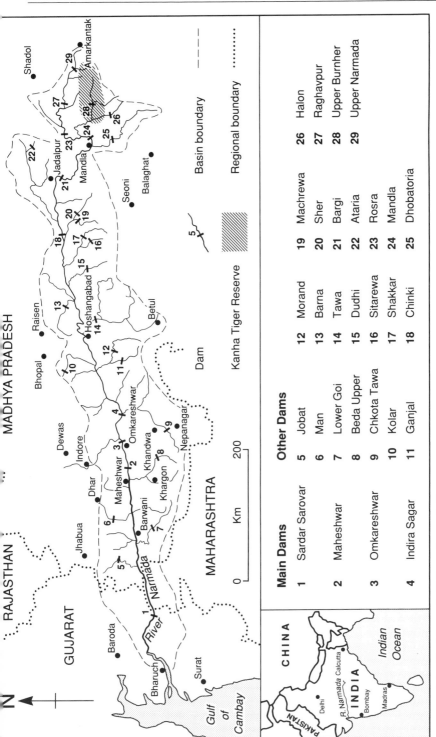

Figure 12.1 The Narmada Valley scheme, India

Basin development

In dry areas, water-supply needs are the driving force behind projects, especially for irrigation. One example of the continuing integrated development of drainage basins is the Narmada River, India. The largest west-flowing river in India, draining a basin of 98,800 km², the Narmada River supports a population of 20 million. Ninety per cent of the annual runoff occurs in the monsoon season between June and September. The river flows through three riparian states, Madhya Pradesh, Gujarat and Maharashtra. Although the original plans were compiled in 1948, inter-state disputes delayed progress until 1979 when the Narmada Water Disputes Tribunal allocated water shares to Madhya Pradesh (65 per cent), Gujarat (32 per cent), Rajasthan (2 per cent) and Maharashtra (1 per cent).

The Narmada project involves 30 large dams (Figure 12.1) and over 3,000 small structures. The benefits include security against disastrous drought problems, irrigation of over 20,000 km² of chronically drought-prone land, reliable water-supply to 4.5–5 million people, and electricity generation to improve the peaking power capacity and support base-load generation during the wet season. Two major projects play key roles. The Indira Sagar Dam will be the centre piece of a power generation and irrigation complex and will regulate flows for downstream users. The Sardar Sarovar project will involve the construction of a 163 m high dam and two powerhouses with an installed capacity of 1450 MW.

The two major reservoirs alone will inundate 1,262 km², including about 500 km of river corridor (*c.* 25 per cent of main river length) and over 500 km² of teak and mixed hardwood forest, although some 50 per cent of this is severely degraded. About 170,000 people will have to be resettled. The Narmada project has become a rallying point for India's fast-maturing environmental movement. On 28 September 1989, 60,000 people from all over India gathered at Harsud in Madhya Pradesh, a meeting which unified a range of environmental groups, tribal groups and including the Gandhian peace-activst, Baba Amte. Subsequently, the project received international media coverage (see, for example, Anon., 1989b). However, in an independent review, Levenhagen (1987) noted major and continuing degradation of land and water resources in the Indira Sagar and Sardar Sarovar project areas, largely due to population pressure and poverty. With environmentally aware planning and appropriate administration, the Narmada Valley project could be revised to incorporate landscape enhancement and restoration measures yielding long-term benefits for both the population and nature conservation.

Inter-basin transfers

In several countries, long-distance water transfers are being seriously considered as a solution to problems of dryland development (Biswas, 1983). Recently,

Falkenmark (1989) has suggested that the problem of water supply in Africa might be solved by inter-basin transfers from the Congo. One of the largest schemes proposed involves the redirection of 60 km^3 of water annually from the River Ob in Soviet Central Asia, reducing the river's flow at its mouth by 25 per cent. The water would be transferred 2,200 km south to support irrigation in the 3 million square kilometre semi-arid triangle of Kazakhstan and Central Asia, containing up to 100 million hectares of potentially irrigable land (Beaumont, 1989). In part the water would be used to counteract problems created by existing abstractions from the main rivers in the region, the Amudarya and Syrdarya. The Aral Sea, into which these rivers discharge, fell by 8 m between 1960 and the early 1980s.

Such large-scale inter-basin transfers could have a wide range of environmental impacts on both the supply and receiving rivers. For example, estimates suggest that the proposed Ob transfers would reduce thermal inputs to the Ob Gulf, increasing ice cover by 10 per cent, delaying spring melt by up to ten days, and causing saline intrusion by one degree of latitude. The reduced flows in the Ob are seen by many as a positive benefit: lowering floodplain groundwater levels, improving drainage, and reducing the area of flooding. However, adverse effects on the land–water ecotone may cause problems for land and water management, and nature conservation, in the longterm (Naiman and Decamps, 1990).

The Hydro Debate

Although only 2.7 per cent of the world's total energy consumption is currently supplied by hydro (as compared to 62.1 per cent from hydrocarbons and 33.1 per cent from solid fuels; Goldsmith, 1989) electricity generation is the largest industrial user of water. In England and Wales, for example, in 1984 cooling systems at thermal power stations used 36 per cent of the water abstracted (Department of the Environment, 1985). World-wide the technically feasible hydro-electric power potential is about 10,000 TWh, slightly less than one-third of the theoretical potential. Only 13.5 per cent of this potential is currently exploited (Table 12.2) and 40% of this is provided by only 150 large dams. In developing countries, 61 large dams contribute about 60 per cent of the installed hydro-power capacity. Considerable opportunities exist for carefully planned hydro-electric power development. In Latin America, plants currently under construction and planned, if and when completed, would increase the proportion of exploitable resources utilized from 10 per cent to 34 per cent.

The technology of hydro-power has also developed rapidly during the twentieth century. By the year 2000 the rated capacity of the hydro-electricity station at Hoover Dam, 1,404 MW, will not be sufficient to include it in the top 100 dams. The largest hydro-electric power dams will be the Turukhansk (20 GW) on the Lower Tunguska in Siberia; Three Gorges (13 GW) on the Changjiang, China; Guri on the Caroni River, Venezuela (rated at 10.3 GW);

Table 12.2 World hydro development, 1988

	Exploitable hydro potential (GWh yr⁻¹)	Total hydro generation in 1988 (GWh)	% exploited in 1988	Total hydro capacity installed and under construction (GW)	% of installed capacity under construction
Japan	130,524	87,384	67	21.17	4
USA and Canada	968,982	536,127	55	134.46	4
Western Europe	910,000	436,269	48	132.70	3
Eastern Europe	163,300	49,107	30	17.82	7
Australasia	202,000	36,945	18	13.26	9
South America	3,189,300	330,558	10	103.4	27
Central America	346,600	32,242	9	12.31	13
S. Asia and Middle East	2,280,700	170,937	7	70.0	36
USSR	3,831,000	219,800	6	76.7	19
China	1,923,304	109,177	6	49.43	33
Africa	1,153,600	35,775	3	17.41	9
World total	15,099,310	2,044,296	13.5	649.2	15.4

and the part-operational Itaipú (currently, 9.1 GW, with 12.6 GW planned) on the Paraná between Brazil and Paraguay.

In China alone a 30-year (1986–2015) development programme will add 140 GW installed capacity from 67 new projects (Anon., 1989a). Many power developments involve a complex of power plants, dams, storage reservoirs and inter-basin transfers. In the James Bay development, Canada, Phase 2 of the La Grande scheme, initiated in 1989, will add three new power plants providing nearly 3.5 GW of new installed capacity (Dagenais, 1989; see Chapter 9). Following the La Grande Phase 2, further developments are planned to add another 17.3 GW of installed capacity by 2006. The largest concentration of development will be the Nottaway–Broadbeck–Rupert river system on which eight power plants will provide an installed capacity of 8.7 GW. The scale of schemes that are planned or under construction can be illustrated by briefly considering two examples reflecting basin and national developments.

Basin developments

Many rivers will be completely harnessed; their valleys will be inundated and dynamic rivers transformed into a chain of slow flowing lakes. The Caroní River, Venezuela, is one such example (Anon., 1989c). Following a feasibility study in 1949, the 360 MW Macagua (I) project was completed in 1961 and in 1986 the final stage of Guri was completed with a total installed capacity of 10 GW. As a result of these works and those planned for completion by the year 2015, runoff from the entire Caroní river basin, yielding a mean annual flow of 4,700 m^{3}s^{-1}, will be impounded by nine dams. The artificial storage of 238 × 10^9 m^3, about 1.6 times the annual runoff, will provide a total installed capacity of 26 GW. Macagua II will close the 3 km wide Caroní River 10 km above its confluence with the Orinoco and a dynamic river corridor will be replaced by a series of eight lakes (Figure 12.2). About 1,000 km of river will be inundated by reservoirs having a combined surface area of 9,300 km^2, equal to 1 per cent of Venezuela's land area and nearly four times the size of Leicestershire! However, the Cachamay and La Llovizna waterfalls, which are important tourist attractions, will be sustained by compensation flows from Macagua II.

National developments

At a national level, Nepal has the greatest number of major projects planned (see Table 12.1). Nepal came to interact with Western civilization only after 1951, and is one of the least developed among the developing countries. In 1984 the GNP per capita was only US$160. By the turn of the century, the population is estimated to rise to 16 million. Foreign aid accounts for practically all the development activities.

The High Himalayas yield a theoretical hydro-electricity potential estimated

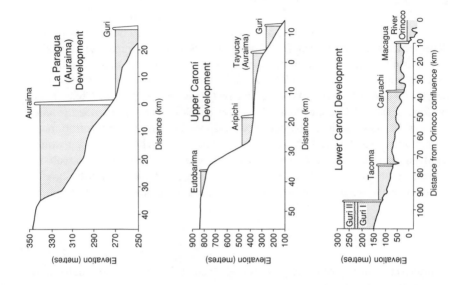

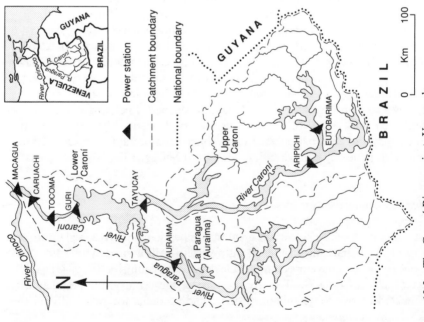

Figure 12.2   The Caroni River project, Venezuela

as 83,000 MW of which the exploitation of 42,000 MW from 66 sites is technically and economically feasible (Sharma, 1989). The present installed capacity is only 161 MW, which is to be increased to 500 MW by 2005. In addition to electricity, water-storage projects will enable the irrigation of 30,000 km^2 of the fertile northern Gangetic plains. Warnock (1989) considers that effective development of the hydropower potential, both for domestic supply and export, and with multiple benefits of improved regulation, provides economic potential far in excess of any other resource. It is not difficult to envisage the realization of the overpowering vision of Nepal as 'an overflowing cornucopia, seen from the vantage point of pure engineering' (Gyawall, 1989). However, such a view ignores the potentially dramatic impacts on landscape and nature conservation, and the long-term implications of these impacts for the sustainability of the developments.

Is hydro an environmentally clean alternative?

With the well-publicized environmental problems of thermal power, some have concluded that hydro-power is the most environmentally compatible form of energy (Gordon, 1983). Currently, hydro-power contributes about 3 per cent of electrical generation capacity. Rogers (1989) argues for the development of the substantial remaining hydro resources in the USA to reduce carbon dioxide emissions from thermal power stations by 22×10^7 t yr^{-1} (about 5 per cent of the nation's total emissions). However, the environmental impacts of hydro-dams in particular and river regulation in general are well established (see, for example, Petts, 1984; Goldsmith and Hildyard, 1984). Such impacts are manifested not least by landscape degradation and reduction of genetic diversity which can arise over periods of tens of years following project completion (Petts, 1987). The scale of the impacts may be illustrated by three examples. On the North American Atlantic seaboard, 415 km of the Saint John River became severely polluted consequent upon hydro-electric developments in 1972 (Ruggles and Wyatt, 1975). In Brazil, the creation of the Tucuruí dam destroyed 2,160 km^2 of tropical rainforest (Monosowski, 1984). In Africa, the Volta River scheme involved the resettlement of 80,000 people (Graham, 1984). The ecological and social impacts of large dams generated considerable concern during the 1980s and it is clear that, although they are different to those produced by thermal power generation, they are no less significant.

Conservation versus development

World-wide opposition has been growing between conservationists and developers. The protectionist approach has intensified conflict but the approach has been beneficial in raising public awareness of the potential environmental damage caused by major water projects. Although observations of human impacts on landscape and predictions of anthropogenic changes have been made for more than 100 years (Marsh, 1864; Bennett, 1938; Thomas, 1956), a widespread appreciation of the nature of human impacts did not develop until the late 1960s. The change was stimulated by rapid growth of our environmental data base and the rise of functional research at this time. The demonstration of widespread pollution in Rachel Carson's *Silent Spring* (1966) led to the view that the villain was multinational capitalism, although, as noted by Bramwell (1989: 247), 'The blindness to the environmental pollution in the Eastern bloc, where capitalism and private exploitation can be punished by death, demonstrates a dyslexia of categories'.

Nevertheless, a philosophical change occurred, inspired in part by the emergence of finite resources as a global issue. Although finite-resource arguements were inherent in the early development of the conservation movement, the arguments became popularized during the oil crisis of the 1970s when the long-term implications of a shortage of resources were impressed clearly on the public mind.

During the 1980s the developing environmental movement began to play a major role in landscape protection in the face of major water engineering projects. In the United States the Federal Energy Regulatory Commission estimates that 32,345 MW of hydro-electricity has been precluded by the Wild and Scenic Rivers Act (Rogers, 1989). The Northwest Power Planning Council has played a leading role by restricting more than 70,800 km of river from hydro-power development since August 1988. Cases of specific projects being stopped or modified as a result of pressure-group action are also growing in number. Pressure from environmentalists to conserve the last remaining virgin forest in the western Ghats of India stopped construction of the Silent Valley project (Palet, 1984). Following world-wide publicity generated by environmental groups, the High Court of Australia ruled that the federal government had the power to prevent the Tasmanian state government from building the Gordon-below-Franklin Dam which would have severely damaged a temperate wilderness and World Heritage area (Cohen, 1984). Construction of the Rafferty Dam on the Souris River, Saskatchewan, has been suspended following an injunction granted by the Supreme Court of Canada, while further environmental studies are carried out (Dagenais, 1989).

The more militant conservationists, including those who work for environment and human rights, and organizations supporting low-income populations, advocate the cessation of all large water projects. Bramwell (1989) argues that today the ecological movement advocates a return to primitivism. Such an extreme opposition to development-orientated philosophies is neither unusual nor unexpected. Nevertheless, unrealistic claims by conservationists of negative impacts, as well as of benefits by developers, has led to relationships becoming increasingly combative and discussions by protagonists on both sides dominated by rhetoric. Exaggerations and misrepresentations have interfered with the decision-making process.

Exploitation or Non-use?

Typically, a state of conflict exists in planning for large water projects because the primary option is between total exploitation, as in the case of the Caroní River, and preservation of wild river, as in the case of Silent Valley. It is informative to consider the World Bank's approach to water projects—the bank finances 3 per cent of the world's dams and is involved to some extent in 10 per cent of them. The World Bank's objective is to seek a balance between preserving the environmental value of the world's more important remaining wildlands, and converting some of them to more intensive, immediate human uses (Ledec and Goodland, 1988). This is stated more formally in the World Bank's *Operational Directive* 4.00, Annex B: Environmental Policy for Dam and Reservoire Projects (April 28, 1989), B1.10: 'Intact Rivers': 'Hydroelectric and other developments should preferably be concentrated on the same river . . . in order to preserve elsewhere a representative sample of rivers in the natural state. This should be considered part of the trade-offs'. The Bank's approach is to encourage developments on already converted rivers whilst preserving the natural landscape as far as possible. Indeed, 600 MW hydropower schemes for Uganda's Murchison Falls proposed in the late 1960s, early 1970s and again in 1988 were not supported by the World Bank because of the damage to these famous falls. The judgement was that the falls were worth more than 600 MW and that there were alternatives.

In March 1989, the World bank promulgated a new official policy to be followed by all staff and borrowers involved in any project related to dams and reservoirs (Goodland, 1989). This is designed to ensure that all environmental aspects of such projects become routinely and systematically integrated into project design and operation. The World Bank recognizes two types of landscape for special consideration. First, conservation units are national parks, wildlife refuges or reserves, both extant and proposed, and the World Heritage Sites. These are *normally* protected from developments, but where this is difficult, it is often *easier* to finance (as part of the water project) the conservation in perpetuity of a tract similar to the tract affected. Second, special units include tropical forests and wetlands. These *should* be conserved but if their loss is unavoidable, then mitigatory and compensatory measures should be included in the project if the units are valuable enough to warrant such measures.

The successful implementation of this approach requires a substantially larger data base on the world's riverine landscapes than exists at the present time. In the face of increasing pressure for new water engineering schemes, an environmental appraisal of all countries and perhaps biogeographic regions is required. Criteria for evaluating sites have been defined by Ratcliffe (1977). Objective criteria include size, diversity or variety, rarity and recorded history. Others such as naturalness, vulnerability or fragility, typicalness, intrinsic appeal and potential value have a subjective element. Appraisals should also give due recognition to the indigenous knowledge of landscape and to the consequences of curtailing a development. However, decisions on new water projects will continue to be made without adequate baseline data. Arguably the existence of an undisturbed river valley should be cause enough to guarantee its protection from development, at least until such baseline data are available.

Large or Small?

It has been argued that large-scale dam projects encapsulate every imaginable social, environmental and economic folly. Big dams have been labelled the world's great man-made disasters. Levenhagen (1987) suggests that large dams increase the gap between rich and poor—the poorest sections of the population bearing all the costs while the rich enjoy the benefits. Underlying the criticism of large water projects is a belief that if there were an accurate accounting of all environmental and social impacts, and full consideration of alternatives, rational judgements would promote alternative ways of providing the services the large dams were intended to supply. Most discussion has focused on small projects and non-structural alternatives.

Considerable potential exists in many areas, including Africa (Biswas, 1986) to develop small-scale irrigation. Small dams can be of high socio-economic merit especially in remote areas, providing water supply and 150–5,000 kW of power, even though of only marginal importance for the national economy. Small projects have several advantages: they do not require major investment nor complex infrastructures and can be developed quickly. However, small projects suffer from poor efficiency and quality control, and lack of government interest and supervision due to their decentralized nature and small size (Biswas, 1986). Economies of scale often argue in favour of large dams and reservoirs even though there is no doubt that mega-projects generate substantial impacts. The economy of scale spreads the capital, operation and maintenance costs over enough customers to keep individual costs low. Moreover, large schemes involving basin or inter-basin management draw supplies from hydrologically different areas and have the added advantage of lowering risk.

Small structures are not free from negative impacts. For example, with regard to the downstream river system, Petts (1980) suggested that even below small dams impacts could be observed until the area controlled by an impoundment was reduced to 35 per cent of the total catchment area. As for the health problems associated with reservoirs, the increase of schistosomiasis and malaria, which become problematic in shallow water areas with constant water level, is not caused mainly by large dams but by the extensive proliferation of numerous shallow impoundments coupled with poor standards of public water supply and sanitation.

Traditionally water management was small-scale and informally organized. It was based on a knowledge of local hydrological conditions. As noted by Bell and Roberts (Chapter 8), the manifestations of such traditional water use in the landscape were largely invisible. Today, non-structural alternatives involve land use, building design, demand management and increased efficiency in water and energy use to meet the needs of flood control, water supply, navigation, recreation, irrigation and power (Blackwelder et al., 1987). For example, flood control measures involve preservation or restoration of floodways and flood-plains, and protection of upstream areas, measures that could carry important conservation and recreational values. In October 1986, the United States Congress passed Public Law 99–662 requiring the Corps of Engineers to present a predominantly non-structural alternative whenever it recommends a new water project. However, in developing countries the large project remains the most attractive option to secure economic growth and food security.

A Technological or Administrative Problem?

The cessation of all large water engineering projects will not reverse the current trend of increasing poverty and environmental degradation. Sustainable development needs large water engineering projects, including large dams and the necessary physical infrastructure, but the goals of these projects and their operation must be radically revised. It is widely acknowledged that large projects offer multi-purpose benefits for economy, society and environment. Feasibility analyses often address multi-objective criteria, but in most cases the full range of opportunities is rarely exploited and the final scheme remains effectively single purpose. In many cases, the social and environmental costs of a large water project result not from the technology used but from the lack of appropriate planning, administration and management.

Sustainable Water Development

Sustainable development requires water engineering projects that are environmentally sound (Sewell and Biswas, 1986). This means making the best use of nature's resources to meet human demands without destroying their sustaining base (David, 1988). Tolba (1982) reported on a growing consensus that, given certain preconditions, both economic development and environmental management can be pursued simultaneously. The impetus for sustainable approaches to water development was given by the World Conservation Strategy (IUCN, 1980). However, despite dialogue to formulate environmental guidelines for water projects, such guidelines are often difficult to implement, have seldom been taken seriously by borrower nations, and are commonly ignored by project officers of development agencies.

Administrative needs Sustainable water development requires the integration of environmental considerations into the management and development processes within a regional framework involving entire river systems. To facilitate such integration, the United Nations Environment Programme (UNEP) launched in 1986 a comprehensive programme for the Environmentally Sound Management

Table 12.3   Main problems of the Zambezi basin incorporated into the Zambezi Action Plan (David, 1988)

(i)   Inadequate monitoring and exchange of information concerning climatic data, water quantity and quality, and pollution control;

(ii)   soil erosion, inadequate soil and water conservation, inadequate floodplain management;

(iii)   deforestation due to population growth and pressure on land;

(iv)   lack of adequate drinking water supply and proper sanitation facilities;

(v)   insufficient community participation, in planning, construction and maintenance of water supply and sanitation systems;

(vi)   inadequate health education;

(vii)   inadequate land-use and river basin planning;

(viii) inadequate development of human resources;

(ix)   inadequate co-ordination and consultation both at the national and river basin levels;

(x)   degradation of the natural resources base;

(xi)   degradation of fauna and flora;

(xii)   inadequate information on environmental impacts of water resources and related development projects;

(xiii) inadequate dissemination of information to the public;

(xiv)   inadequate protection of wetlands.

of Inland Waters (EMINWA), involving land and water management and international co-operation (David *et al.*, 1988). The Zambezi Action Plan (David, 1988) is the first programme to arise out of EMINWA and seeks to facilitate the co-ordination of management efforts involving six countries within which five to eight ministries have major water responsibilities. The main problems recognized for the Zambezi basin (Table 12.3) are common to many basins in the Third World. Clearly, the success of EMINWA depends on the development of appropriate institutional arrangements and environmental legislation, harmonized to ensure regional uniformity, and its successful enforcement.

Scientific needs Sustainable development requires the incorporation of scientific knowledge at the planning stage and the use of this knowledge in formulating management strategies at both the basin and local scales. Environmental assessments must provide a primary input to all levels of planning, not only for site assessment but also for technology assessment (for example, hydro-power or thermal power). Particular attention must be given to the allocation of water to sustain environmental processes within the downstream river corridor and the application of reservoir-level control rules that give due regard to the requirements of the lentic and marginal ecosystems.

International awareness of the need to foster scientific research on river regulation was such that an International Symposia Series was initiated in 1979

(Ward and Stanford, 1979; Lillehammer and Saltveit, 1984; Craig and Kemper, 1987; Petts *et al.*, 1989a), and a dedicated international journal, *Regulated Rivers*, was founded in 1987. Two evolving areas of research are the development of tools to restore damaged rivers (eg. Gore, 1985) and the provision of environmentally sound alternatives for river regulation (Gore and Petts, 1989; Petts *et al.*, 1989b; Petts 1990). These provide a framework for evaluating the feasibility of environmentally sound water development, including not only landscape protection but also the restoration and enhancement of landscapes. However, scientists have been slow to communicate effectively their findings to decision-makers and the application of scientific knowledge in developing water projects has been small-scale and largely responsive. Thus, Monosowski (1984), in a review of the Environmental Impact Assessment for the Tucuruí Project, Brazil—one of the first environmental asessments to be undertaken on a tropical dam—emphasised three major problems. These are, first providing scientific information that is appropriate for planning and management; second, translating the scientific knowledge into a firm and integrated action plan; and third ensuring co-ordination between government agencies.

Towards the twenty-first century

The relationship between water, engineering and landscape has experienced a three-phase development. The first phase was the management of perennial water sources for local agriculture and domestic supplies and the opportunistic use of seasonal floods and rains for agriculture. The second phase involved the management of rivers for navigation and water power, informal regulation of seasonal floods for irrigation agriculture, and drainage of wetlands. In Europe, this phase lasted from about 1600 until about 1900 (Petts *et al.*, 1989c). During the third phase, rivers have been completely regulated by large structures, often as part of a complex basin or inter-basin development, for hydro-electric power generation, water supply and flood control. The progressive development of the relationship between water, engineering and landscape is needed to provide solutions to water problems in the twenty-first century. In this fourth phase, landscape protection and environmental enhancement would be key components of each water project.

Large government-funded and internationally financed water projects have continued to be advocated by various bilateral and multilateral donors and leaders of several Third World countries whose goals are as much political as economic. They emphasise that large water projects are required for urban-industrial development and food self-sufficiency. It is still a popular belief that water represents a natural resource capable of development at a cost far below that of alternatives. On the one hand, the spectacle of fresh water running to the oceans is portrayed as wasteful, nations being seen to be pouring their natural wealth into the sea (see, for example, Dixon *et al.*, 1989). On the other hand, wetlands are seen as wastelands and a hazard to human health, floods as an unacceptable threat to land and life. One generally held assumption (see Goodland, 1989) is that the standards of living of the poorest peoples can rise to acceptable levels only by using more water for energy production and intensification of irrigation. Water rather than land is seen as the limiting resource for economic development (Schuh, 1987) and the change from local rural autonomy to the nation-state has led to an excessive reliance on large-scale engineering. Careful management of natural resources has been neglected.

Irrigated food production is the major consumer of the world's available fresh water but the efficiency of irrigation schemes is only about 30 per cent. Clearly, opportunities exist to improve the efficiency of water use but the scope for improvement may be less than it would appear (Tak et al., 1989). This is because of seasonal constraints and because basin efficiency is lower than scheme efficiency, drainage from upstream projects being used by downstream areas. The 'inescapable' conclusion is that in the immediate future the continued expansion of water-engineering projects for supply is needed to meet growing demands in the developing countries and drylands. Furthermore, water projects having gestation periods of more than 15–20 years in countries with high population growth will have to proceed, because the human risks of not harnessing these resources in a timely manner may be too high.

In terms of energy, one scenario to the year 2020, to meet the increasing demand in developing countries, requires a 3.5-fold increase in power generation capacity (Goldemberg et al., 1988). This scenario requires 565 GW of installed hydro-power capacity compared with an actual level of 154 GW in 1986; other scenarios envisage higher demand. Some new renewable energy sources may become competitive in the long term, such as tidal power and wind power. However, even with the greatest feasible conservation efforts, an increase in electrical supply is required and for developing countries the increase forecast is substantial.

Practically, water power is the only renewable, inexhaustible source of energy which can be exploited on a large scale at a competitive price. Hydro-power is attractive because, although initial capital costs are high and the lead time can be 15–30 years, the profits eventually realized are usually favourable, owing to the long life expectancy of plants and the simplicity of operating them. Average production costs are generally only a fraction of those from other sources. Furthermore, geographically tied hydro-plants are able now to take advantage of power markets further afield as a result of the increasing range, load transfer capability and efficiency of power transmission. Economic arguments lead to the exploitation of the hydro-electric power source on the maximum feasible scale. Boiteux (1989) considers the technical audacity of the modern engineer will continue to generate sites with exceptional opportunities.

Prospect

The modernist vision of development involved mega-projects to control nature, projects that directly or indirectly led to the extraction of wealth from rural areas and its dispersal through cities. The current vision has concern for the quality of life, focuses on investment in the environment, and is expressed by symbols of social advancement: restored landscapes and protected wilderness areas. Implicit in many approaches to water development is an acceptance of the complete exploitation of landscapes that are degraded or denuded, as a trade-off to preserve a few 'natural' landscapes. Similarly, intensification of agriculture is seen to be beneficial for landscape, by reducing pressure to expand into marginal areas and sustaining intact wildlife habitat. Too often the different values— actual and potential—of different landscapes are not appreciated. An improved approach would be to develop water resources while simultaneously restoring or enhancing degraded or denuded landscapes, as well as preserving special ones.

All water-engineering projects change landscapes and the sustaining processes for these landscapes. The significance of the changes relates not only to the scale of the project but also to the vulnerability of the affected ecosystems. In the past, the displacement and resettlement of people living in the area to be flooded by a reservoir has been most significant in affecting project development. Landscape, biological diversity and ecological functioning of river corridors are factors that must be incorporated into the decision-making process. In addition, the long-term fate of water projects must be considered. Large dams are built to extremely high standards of safety and problems could theoretically arise when they exist beyond the economic life for which they were designed. Attention is now beginning to be directed to making provision for safely decommissioning dams (Leyland, 1990); the problem of landscape restoration in reservoir basins is a theme for future research.

Large water-engineering projects can provide the foundation for attaining sustainable economic growth, if they are developed sparingly and as part of a comprehensive catchment, national or regional plan which incorporates both development and conservation objectives. Clearly, there is a need for better planning design and operation together with proper institutional managerial arrangements. Catchment management should not provide costly master plans, but should provide a flexible framework for examining various options which include large-scale water engineering.

Today, the traditional paradigm 'man *versus* environment' is changing to 'people *within* environment'. The change from reductionist and isolationist scientific research to truly interdisciplinary and collaborative studies is being paralleled by a new acceptance that for economic development to be sustainable, water and land management must be environmentally sound. This is especially true with regard to energy generation, and a view that has been reinforced by the concern for atmospheric pollution and climatic change. Conventionally, engineers investigate technical problems, economists analyse costs and benefits, sociologists examine social issues, and scientists study effects on ecosystems. Decisions must be based on a rational assessment of all factors giving due regard to local, national and global issues in both the short and long term. Such holistic decision-making is needed if sustainable water and landscape development is to be achieved.

References

Anon. (1989a) 'An overview of Chinese hydropower construction', *Water Power and Dam Construction*, September, 27–9.

Anon. (1989b) 'Damnation', *Wildlife*, 7 (12), 830–1.

Anon. (1989c) 'Hydro development in Venezuela', *Water Power and Dam Construction*, December, 16–24.

Beaumont, P. (1978) 'Man's impact on river systems: a world-wide view', *Area*, 10, 38–41.

Beaumont, P. (1989) *Environmental Management and Development in Drylands*, London, Routledge.

Bennett, H.H. (1938) *Soils and Men*, Washington, DC, US Department of Agriculture.

Biswas, A.K. (ed.) (1983) *Long-distance Water Transfer*, Dublin, Tycooly International.

Biswas A.K. (1986) 'Water development policies', *Resources Policy*, 12 (4), 290–2.

Blackwelder, B., Harding, B.L. and Colborn, T. (1987) 'Alternatives to traditional water development in the United States', *Ambio*, 16 (1), 32–7.

Boiteux, M. (1989) 'Hydro: and ancient source of power for the future', *Water Power and Dam Construction*, September, 10.

Bramwell, A. (1989) *Ecology in the 20th Century. A History*, London, Yale University Press.

Carson, R. (1966) *Silent Spring*, Harmondsworth, Penguin.

Cohen, B. (1984) 'The Franklin Saga' in V. Martin and M. Inglis, *Wilderness, the Way Ahead*, Forres, Scotland, Findhorn Press. 47–54.

Craig, J.F. and J.B. Kemper (eds) (1987) *Regulated Streams, Advances in Ecology*, New York, Plenum Press.

Dagenais, C. (1989) 'World energy congress focusses on energy for tomorrow', *Water Power and Dam Construction*, September 20–21.

David, L.J. (1988) 'Environmentally sound management of the Zambezi river basin', *Water Resources Development*, 4 (2), 80–102.

David, L.J., Golubev, G.N. and Nakayama, M. (1988) 'Environmentally sound management of large international basins. The EMINWA programme of UNEP', *Water Resources Development*, 4 (2), 103–7.

Department of the Environment (1985) *Digest of Environmental Protection and Water Statistics*, London, HMSO.

Dixon, J.A., Talbot, L.M. and Le Moigne, G.J.-M. (1989) Summary of the seminar on *Dams and Environment: considerations in World Bank Projects*, Washington, DC, World Bank, May.

Falkenmark, M. (1989) 'The massive water scarcity now threatening Africa—why isn't it being addressed?', *Ambio*, 18 (2) 112—18.

Goldemberg, J., Johansson, T., Reddy A. and Williams, R. (1988) *Energy for a Sustainable World*, new Delhi, Wiley Eastern Ltd.

Goldsmith, E. and Hildyard, N. (eds) (1984) *The Social and Environmental Effects of Large Dams*, 2 vols, Camelford, Wadebridge Ecological Centre.

Goldsmith, K. (1989) 'The role of hydropower in the world's energy supply', *Water Power and Dam Construction*, September, 22–4.

Goodland, R. (1989) 'The World Bank's new policy on the environmental aspects of dam and reservoir projects', unpublished paper presented at the Workshop on the Environmental Implications of Large Dams, 12–13 June, Washington, DC World Bank.

Gordon, J.L. (1983) 'Recent developments in hydropower', *Water Power and Dam*

Construction, September, 21–3.

Gore, J.A. (ed.) (1985) *The Restoration of Rivers and Streams*, Barton, Mass., Butterworth.

Gore, J.A. and Petts, G.E. (eds) (1989) *Alternatives in Regulated River Management*, Boca Raton, Fla, CRC Press.

Graham, R. (1984) 'Ghana's Volta Resettlement Scheme' in E. Goldsmith, and N. Hildyard (eds), *The Social and Environmental Effects of Large Dams*, Camelford, Wadebridge Ecological Centre, Vol. 2, pp. 131–9.

Gyawall, D. (1989) 'Water in Nepal'. *Occasional Paper 6*, East West Environment and Policy Institute.

International Union for the Conservation of Nature (1980) *World Conservation Strategy: Living Resource Conservation for Sustainable Development*, Gland, Switzerland, IUCN.

Ledec, G. and Goodland, A.C. (1988) *Wildlands: Their Protection and Management in Ecnomic Development*, Washington, DC, World Bank.

Levenhagen, D.W. (1987) *Overview Environmental Impact Report. Sadar Sarovar and Narmada Sagar Complex Project Areas. Narmada River Basin India* Consultants' Report, Washington, DC, World Bank.

Lillehammer, A. and Saltvelt, S.J. (eds) (1984) *Regulated Rivers*, Oslo, Universteitsforlaget.

Leyland, B. (1990) Large dams! Implications of immortality *Water Power & Dam Construction*, February, 34–37.

Marsh, G.P. 1864 *Man and Nature* (ed.) D. Lowenthal [1965]), Cambridge, Mass., Balknap Press of Harvard University Press.

Mermel, T.W. (1989) 'The world's major dams and hydro-plants', *Water Power and Dam Construction*, July, 35–41.

Monosowski, E. (1984) 'Brazil's Tucuruí Dam: development at environmental cost' in E. Goldsmith, and N. Hildyard (eds), *The Social and Environmental Effects of Large Dams*, Camelford, Wadebridge Ecological Centre, Vol. 2, pp. 191–200.

Naiman, R.J. and Decamps, H. (eds) (1990) *Ecology and Management of Aquatic-Terrestrial Ecotones*, Carnforth, Parthenon.

Palet, R. (1984) 'The Silent Valley story' in V. Martin and M. Inglis, *Wilderness, the Way Ahead*, Forres, Scotland, Findhorn Press, 54–60.

Petts, G.E. (1980) 'Morphological changes of river channels consequent upon headwater impoundment', *Journal of the Institution of Water Engineers and Scientists*, 34, 374–82.

Petts, G.E. (1984) *Impounded Rivers*, Chichester, Wiley.

Petts, G.E. (1987) 'Time-scales for ecological change in regulated rivers' in J.F. Craig and J.B. Kemper (eds), *Regulated Streams: Advances in Ecology*, New York, Plenum.

Petts, G.E. (1989) 'Perspectives for ecological management of regulated rivers' in J.A. Gore and G.E. Petts (eds), *Alternatives in Regulated River Management*, Boca Raton, Fla., CRC Press. pp 3–26.

Petts, G.E. Armitage, P. and Gustard, A. (1989a) *Fourth International Symposium on Regulated Streams*. Special Volume of *Regulated Rivers*, 3.

Petts, G.E., Imhof, J.G. Manny, B.A., Maher, J.F.B. and Weisberg, S.B. (1989b) Management of fish populations in large rivers: a review of tools and approaches. *Canadian Special Publication of Fisheries and Aquatic Sciences*, 106, 578–88.

Petts, G.E., Moller, H. and Roux, A.L. (1989c) *Historical Changes of Large Alluvial Rivers: Western Europe*, Chichester, Wiley.

Petts, G.E. (1990) 'The Role of ecotones in aquatic landscape management' in R. Naiman and H. Decamps (eds) *The Roles of Ecotones in Aquatic Landscapes*, Cambridge,

Cambridge University Press, Chapter 11.

Ratcliffe, D.A. (ed.) (1977) *A Nature Conservation Review. The Selection of Biological Sites of National Importance to Nature Conservation in Britain*, 2 vols, Cambridge, Cambridge University Press.

Rogers, W.L. (1989) 'The environmental benefits of further US hydro development', *Water Power and Dam Construction*, August, 10–11.

Ruggles, C.P. and Wyatt, W.D. (1975) 'Ecological changes due to hydropower development in the St John River', *Journal of the Fish Research Board of Canada*, 32, 161–70.

Sewell, W.R. and Biswas, A.K. (1986) 'Implementing environmentally sound management of inland waters', *Resources Policy*, 12 (4), 293–307.

Sharma, C.K. (1989) 'Nepal's hydro schemes: progress and plans', *Water Power and Dam Construction*, March, 22–3.

Schuh, G.E. (1987) 'Importance of environmental considerations in the construction and management of dams', opening statement at seminar on Dams and the Environment, 18 June, World Bank, Washington, DC.

Shuh, G.E., Le Moigne, G., Cernea, M. and Goodland, R. (1988) 'Social and environmental impacts of dams: the World Bank experience', *Transactions of the Sixteenth Congress on Large Dams*, International Commission on Large Dams, Paris, France, 419–36.

Tak, H. an der, Rangeley, B., Besant-Jones, J., Goodland, R., Leise, B. and Partridge, B. (1989) 'Large dam controversy', draft report presented at the Workshop on the Environmental Implications of Large Dams, 12–13 June, World Bank, Washington, DC.

Tolba, M.K. (1982) *Development without Destruction*, Dublin, Tycooly International.

Thomas, W.L. (ed.) (1956) *Man's Role in Changing the Face of the Earth*, Chicago, University of Chicago Press.

Voeikov, A.I. 1901 'De l'influence de l'homme sur la terre', *Annales de Geographie*, 10, 97–114, 193–215.

Ward, J.V. and Stanford, J.A. (eds) (1979) *The Ecology of Regulated Streams*, New York, Plenum Press.

Warnock, J.G. (1989) 'The hydro-resources of Nepal', *Water Power and Dam Construction*, March, 26–30.

White, G.F. (1977) *Environmental Effects of Complex River Development*, Boulder, Colo, Westview.

Index